MORE THAN FISCAL

THE INTERGENERATIONAL REPORT, SUSTAINABILITY AND PUBLIC POLICY IN AUSTRALIA

MORE THAN FISCAL

THE INTERGENERATIONAL REPORT, SUSTAINABILITY
AND PUBLIC POLICY IN AUSTRALIA

**EDITED BY ANDREW PODGER,
JANE HALL AND MIKE WOODS**

Australian
National
University

ANU PRESS

Australian
National
University

ANU PRESS

Published by ANU Press
The Australian National University
Canberra ACT 2600, Australia
Email: anupress@anu.edu.au

Available to download for free at press.anu.edu.au

ISBN (print): 9781760465773
ISBN (online): 9781760465780

WorldCat (print): 1374546376
WorldCat (online): 1374545094

DOI: 10.22459/MF.2023

Cover design and layout by ANU Press

This book is published under the aegis of the Public Policy editorial board of ANU Press.

Contents

List of Illustrations

Figures

Tables

Preface

The Academy of the Social Sciences in Australia has long had an interest in promoting more evidence-based public policy and has frequently drawn on its membership and the wider expert community to actively engage with public policy practitioners in government.

Intergenerational reports (IGRs) offer the opportunity to examine longer-term issues and trends, beyond short-term political agendas, and to identify the areas that deserve serious attention for long-term structural reform. Their very nature should also facilitate closer interaction between governments and external experts.

With that in mind, the academy hosted a workshop in September 2021 of both practitioners involved with the preparation of the 2021 IGR and external experts to assess the report and to advise on how future IGRs might be improved in light of this assessment.

This book is based upon the papers presented by the external experts at the workshop, revised following discussion and further analysis. They do not purport to represent the views expressed by the government practitioners who participated, as their involvement was strictly based on the Chatham House Rule. The views expressed by the authors are their own and, in some cases, differ from those of other authors.

Drawing on the material from the experts, the final chapter of the book has been written by the president of the academy, Richard Holden, and summarises the academy's conclusion about the 2021 IGR and recommendations for future IGRs. The academy concluded that the 2021 IGR represented a substantial improvement on the previous 2015 IGR but still has significant shortcomings.

There is a danger that IGRs have become too mechanical, too narrow and too subject to the views of the government of the day. They don't shed enough light on the future or provide the wake-up call for public understanding of looming issues that such reports were intended to foster. Nor, in all the focus on expenditure, do they consider the benefits of that expenditure.

It is recommended that future IGRs be prepared with greater independence from politics, that they cover all Australian governments (not just the Commonwealth), that the analysis be more open and include sensitivity analyses and scenario assessments, and that there be a much wider 'wellbeing' approach to long-term 'sustainability' rather than focus only on fiscal sustainability. Such an approach should highlight the long-term issues the Australian public needs to address.

The academy's assessment of the 2021 IGR identified several fiscal and broader policy issues not highlighted in the report that warrant greater attention over the next few years. They include the need to consider revenues as well as expenditures as avenues for addressing fiscal sustainability and the danger of increasing inequality. While productivity and workforce participation are highlighted, there is little discussion of options for improvement, nor advice on the future direction of Australia's migration program or on building capacity for economic resilience to respond to future shocks.

We hope the book attracts close attention from public officials and politicians, and generates constructive debate in the community.

Andrew Podger, Jane Hall and Mike Woods

Contributors

Robert Breunig FASSA is one of Australia's leading public policy economists. His research is motivated by important social policy issues and debates, and his work is characterised by careful empirical study and appropriate use of statistical techniques. Professor Breunig's research agenda has led to many partnerships with government organisations in Australia and overseas, and he has been a consultant to the private sector on marketing, mergers, bank competition and customer loyalty programs.

Diane Gibson FASSA is currently a distinguished professor (health and ageing) at the University of Canberra. Professor Gibson has held senior management roles in both the university and public service sectors and has made significant national contributions to ageing-related research, policy and practice. In addition to being a fellow of the Academy of Social Sciences in Australia, she is a fellow and national board member of the Australian Association of Gerontology, and a previous editor-in-chief of the *Australasian Journal on Ageing*.

John Goss is currently an adjunct associate professor with the Health Research Institute at the University of Canberra. He was previously principal health economist at the Australian Institute of Health and Welfare from 1990 to 2010, responsible for health and welfare expenditure collection, publication and analysis by the institute. He has been an adviser to the Organisation for Economic Cooperation and Development (OECD), the World Health Organization and the Chinese National Health Development Research Centre on health expenditure and projections of health expenditure. He is the author of *Projection of Australian Health Care Expenditure by Disease, 2003 to 2033* (Australian Institute of Health and Welfare, 2008), a 2008 report that was commissioned by the National Health and Hospitals Reform Commission.

Jane Hall FASSA is a distinguished professor of health economics at the University of Technology Sydney and immediate past president of the Academy of the Social Sciences in Australia.

Steven Hamilton is an assistant professor at George Washington University in Washington, DC, and visiting fellow at the Tax and Transfer Policy Institute at The Australian National University (ANU). His research is in public finance and the evaluation of government programs. He is a former Treasury official, where among other things he worked on budget policy.

Richard Holden FASSA is a professor of economics at the University of New South Wales (UNSW) Business School, and president of the Academy of the Social Sciences in Australia. He received a PhD from Harvard University and was a faculty member at the Massachusetts Institute of Technology (MIT) and the University of Chicago before returning to Australia. He is also a fellow of the Econometric Society.

Diane Hosking is the head of research at National Seniors Australia. Diane completed her PhD in cognitive ageing at the University of Adelaide and CSIRO Human Nutrition. She took up a postdoctoral position at ANU as a research fellow at the Centre of Excellence in Population Ageing Research before joining National Seniors in 2019.

John McCallum FASSA is a social gerontologist educated at University of Queensland, Nuffield College Oxford and Andrus Gerontology Centre LA, and has a special interest in Asia, in particular Japan. He has had university leadership roles as dean, deputy vice-chancellor and the director of TAFE. After his university career he worked at the National Health and Medical Research Council and was the CEO of National Seniors Australia from 2016 to 2023.

Peter McDonald FASSA holds honorary professorial positions at the University of Melbourne and ANU and is the chief investigator of the ARC Centre of Excellence in Population Ageing Research. In 2015, he received the Irene B. Taeuber Award of the Population Association of America and, in 2022, the Laureate Award of the International Union for the Scientific Study of Population (IUSSP). He was the president of IUSSP from 2010 to 2013.

Rachel Ong ViforJ is an Australian Research Council future fellow and a professor of economics at Curtin University. She is also the managing editor of *Australian Economic Papers*. Her research interests include the role of housing in Australia's ageing population, intergenerational housing concerns and the links between housing and wellbeing outcomes.

Lindy Orthia is a research officer and communicator at the advocacy organisation National Seniors Australia. In her academic roles outside of this she has edited three books and published over 40 peer-reviewed papers and chapters.

David Pearce is the principal and executive director at the Centre for International Economics. He has around 35 years' experience as an applied economist, having worked in a wide variety of industries including agriculture, mining, natural resources, climate and the environment, water, electricity, construction, education, finance as well as international trade and development. David's experience extends beyond Australia to include projects in China, Vietnam, Indonesia, India, Papua New Guinea, Laos, the Philippines, Sri Lanka and Bulgaria. David has undertaken a wide range of projects on climate issues over the past 30 years.

John Piggott AO FASSA is the director of the ARC Centre of Excellence in Population Ageing Research at UNSW, where he is a scientia professor of economics. He has published widely on retirement and pension issues, and in public finance more generally; his research has appeared in leading international economics and actuarial academic journals. He was a panellist on the Henry tax review, and is actively involved in tax and retirement policy debate.

Andrew Podger AO FASSA is an honorary professor of public policy at ANU. He is a former senior public servant. He has published widely on social policy and public administration. He is also a fellow of the (US) National Academy of Public Administration.

Dennis Trewin AO FASSA was the Australian statistician and head of the Australian Bureau of Statistics from July 2000 to January 2007. Prior to that he was the deputy Australian statistician and, from 1992 to 1995, the deputy government statistician in New Zealand. Internationally, Dennis has been president of the International Statistical Institute and the International Association of Survey Statisticians.

Peter Whiteford FASSA is a professor in the Crawford School of Public Policy at ANU. He has also worked with the Organisation for Economic Cooperation and Development (OECD) and the Australian government. He has published widely on inequality, child poverty, family assistance and welfare reform.

Mike Woods is a professor of health economics at the University of Technology Sydney. He chairs the editorial board of the biannual report *Australia's Aged Care Sector*. He has been a member of the board of the Australian Digital Health Agency and the Aged Care Financing Authority, deputy chair of the Australian Productivity Commission, and secretary of the ACT Treasury.

1

Making the Intergenerational Report More Relevant and Useful

Andrew Podger, Jane Hall, Mike Woods
and Dennis Trewin

Key points

- The 2021 Intergenerational Report (IGR) is a significant improvement on the previous (2015) report.

- Nonetheless, it has many shortcomings: it is not as independent or authoritative as it might have been; its focus is largely limited to the Commonwealth government, as was the case with previous reports; it fails to highlight many of the issues the public needs to address, given its 40-year projections apply only to existing policies; its focus on fiscal pressures omits serious discussion of the structural deficit it identifies and any consideration of revenue issues; and its sensitivity analysis is limited.

- Future IGRs could take one of two approaches:
  - focusing primarily on fiscal sustainability; or
  - broadening the concept of 'sustainability' by drawing on 'wellbeing' frameworks.

- Major improvements could be made even within a narrow fiscal sustainability perspective: greater objectivity; reference to the whole Australian public sector; highlighting of issues beyond the budgetary bottom line; and inclusion of more sensitivity analyses and scenario assessments, including for the revenue side of the ledger.

- The second approach could build on these enhancements by drawing on international work on 'wellbeing' and facilitating the identification of broader policy issues the nation needs to address in the longer term. This approach would require considerable investment including rebuilding Australian Bureau of Statistics' (ABS) capability in wellbeing measurement.

Introduction

The *Charter of Budget Honesty Act 1998* (Cth) requires the publication of an intergenerational report (IGR) at five-year intervals, assessing the 'long-term sustainability of current government policies over the 40 years following the release of the report, including by taking account of the financial implications of demographic change' (Commonwealth of Australia 1998:section 21). The Act was the product of wider public governance, economic and financial management reforms across many countries (including Australia and New Zealand) in the course of the 1980s and 1990s.

Australian IGRs have been published in 2002, 2007, 2010, 2015 and 2021. This book reviews the most recent (2021) IGR, both in an international context and relative to the four Australian IGRs that have preceded this most recent set of projections and analyses.

This opening chapter provides a brief overview of developments and changes to IGRs since 2002 before presenting a summary assessment of the findings in the body of the book about the 2021 IGR. It then identifies and weighs up options for the scope of future IGRs so that they could be more relevant and useful in drawing public attention to the significant social, economic and environmental issues facing the nation in the longer term.

Subsequent chapters explore different facets of Australia's future sustainability in greater depth and collectively point to ways that future IGRs might better contribute to the identification of the key long-term fiscal and other policy challenges facing the nation and to promote more evidence-based deliberation of those issues.

- Chapter 2 (Mike Woods) describes the international and national origins of Australia's long-term fiscal projections and discusses some of the limitations of the processes used to date.
- Chapter 3 (Steven Hamilton) reviews the economic and budgetary analysis in the 2021 IGR.
- Chapter 4 (Peter McDonald) examines the demographic assumptions and projections behind all five IGRs.
- Chapter 5 (Andrew Podger, Robert Breunig and John Piggott) reviews how the 2021 IGR covers retirement incomes.
- Chapter 6 (Peter Whiteford) examines the assumptions behind the projections of social security expenditures.
- Chapter 7 (Rachel Ong ViforJ) analyses long-term trends in housing, a subject not explored in the 2021 IGR.
- Chapter 8 (John McCallum, Lindy Orthia and Diane Hosking) examines long-term social developments including those referred to in the IGR and those omitted.
- Chapter 9 (Diane Gibson, John Goss and Jane Hall) reviews projections of health and aged-care expenditures.
- Chapter 10 (David Pearce) examines the way that the IGR considers climate change.

The final chapter (by Richard Holden, the national president of the Academy of the Social Sciences in Australia) summarises the academy's recommendations to the government about the role and processes for future IGRs, and as such sets a longer-term agenda for these reports. In the short term, the academy also hopes that a number of these recommendations can be taken up in the IGR the current (Albanese) government has announced it intends to issue later in 2023.

Developments and changes to IGRs since 2002

The annex to this chapter summarises how the five IGRs published to date have developed and changed over time. The key developments and changes are set out below.

First, in terms of authorship and independence, the first four IGRs were authored by Treasury but circulated by the treasurer, initially in parliament. However, there does seem to have been increasing political influence over these first four reports. The 2010 IGR was the first to contain a foreword by the treasurer. It also introduced a broader focus by including a new chapter dealing with wellbeing and considered the environment and climate change risks in some detail in another chapter. The 2015 IGR removed these chapters and based its analysis of economic and fiscal sustainability mainly on the then government's proposed policy (while also still describing the projected fiscal outcome for legislated policy and existing policy). The 2021 IGR was the first to be authored by the treasurer, although it was based on existing policy and, unlike the 2015 report, did not make projections based on the government's proposed policy.

Second, in terms of assumptions and sensitivity analysis, a range of assumptions are identified and well documented in each report. Sensitivity analysis of the key assumptions is also included in each report. The number of variables used in the first four reports was quite large, while the 2021 IGR took a different approach focusing on what were deemed the most important variables for sensitivity analysis, namely labour productivity, migration and bond yields.

The assumed labour productivity has been based each time on the average over the previous 30 years, resulting in successive estimates of 1.75 per cent, 1.75 per cent, 1.6 per cent, 1.5 per cent and 1.5 per cent. The problem is if there is a downward trend in productivity, as there has been over the last two decades, this methodology presents a lagged measure with an upward bias for estimating current and projected productivity. For this reason, the 1.5 per cent labour productivity assumption in the 2021 IGR may be optimistic. The 2021 IGR noted that several countries had recently reduced their labour productivity rate to 1.2 per cent, and presented an alternative scenario based on this assumption as part of its sensitivity analysis.

Until the 2021 IGR, population growth rates increased over successive IGRs. This is largely due to net migration being larger than anticipated and projected levels consequently being increased. Although the 2021 IGR assumes that migration will eventually return to previous levels, the close to zero migration seen during the COVID-19 pandemic years will have a long-term impact on population, so projected population growth is somewhat lower than for the 2015 IGR.

Third, there have been changes in the highlighted areas of expenditure growth and other factors and outcomes. Expenditure growth in health and aged care is highlighted in all the reports. The age pension was also highlighted in 2007 but removed in 2021. The National Disability Insurance Scheme (NDIS) has been highlighted since 2015.

Climate change was identified as a risk to economic and fiscal sustainability in 2007 and considered in some detail in both 2010 and 2021 (in the context of quite different prevailing policies in each case), but was omitted in 2015. As mentioned, wellbeing was also addressed in 2010 but not in subsequent IGRs.

Finally, the findings in terms of the 40-year deficit projections have changed. Ignoring the 2015 IGR, which was based on projected fiscal policy, the 40-year deficits have gradually declined over time from 5.0 per cent of GDP in the 2002 IGR to 2.3 per cent in the 2021 IGR. However, the 2021 IGR's projected 40-year net debt of 34 per cent of GDP is the highest. While there have been some differences in the demographic and non-demographic assumptions between the IGRs, the predominant reason for the high projected net debt in the 2021 IGR is the debt already accumulated through fiscal stimulus policies to address both the global financial crisis and the COVID-19 pandemic.

A summary assessment of the 2021 IGR

The 2021 IGR is a significant improvement on the previous (2015) report. First, it omits the blatantly partisan use of the IGR process that occurred in 2015 to support the government's then policy proposals that had not been agreed by the parliament. The 2021 analysis is also enhanced by its recognition of a wider range of factors that may impact fiscal sustainability, including climate change and measures to address that change, and including additional sensitivity analysis of the assumptions behind the projections.

But the academy fellows and other researchers contributing to this volume still find the 2021 report has many shortcomings. It was published as the treasurer's report, although under the legislation it could have been authored by the Treasury (as occurred previously). It is therefore not as independent or authoritative as it might have been. Its focus only on the Commonwealth also limits its usefulness, particularly as many key areas of expenditure and expenditure growth (and policy more broadly) are shared between the Commonwealth and the states and territories (see Chapter 2).

Rather than highlighting the issues the public needs to address in considering a 40-year projection of existing policies, the most recent report presents no clear agenda of policy issues that will impact on national wellbeing other than to address continuing fiscal pressures. Even its identification of that issue omits serious discussion of the structural deficit its analysis reveals (and arguably understates) and how that deficit might be addressed (see Chapter 3). It also ignores the impact of the then government's revenue cap on the fiscal balance, implicitly leaving the task of future fiscal repair to containing expenditures and/or improving economic growth. Moreover, the impact of the cap on the future mix of revenues, evident in the projections in the report based on existing tax policies, is not mentioned nor the economic implications of such a change in the tax mix. The report also overstates the impact of demographic developments on expenditure growth (though less so than previous IGRs—see Chapter 4) and does not explore other drivers or any policy options to contain expenditures and repair the fiscal balance (for example, in health and aged care—see Chapter 9).

The projected worsening fiscal balance is presented as an intergenerational equity issue, but the report fails to explore whether within-generation inequity is likely to worsen under existing policies. Several chapters in this volume (particularly Chapters 5, 6, 7 and 8) demonstrate how existing policies are likely to increase inequality substantially. This is arguably even more concerning than any emerging inequity between generations.

While recognising the likely impact of climate change (and of policies to mitigate and adapt to that change), the report does not attempt to include this in its modelling of the fiscal balance (see Chapter 10). Readers are left with little appreciation of the scale of this impact, nor (most importantly) of the trade-offs involved between costs of action taken in the shorter term and the benefits of such action in the longer term (economic, social and environmental).

The report's sensitivity analyses remain limited notwithstanding the role that assumptions such as on productivity and migration play in the projections. The report fails to consider or use scenario assessments either, to gauge the impact of possible future 'shocks' despite the recent evidence (e.g. the COVID-19 pandemic) of the importance of these (see Chapter 3). There is also no discussion of the policies required to support greater resilience against future shocks, including the case for earlier budget repair.

Addressing the scope of future IGRs: Issues of sustainability and wellbeing

The *Charter of Budget Honesty Act* leaves open how widely the reports are able to define the scope of 'long-term sustainability', and how far beyond 'taking account of the financial implications of demographic change' the IGRs might go. Broadly, future IGRs could take one of two approaches:

- Focus primarily on fiscal sustainability, as has been the case not only for the 2021 report but also the first two reports in 2002 and 2007 and IGR 2015, while significantly improving the value of the report for policy dialogue.
- Broaden the concept of 'sustainability' as was attempted in the 2010 IGR, drawing on 'wellbeing' frameworks developed by the Organisation for Economic Cooperation and Development (OECD) and a number of member countries, notably New Zealand, (including the work undertaken by the Australian Treasury and the Australian Bureau of Statistics more than a decade ago).

Retaining a focus on fiscal sustainability

Major improvements could be made to future IGRs while still pursuing a narrow fiscal sustainability perspective. In particular, the objectivity of the reports could be enhanced by making them the responsibility of an independent authority rather than the treasurer, and 'fiscal sustainability' could refer to the whole Australian public sector including state, territory and local governments.

There are several options open for pursuing these improvements. In New Zealand (a unitary government, of course), the Statements on the Long-term Fiscal Position are prepared and published by the Treasury and the legislation requires the Treasury secretary to sign a statement of responsibility certifying that Treasury has used its best professional judgements about the risks and the outlook. The NZ public service has long had firmer protection from political pressures than the Australian public service (for example, departmental secretaries are employed by the public service commissioner and not appointed by the prime minister). The NZ Treasury's Statements are also complemented by long-term insights briefings that line departments are required to develop independently after public consultations and then publish. The statements are also prepared after public consultations.

A similar approach could be adopted in Australia, though government departments in Australia have not in recent years had the same degree of independence as those in NZ. Other options include the Parliamentary Budget Office (PBO) and the Productivity Commission (PC); alternatively, the Treasury might author the report while drawing on work commissioned from the PC. The PC is well placed to explore state, territory and local government revenues and expenditures given its experience with working across jurisdictions. It might also be better placed than the Treasury to publicly canvass some of the policy issues arising from the fiscal projections, taking advantage of its considerable experience in public consultations.

IGRs that are focused on fiscal sustainability could also highlight issues beyond the budgetary bottom line that the projections raise. Recent NZ statements not only explore the long-term fiscal pressures and the need for prudent management, but also illustrate options for how spending or revenue might be adjusted to move the nation's finances to a more sustainable footing. Increasingly, they have encompassed associated factors such as whether reducing or removing barriers to social and economic participation might offer fiscal benefits as well as improved social outcomes. The most recent NZ report (The Treasury 2022a) incorporates NZ Treasury's own Long-term Insights Briefing into the Statement on the Long-term Fiscal Position and canvasses a range of the policy choices facing future governments on the level of debt, speed of adjustment and associated policy options (including to manage growth in expenditure over time, to improve the quality of public spending and to increase revenues). While the report does utilise a framework for wellbeing analysis of the policy options examined, there is a separate report on wellbeing (see below).

Issues raised in the analysis of Australia's 2021 IGR in subsequent chapters of this book suggest future IGRs that remain focused on fiscal sustainability would be more useful if they canvassed broad policy options to raise revenues and to contain expenditures, as well as related policies concerning inequality, productivity, migration and labour.

The IGRs would also be improved if they presented more detailed sensitivity analysis around key assumptions including migration levels, productivity and workforce participation, and if they included some explorations of scenarios of possible future shocks including natural disasters. The latter is a more recent innovation in the NZ statements and allows explanation of the role of prudent fiscal policy in building resilience.

Broadening the concept of 'sustainability'

Most contributors to this volume see considerable advantage in pursuing this second approach, drawing on the international work on 'wellbeing' undertaken since the 2010 IGR (and the academy's 2014 study, *Measuring and Promoting Wellbeing* [Podger and Trewin 2014]).

The OECD's work in this area began around 2002 (for example, OECD 2002) and was subsequently influenced by the Stiglitz, Sen and Fitoussi report (2009) commissioned by the then French president Nicholas Sarkozy, who was concerned that existing measures of national progress (in particular GDP) were insufficient. The framework developed by the OECD identified a range of measures of human wellbeing, including measures of both quality of life and material living conditions, and also referred to 'sustainability of wellbeing', which requires preserving different types of capital: economic, human, social and natural (OECD 2011).

The ABS has long been a leader in the field of social indicators, and around the turn of the century contributed to the OECD work on wellbeing measures. The ABS pioneered the development of broader measures through its Measures of Australia's Progress (MAPs) project, which issued its first publication in 2002 (ABS 2002). The Australian Treasury also developed a wellbeing framework for its work in advising ministers, drawing heavily on Amartya Sen's focus on people's 'opportunities' and making use of the ABS MAPs data. This early work contributed to the attempt in the 2010 IGR to assess wellbeing and the sustainability of wellbeing in its projections of existing policies. That approach was abandoned for the 2015 IGR and Treasury also dropped its wellbeing framework; budget limits also led to the ABS ceasing its MAPs publications from 2015.

New Zealand, under both conservative and progressive governments, has subsequently taken over Australia's leadership mantle in building and drawing upon wellbeing frameworks. NZ Treasury's work is supported by Stats NZ, which regularly publishes measures of NZ's current and future wellbeing, and NZ's impact internationally, along with contextual data (Stats NZ 2022). Future wellbeing measures use the OECD's four types of capital mentioned above. The 2021 Statement on the Long-term Fiscal Position is complemented by a new Wellbeing Report, which uses a version of the OECD's framework (The Treasury 2022b). The report is intended to inform Treasury's policy and investment advice to governments over time, and future iterations will build on the foundation of this new report.

If future Australian IGRs are to make use of a wellbeing approach, almost certainly considerable investment will be needed to reinstate the ABS capacity so it can produce the supporting data along the lines of its former MAPs. Careful consideration will also need to be given to the selection of domains and measures to ensure that IGRs do highlight the most important longer-term issues for fiscal and broader sustainability that need government and public attention.

In summary, this second approach, if adopted, should build upon the enhancements suggested under the first approach but not attempt to cover every public policy issue that might affect wellbeing now or in the future.

Which is the preferred approach?

Each approach has its advantages and its limitations. The first approach has the advantages of a firm focus and requires fewer assumptions and technical hurdles than the second. The second approach has the advantage of being holistic, recognising that no single dimension of sustainability (even fiscal sustainability) can be properly explored without appreciation of the other dimensions.

While the second approach would require considerable investment, there remains relevant expertise in the ABS and Treasury and that capability could be enhanced in those two institutions and in a third body such as either the PBO or the PC, should they be tasked with producing or contributing to the future IGRs. A first step on the path of enhancement could be through renewed interaction with NZ and others who have developed the wellbeing approach further over the last decade.

References

ABS (Australian Bureau of Statistics) 2002, *Measures of Australia's progress,* Canberra.

Commonwealth of Australia 1998, *Charter of Budget Honesty Act 1998*, available at: www.legislation.gov.au/Details/C2012C00230 (accessed 17 February 2023).

OECD (Organisation for Economic Cooperation and Development) 2002, *Social capital: The challenge of international measurement.* Report of an International Conference Convened by the Organisation of Economic Cooperation and Development and the United Kingdom Office for National Statistics, London, 25–27 September 2002, available at: www.oecd.org/education/innovation-education/2380584.pdf (accessed 24 August 2022).

OECD 2011, *How's life? Measuring wellbeing,* OECD Publishing, Paris.

Podger, A and Trewin, D (eds) 2014, *Measuring and promoting wellbeing: How important is economic growth?* ANU Press, Canberra, doi.org/10.22459/MPW. 04.2014.

Stats NZ 2022, *Wellbeing data for New Zealanders,* available at: statisticsnz.shiny apps.io/wellbeingindicators/ (accessed 24 August 2022).

Stiglitz, J, Sen, A and Fitoussi, J-P 2009, *Report by the Commission on the Measurement of Economic Performance and Social Progress,* Paris.

The Treasury (NZ) 2022a, *He Tirohanga Mokopuna 2021: The Treasury's combined statement on the long-term fiscal position and long-term insights briefing,* New Zealand Government, Wellington.

The Treasury (NZ) 2022b, *Te Tai Waiaora: Wellbeing in Aotearoa New Zealand 2022,* New Zealand Government, Wellington.

Annex: Developments and changes to IGRs since 2002

IGR	Important aspects of style and methodology, and key findings
2002	Authored by Treasury but circulated by the treasurer (Peter Costello).
	Introduces the importance of population, participation and productivity as key concepts in future economic growth and projecting expenditure and revenue outcomes.
	Analyses the impact on main areas of expenditure and revenue. Identifies health and aged care as the main areas of expenditure growth.
	Assumes a population of 25.3 m in 40 years (2041–42) and annual labour productivity growth of 1.75 per cent, the 30-year average.
	Discusses budget risks of the environment including climate change.
	Assumes no changes to existing policy settings.
	Detailed sensitivity analysis of assumptions on migration, fertility, life expectancy, labour force participation of older males, productivity, unemployment rate and health spending.
	Projects a deficit in 40 years (2041–42) of 5.0 per cent of GDP from a current surplus of 0.2 per cent using baseline assumptions.
	The current net debt to GDP ratio was 4.6 per cent. No projection was made of the debt in 40 years' time. Rather, it was stated that there was no target but net debt should be maintained at prudent levels.

IGR	Important aspects of style and methodology, and key findings
2007	Authored by Treasury but circulated by the treasurer (Peter Costello).
	Minimal changes to the structure of the report.
	Assumes a population of 28.5 m in 40 years (2046–47), higher than previously, mostly because of increased net migration level assumptions. Assumed annual productivity growth remains at 1.75 per cent.
	Continues to assume no change to existing policy settings.
	Identifies the age pension as well as health and aged care as major area of expenditure growth. Specifically addresses climate change as a long-term risk for economic and financial sustainability.
	Discusses broad policy choices to address fiscal sustainability issues.
	Sensitivity analysis on same variables as 2002 IGR except health spending.
	Projects a deficit in 40 years (2046–47) of 3.25 per cent of GDP.
	Net debt as a percentage of GDP was projected to increase from the current negligible level to 30 per cent in 40 years.
2010	Foreword by the treasurer (Wayne Swan) included, although report still authored by Treasury.
	The main changes to the structure of the report are the addition of chapters on 'Climate Change and the Environment' and 'Sustainable Society'. The latter chapter includes discussion of the future for different aspects of wellbeing.
	Assumes a population of 35.9 m in 40 years (2049–50), reflecting assumption of higher levels of migration. Assumed annual productivity growth was reduced to 1.6 per cent, the new 30-year average.
	Continues to assume no changes to existing policy settings (although it discusses the benefit of changes to the government's fiscal strategy).
	Sensitivity analysis on the same variables as 2007.
	Projects a deficit in 40 years (2049–50) of 2.75 per cent of GDP in part due to slower ageing of the population.
	Net debt as a percentage of GDP was projected to increase from the current 3 per cent to 20 per cent in 40 years.
2015	Foreword by the treasurer (Joe Hockey) included, although still authored by Treasury.
	The main changes to the structure of the report are the removal of the chapters on 'Climate Change and the Environment' and 'Sustainable Society'. A new chapter on 'Preparing for the Future'. This provides consideration of the policy settings required to build jobs, growth and opportunity, and raise living standards.
	Assumes a population of 39.7 m in 40 years (2054–55) and a fall in productivity to 1.5 per cent.
	Adds NDIS as a main area of expenditure growth.
	Analysis of fiscal sustainability is based on three scenarios: (1) previous policy, (2) legislated policy and (3) the government's proposed policy. Legislated policy is closest to what was used for previous reports.
	Much of the analysis is based on the government's proposed policy.
	Sensitivity analysis on the same variables as 2007.

IGR	Important aspects of style and methodology, and key findings
	In 40 years, projects a deficit of (1) 11.7 per cent, (2) 6 per cent or (3) a surplus of 0.5 per cent of GDP depending on the scenario.
	Based on the government's proposed policy, net debt as a percentage of GDP was projected to reverse from the current 15 per cent (largely due to fiscal stimulation for the global financial crisis) and to become an accumulated net asset of 15 per cent in 40 years. The basis for projections using either previous policy or legislated policy was not clear.
2021	Published by the treasurer (Josh Frydenberg) rather than Treasury. Treasurer's statement had a link to the report.
	The main change to the structure of the report was the removal of the chapter on 'Preparing for the Future'. The analysis on the environment and climate change was much more extensive than in the previous report.
	Assumes a population of 38.8 m in 40 years (2060–61), lower than in the previous report because of COVID-19 impacts on migration and a lower (but more realistic) fertility rate but assumes migration gets back to previous levels. Assumed productivity remains at 1.5 per cent but recognises this is significantly higher than the recent productivity cycle and higher than assumed by other like countries.
	Removes age pension as one of the main areas of expenditure growth.
	Analysis of fiscal sustainability is based on current policy.
	Sensitivity analysis is limited to migration and labour productivity, but bond yields are added.
	Projects a deficit of 2.3 per cent in 40 years (2060–61).
	Net debt as a percentage of GDP was projected to increase from the current 30 per cent (higher than in 2015 because of the COVID-19 stimulus) to 34 per cent in 40 years.

2

Origin and Evolution of Australia's Intergenerational Reports

Mike Woods

Key points

- The preparation of long-term fiscal projections by the Australian government and governments of many other countries had its origin in the governmental reforms of the 1980s and 1990s and in the growing awareness of the demographic destiny and associated fiscal stress that was awaiting in the new century.

- The Organisation for Economic Cooperation and Development (OECD) has played an important role in arguing that long-run fiscal perspectives are required to assess such matters as the impact of ageing on government spending, public debt sustainability and the budgetary impacts of structural reforms.

- There is a diversity of approaches in the development of long-term fiscal projections. Projection timeframes vary but the most common periods are for 40 to 50 years. Periodicity varies, but annual reporting is the most common, though Australia to date has produced most reports on a five-yearly basis, as has New Zealand. These two countries are also exceptions in having legislative bases for their reports. Reports also vary considerably across countries in other respects, such as the objectivity, institutional independence and scope of their reports.

- In most countries, the aim of their reports is to objectively analyse the consequences of current policy in the light of the most likely future outlooks. This is primarily achieved through granting a measure of independence to the authoring institution. New Zealand's legislation, for example, has been framed to ensure the independence of Treasury's assessment and reporting of the fiscal outlook. In contrast, Australia's reports have tended to reflect the policies and perspectives of the government of the day.

- A shortcoming of Australia's intergenerational reports (IGRs) is that the budgetary analyses are limited to Commonwealth responsibilities even though the states and territories comprise a significant share of total public sector outlays—especially for the delivery of public hospital services.

- In terms of report scope, some countries have remained firmly focused on the demographic outlook and its fiscal implications. Others have attempted to expand the relevance of their reports to both policymakers and the wider community, such as by broadening the concept of sustainability and drawing on the wellbeing frameworks developed by the OECD and some member countries such as New Zealand.

Introduction

This chapter outlines the origins of the preparation of long-term fiscal projections by governments in Australia and internationally and the varying roles and methodologies that those countries have adopted for their reports. The chapter provides a contextual overview for the subsequent chapters that focus on many of the fiscal, economic, social and environmental projections contained in the Australian government's 2021 Intergenerational Report (IGR) (Commonwealth of Australia 2021). The chapter also contributes to the discussion commenced in Chapter 1—whether future reports should focus primarily on a country's long-term fiscal sustainability or broaden the concept of sustainability to that of the future wellbeing of the community as a whole.

Background: The significant governmental reforms of the 1980s and 1990s and a growing awareness of the destiny of demography

Australia's commitment to the periodic production of IGRs, which was formally enshrined in legislation in 1998, emerged as part of the wider public governance, economic and financial reforms that were taking place across many countries in the 1980s and 1990s.

During that period the perceived failings of big government were being contrasted with the powerful incentives for effectiveness and efficiency that were embedded in market forces. In Australia, several phases of reforms were initiated. The first phase was managerialism, which was based on a results-driven private sector approach and included financial management improvement and a focus on establishing government business organisations. Markets were the central concept of the second phase, which included outsourcing and privatisation. The third phase has been described as integrated governance with central control and a performance-based orientation (Edwards et al. 2012:36, 37).

Alongside these reforms, there was a growing awareness of the prospective social, environmental and economic consequences of a forthcoming shift in the demographic profile of many mainly developed countries. Fertility rates were declining and lifespans were increasing. It became evident that population ageing was already entrenched in the structure of those existing demographics and that its impacts would accelerate in the early decades of the twenty-first century.

Some of this new thinking was brought together in 1982 when the United Nations held its first 'World Assembly on Aging'. As the report of that assembly noted:

> At certain stages of development, trends of population growth, age distribution and demographic structure could create additional difficulties for sustained development, if they were out of balance with social, economic and environmental factors. On the other hand, if taken into account and properly planned for, these trends could enhance development. (United Nations 1982:44)

There is much truth in the notion that 'demography is destiny'. Although that particular phrase is of uncertain origin, it encapsulates the structural certainties of two of the drivers of populations: fertility and mortality. This is not to say that they are immune to change or are shielded from policy intervention, as is evidenced by investments in health research, which have contributed to reductions in age-specific mortality. Similarly, social expectations, cultural norms and developments in birth control have reduced fertility rates in many countries, as have policy interventions such as the population planning policies of the Communist Party of China. Migration policies also vary considerably and, at the margin and over time, can affect demographic profiles and either entrench cultural homogeneity or lead to more multicultural societies.

The World Assembly was an early international response to the destiny that was being foretold by the established demographic trends. The concluding remarks of the secretary-general of the United Nations noted that this gathering of nations:

> was one of the few occasions on which an issue of global impact and importance had been considered by the international community at a relatively early stage, before it was too late. (United Nations 1982:45)

Although the consideration may have been timely, it did not translate into widespread action. Nonetheless, many governments did start modelling the lower rates of revenue raising that would result from declining proportions of workers in their populations and the higher levels of expenditure on healthcare services and income support that would be needed for their growing elderly populations.

By the mid-1990s, only four Organisation for Economic Cooperation and Development (OECD) members were preparing some form of long-term fiscal projections—New Zealand, Norway, the United Kingdom and the United States—but many other countries adopted the practice shortly afterwards. In 1998 Australia made a legislative commitment to produce an IGR and the first of these was published in 2002 as part of the 2002–03 Commonwealth government budget (Commonwealth of Australia 2002).

The OECD itself undertook an active role in developing a global understanding of the importance of ageing and the need for countries to analyse their demographic outlooks and make early adjustments to many of their policy settings. By 2009, an OECD analysis of the long-term projections being published by 27 of its member countries argued that such projections:

> raise the profile of fiscal sustainability, provide a framework to discuss the fiscal sustainability of current policies and the possible fiscal impact of reforms, and centralise responsibility for long-term policy analysis. (Anderson and Sheppard 2009:9)

However, they also posed the question: 'What evidence is there regarding the effectiveness of fiscal projections in managing the political incentives that result in a projected mismatch of government obligations and revenues?' (2009:8) The authors were unable to come to a definitive answer and the question remains relevant today.

Approaches to reporting on long-term fiscal projections

Countries have adopted a diversity of approaches in their development of long-term fiscal projections, including in terms of their timeframes, periodicity and legislative basis. As discussed later, they also vary considerably in other respects such as their objectivity, institutional independence and scope.

The great majority of fiscal projections that were being produced in the first decade of this century, including those from New Zealand and Australia, adopted a timeframe of 40 to 50 years for their analyses, with the US being a notable outlier at 75 years. The majority, including the US, also reported on an annual basis, though New Zealand and Australia were two of the five that produced periodic reports (every 3–5 years). Similarly, although various European countries were bound to produce reports by requirements of the European Union Stability and Growth Pact, New Zealand and Australia were exceptions in having formal legislation that set out fiscal management principles and required the preparation and publication of long-term fiscal projections (Anderson and Sheppard 2009).

The diversity of approaches can be illustrated through a brief overview of three models.

United States — Statement of Long-Term Fiscal Projections

In the later decades of the last century, the US government was very focused on its fiscal gap and the need to reduce the budget deficit, in large part by targeting discretionary expenditure. The *1990 Budget Enforcement Act* replaced the earlier legislated policy of setting deficit targets and sought, instead, to enforce agreed-upon levels of discretionary spending and ensure the budget neutrality of new spending and taxation laws (Muhleisen and Towe 2004).

Through the 1990s, the Congressional Budget Office (CBO) produced its series of annual reports on the state of the economy and the budget and included an outlook for the following decade. However, the report released in 1996 represented a marked change in long-term thinking and acknowledged that a 10-year timeframe was no longer sufficient. The CBO drew attention to the expected longer-term increase in the number of the elderly accessing federal Social Security, Medicare and Medicaid, and the increasing per person cost of Medicare, together with the slowing in the rate of growth of the labour force and related collection of payroll taxes, which support the programs. The 1996 report set out projections and sensitivity analyses for the 55-year period to 2050 (CBO 1996).

The CBO warned that the mounting deficits would be exceptionally large, even before considering the effects of economic feedbacks and concluded that: 'If those pressures are not dealt with by reducing spending or increasing taxes, the mounting deficits could seriously erode future economic growth' (CBO 1996:xiii). Over two decades later, the 2020 Financial Report of the US government, prepared by the Department of the Treasury, was still coming to similar conclusions: 'The current fiscal path is unsustainable' (US Department of the Treasury 2021:8).

New Zealand — Statement on the Long-Term Fiscal Position

In the 1980s and 1990s, New Zealand was a leader in public governance and financial reforms. Its *Fiscal Responsibility Act 1994* accompanied the opening of the economy, deregulation, asset sales and the market-led restructuring of the public sector.

The Act established a set of fiscal management principles that had a focus, similar to that of the US, on achieving and maintaining prudent levels of total Crown debt and Crown net worth as well as on managing fiscal risk and maintaining a degree of tax rate stability (New Zealand 1994:section 4(2)). The Act also created the obligation to produce a Budget Policy Statement, which specified the government's long-term objectives for fiscal policy for a forward-looking period of 10 or more years and to produce a Fiscal Strategy Report (sections 6 and 7).

The New Zealand Act received international recognition when it was first legislated, and many of its features were emulated by other countries, including the United Kingdom and Australia. The International Monetary Fund's 2007 update of its *Manual on Fiscal Transparency* held the New Zealand initiative in high regard, stating that it was 'a benchmark piece of legislation, which sets legal standards for transparency of fiscal policy and reporting, and holds the government formally responsible to the public for its fiscal performance' (International Monetary Fund 2007:95).

The substance of the 1994 legislation was incorporated into *New Zealand's Public Finance Act 1989* in 2004 (New Zealand 2021). Section 26N of the revised 1989 Act requires the retitled Statements on the Long-term Fiscal Position to:

- be prepared by the Treasury
- be published at least every four years
- have a 40-year trajectory of government finances
- state all significant assumptions underlying the projections.

Although there were many differences in approach, scope and period of analysis between the New Zealand and US projections, the headline messages were aligned. The New Zealand Treasury determined that fiscal pressures would continue to build, with population ageing slowing revenue growth and increasing expenses (a message reinforced in its 2021 Statement, though with an overlay of the impact of the debt incurred in response to the COVID-19 pandemic) (New Zealand Treasury 2021).

Australia — Intergenerational Report

The Australian government's approach to fiscal sustainability followed the initiatives of New Zealand. The purpose of its *Charter of Budget Honesty Act 1998* (Commonwealth of Australia 1998a) is to improve fiscal policy outcomes (section 1), and one of the fiscal management principles requires the government to 'ensure that its policy decisions have regard to their financial effects on future generations' (section 5(1)(e)).

Unlike the case of New Zealand, section 20 of the Act requires the Australian treasurer to publish an intergenerational report within five-yearly intervals and section 21 requires the report to 'assess the long-term sustainability of current government policies over the 40 years following the release of the report, including by taking account of the financial implications of demographic change'.

Although the New Zealand and Australian government statements are closely aligned in their primary intent, frequency of publication and legislative underpinnings, there are noteworthy differences. These relate to the level of independence of the reports from the government of the day and the scope of issues under analysis.

The sought-after benefits of long-term fiscal projections

The benefits of producing long-term fiscal projections are invariably lauded in the opening passages of the reports in which they are published. As argued in an OECD working paper:

> Questions around the impact of ageing on government spending, public debt sustainability, the sensitivity of fiscal positions to interest rate normalisation, the budgetary impacts of structural reforms, etc., all require a long-run perspective. (Guillemette and Turner 2017:5)

The Australian government's 2021 IGR affirmed that its role was to examine the long-term sustainability of current policies and how demographic, technological and other structural trends may affect the economy and the budget over the next 40 years. (It also cautioned, however, that the 2021 report was prepared in particularly uncertain times given the COVID-19 pandemic and drew particular attention to the importance of its sensitivity analyses of key variables.)

Despite the lofty objectives, Australia's IGRs have been received with somewhat muted applause from the outset. A critique of the first (2002) IGR by two noted academics (Dowrick and McDonald 2002) drew attention to several significant limitations. These include that 'only relatively small variations from recent trends are tested' and that 'there is a range of possible policy initiatives that could significantly alter the assumptions of the model'. They highlighted that 'the report does not deal with State and Territory budgets or with household budgets', and considered that the resulting distributional issues should have been addressed more explicitly. They were also critical of the fact that the workings of the model and numerous minor assumptions were not made explicit, which meant that they were not in a position to re-run the model with different assumptions (Dowrick and McDonald 2002:1, 2).

Objectivity of the analyses

A commonly held position is that long-term fiscal projections should objectively inform the community and hold the government to account for its management of future risks and its policy positions. However, there have been instances where the political narrative has become more evident in the crafting of the reports.

The OECD's Committee of Senior Budget Officials recommends that one of the principles of a sound budgetary governance framework is to identify, assess and prudently manage longer-term sustainability and other fiscal risks. On this basis it argues that governments should publish a report on the long-term sustainability of the public finances regularly enough to make an effective contribution to both public and political discussion (OECD 2015:10). Similarly, the US Treasury considers that an important purpose of its Financial Report is to aid the public understanding of the current fiscal policy, to stimulate public discourse on what is required to achieve fiscal sustainability and to comprehend the merits of policy reform (US Department of the Treasury 2021:8).

New Zealand's enabling legislation places responsibility for the preparation of its statement on its Treasury. The Treasury acknowledges the balancing act it plays:

> While we provide ongoing advice to the government of the day, we also take into account how New Zealand's economy and state sector need to evolve over coming decades in response to a changing world. (New Zealand Treasury 2016:3)

Australia's federal Charter of Budget Honesty also supports the ideal of informing the public and making the government accountable for its policies and performance:

> The purpose of the Charter is to improve fiscal policy outcomes. The Charter provides for this by requiring fiscal strategy to be based on principles of sound fiscal management and by facilitating public scrutiny of fiscal policy and performance. (Commonwealth of Australia 1998a:section 1)

But the degree to which the public is informed, and the government is held accountable, depends greatly on the transparency of the consultations held in developing the projections, the level of specification of assumptions, the publication of the modelling, and the justifications given for the myriad of judgements that are required to be made. The concerns raised by Dowrick and McDonald in 2002 remain relevant today.

The Australian government's IGRs have had a tendency to promote the specific policies of the government of the day. For instance, the 2010 IGR devoted considerable space to explaining the then government's support of policies relating to climate change and other environmental issues as well as to its wellbeing policies (Commonwealth of Australia 2010).

In a departure from earlier practice, the 2015 report was more overtly political in its intent. It offered three sets of fiscal projections based on the following scenarios:

- previous policy—being the set of policies in place prior to the 2014–15 budget (in effect, the policies of the previous government)
- currently legislated position—based on the laws passed by the Australian parliament (in effect excluding the government's proposals that were blocked by the parliament at that time)
- proposed policy—which anticipated the full implementation of the government's proposed policies.

The report was strident in its tone:

> The first two scenarios show an unequivocal deterioration in fiscal sustainability. The third scenario shows that the government's current set of policies would bring the budget back to a sustainable path over the medium to long term. (Commonwealth of Australia 2015:xiii)

Two academics described the 2015 IGR as offering Australians a limited and political view of the country's future (Woods and Kendig 2015).

At issue, therefore, is not whether there should be public and political discourse on a report's projections or even on any policy scenarios it may analyse, as the two are intertwined, but whether the reports themselves should have a political bias. In most countries the aim is to objectively analyse the consequences of current policy in the light of the most likely future outlooks (demographic, macro- and micro-economic, environmental, etc.) to determine whether those policy settings are fiscally sustainable. As discussed next, the objectivity of a report can depend on the independence of its authorship.

Independence of the agency, or at least for its production of the report

Some countries have established technocrat bodies to contribute to the preparation of long-term fiscal projections while others have strengthened the independence of the authorship of the report by an agency that is otherwise subject to ministerial direction.

The European Union's Economic Policy Committee has established a Working Group on Ageing Populations and Sustainability. As stated on its website, this technical Working Group has been constituted to:

> contribute to improving the quantitative assessment of the long-term sustainability of public finances and economic consequences of ageing populations of the EU Member States, so as to assist policy formation. (European Union 2022)

In contrast, New Zealand's Statement on the Long-Term Fiscal Position is prepared by the Treasury, which is an agency subject to ministerial direction. However, New Zealand's legislation has been framed to ensure the independence of the assessment and reporting of the fiscal outlook. The Treasury secretary is required to certify that the assessment of risks and the outlook represent Treasury's best professional judgements. The preparation of the statement involves wide consultation and the data that underpin the judgements is published.

As noted above, Australia's legislation requires the treasurer, a minister of the elected government, to publish its intergenerational report and, at least in the case of the 2015 IGR, the report's independence and objectivity have been called into question.

Although the 2021 IGR has gone some way toward re-establishing the reputation of the reports, Australia could take steps to shore-up the objectivity of future reports. One simple approach would be to adopt the highly regarded New Zealand governance model through a legislative amendment to the *Charter of Budget Honesty Act*.

An alternative approach, which would also require legislation, would be to entrust the task to the Parliamentary Budget Office (PBO) or a legislatively independent body such as the Productivity Commission. The former's website describes its role as follows:

> The PBO improves transparency around fiscal and budget policy issues … and publishes a report after every election that shows the fiscal implications of major parties' election commitments (Parliament of Australia 2022).

Australia's Productivity Commission is an independent policy research and advisory agency established under its own legislation (Commonwealth of Australia 1998b). Its remit spans economic, social and environmental issues and its three operational pillars are its independence, transparency and community-wide perspective (Productivity Commission 2023).

In 2005, at the request of the Council of Australian Governments (COAG), the Productivity Commission examined the productivity, labour supply and fiscal implications of likely demographic trends over the next 40 years for all levels of government—federal and states and territories (including their subsidiary local governments, where practicable). Consistent with the commission's commitment to transparency, its 2005 report was accompanied by the publication of all modelling and the 14 associated technical papers. The commission also undertook extensive consultation and published the 74 submissions it received, including on a draft of the report that it circulated for comment. Given the long timeframes over which the projections are made and the uncertainty that necessarily ensues, the Productivity Commission also noted:

> In the face of such uncertainty, the appropriate stance is to model a variety of possible futures so that policymakers can determine the best overall responses. Consequently, sensitivity analysis is used throughout this study. (Productivity Commission 2005:3)

Mirroring the New Zealand approach, the Commission observed:

> apart from ignoring the likely reactions of government, the projections are the Commission's best judgements about what Australia will be like as it ages over the next 40 years. (Productivity Commission 2005:3)

A further option could be for the Australian Treasury to be empowered to lead the production of an independent IGR along the New Zealand model as noted above, but have it draw on the expertise of the Productivity Commission and Australian Bureau of Statistics to contribute, including in terms of public consultations, specialist analyses and modelling.

Long-term fiscal reports play a legitimate role in aiding policy and political debate, but the community is best served when the analysis of risks and the modelling of outlooks are undertaken independently and objectively, are transparent and draw on the best available expertise.

Jurisdictional scope

There are differences in the jurisdictional coverages of long-term fiscal projections, and these are primarily the consequence of more fundamental constitutional differences between countries. New Zealand has a central government supported only by local councils and therefore its Statement on the Long-term Fiscal Position encompasses all of the country's main public sector functions.

In the context of Australia as a federation, the Australian government's IGR is focused on the fiscal projections of its own functions and generally excludes those of the states and territories. The underlying demographic, economic and related projections, however, necessarily relate to the whole country/economy.

Separately, state and territory governments may prepare their own long-term fiscal projections. The New South Wales government is required by section 8 of its *Fiscal Responsibility Act 2012* (New South Wales 2012) to include, in the annual budget papers, an assessment of the impact of the budget on the state's long-term fiscal gap and, on a five-yearly basis, to include an updated report on long-term fiscal pressures and a reassessment of that gap.

Australia does produce nationally aggregated public sector financial statistics such as the Government Finance Statistics, which are collected and published by the Australian Bureau of Statistics (ABS 2021). This series provides a quarterly report on the finances of the general government and public non-financial corporation sectors for the various levels of government in Australia. It is accompanied by a contextual commentary on the data, but that commentary does not extend to any form of forward-looking impact analysis.

The Productivity Commission's 2005 report recognised the limitations of the IGR's jurisdictional scope and included coverage of all levels of government in its analyses. This enabled it to draw meaningful conclusions on the overall public sector fiscal outlook over the 40-year projection period. Unsurprisingly, the Commission determined that the major source of budgetary pressures would be health costs and that, although much of this would be borne by the federal government: 'there are significant potential burdens faced by State and Territory Governments' (Productivity Commission 2005:XII).

The divided responsibility for the delivery of health services between the Australian government and the states and territories is a particular limitation on the usefulness of the IGR. In 2017–18 the Australian government was responsible for 42 per cent of total expenditure on health, with a further 27 per cent being funded by state and territory governments. The remainder was paid for by individuals (17 per cent), health insurance providers (9 per cent) and other non-government entities (6 per cent) (AIHW 2020:36). Without an aggregation of federal and state/territory data, it is not possible to properly assess the public sector fiscal impact of drivers of health expenditure, of which demographics is only one (Chapter 9 examines in more detail the 2021 IGR analysis of the fiscal impact of health expenditure).

Defining the scope of sustainability more broadly

As noted earlier, a major driver of the development of the initial long-term fiscal projections by governments late last century was a growing concern about the impact of population ageing. As that destiny unfolds, some reports remain firmly focused on demography and its fiscal implications while others have attempted to expand their relevance to both policymakers and the wider community. Chapter 1 of this volume posed the question of whether future IGRs should broaden the concept of sustainability by drawing on the wellbeing frameworks developed by the OECD and some member countries such as New Zealand.

Chapter 1 refers to the OECD's work on this issue, which began around the turn of the century. The OECD's framework included consideration of the quality of life and material living conditions and broadened the concept of capital to encompass economic, human, social and natural capital. The US Treasury's Statements of Long-Term Fiscal Projections consider only a limited number of variables when calculating the present value of its 75-year projections. Demography is at the centre, the receipts and non-interest expenditure items are high-level aggregations, and the assessed impact on the budget deficit is seen as the core output.

The European Commission's 2021 Ageing Report, its seventh, is similarly centred on demography and future fiscal sustainability. It contains 50-year projections of the budgetary impacts of the retirement of the baby boomers and the increasing life expectations of the population. Its ageing reports do, however, feed into policy debates at the EU level that have a slightly wider scope: 'they are used in the context of the coordination of economic policies to identify relevant policy challenges and options' and 'support the analysis of the macroeconomic impact of population ageing, including on the labour market and potential economic growth' (European Commission 2021:1).

From its inception, New Zealand's Statement on the Long-term Fiscal Position has had a broader perspective, with expenditure modelling extending beyond health and income support to include education, transport and communications and other heads of expenditure (New Zealand Treasury 2006). The New Zealand Treasury's 2016 Statement also forewarned of threats to the country's natural resources from climate change, a reduction in water quality and the impact of natural disasters, all of which would add to long-term fiscal pressures. It placed a new weight on social inclusion: 'unlike previous Statements, this time we also consider whether improving social outcomes provides fiscal benefits in addition to improving living standards' (New Zealand Treasury 2016:3). New Zealand Treasury advocated for: 'reducing and removing the significant barriers to social and economic participation for the minority of New Zealanders who face these challenges' (New Zealand Treasury 2016:6).

The rationale for this expanded approach was Treasury's recognition that there was a dynamic relationship between New Zealand's long-term public finances and intergenerational wellbeing, with the latter relying on the growth, distribution and sustainability of the four capitals. In New Zealand's case, they were defined as: 'financial and physical capital; human capital (e.g. health and skills); social capital (e.g. institutions and trust); and natural capital (e.g. water and biodiversity)' (New Zealand Treasury 2016:6).

New Zealand has recently expanded its financial management and budgetary stewardship reporting arrangements to include a new Long-term Insights Briefing. The briefing first accompanied the 2021 Statement with the aim of informing the public about medium- and long-term trends, risks and opportunities affecting the country, together with 'information and impartial analysis, including policy options (but not recommendations) to respond to these trends, risks and opportunities. This report must be done independently of Ministers' (New Zealand Treasury 2021:3). The Treasury must also consult publicly on the preparation of the insights briefing.

The scope of the Australian government's first IGR, in 2002, included separate modelling for health, aged care, income support (five categories), education and training, Commonwealth superannuation and defence. There was also a one-page summary of various future fiscal impacts of environmental challenges, though there was no attempt to model these (Commonwealth of Australia 2002).

The 2010 IGR expanded its coverage of environmental issues by devoting a chapter to climate change, water and land matters. It stated that: 'Climate change is the largest threat to Australia's environment and represents one of the most significant challenges to our economic sustainability' (Commonwealth of Australia 2010:71). The 2021 IGR also included a chapter on the environment, which, while covering climate change and some broader environmental issues, was largely descriptive and made note of the government's initiatives in this area. The 2010 IGR also canvassed the possibility of considering a broader social agenda: 'In this report wellbeing and sustainability are assessed through the prism of the stock of economic, environmental, human and social resources' (Commonwealth of Australia 2010:83).

Chapter 3 makes clear another limitation of the scope of Australian IGRs. The 2021 IGR continues the practice of focusing on the expenditure side of the budget, rather than also on revenue. The assumption it adopts of maintaining a tax-to-GDP ratio of 23.9 per cent of GDP is seen as a binding constraint (rather than as a policy position that can be challenged) and does little to allow sensitivity analyses of various revenue options and projections over the next 40 years. This policy constraint is a significant driver of the future fiscal unsustainability that is a central message of the report.

The 2010 IGR illustrates some of the opportunities open to the government to adopt a more comprehensive analysis of the wellbeing prospects facing the Australian community. As will become evident in the following chapters, the authors are in general agreement that the concept of sustainability should be broadened to enable subsequent IGRs to better prepare for Australia's future.

References

ABS (Australian Bureau of Statistics) 2021, *Government finance statistics, Australia*, available at: www.abs.gov.au/statistics/economy/government/government-finance -statistics-australia/sep-2021 (accessed 26 January 2022).

AIHW (Australian Institute of Health and Welfare) 2020, *Australia's health 2020: In brief*, available at: www.aihw.gov.au/getmedia/2aa9f51b-dbd6-4d56-8dd4-06a 10ba7cae8/aihw-aus-232.pdf.aspx?inline=true (accessed 26 July 2022).

Anderson, B and Sheppard, J 2010, 'Fiscal futures, institutional budget reforms, and their effects: What can be learned?' *OECD Journal on Budgeting* 9(3): 7–117, doi.org/10.1787/budget-9-5kmh6dnl056g.

CBO (Congressional Budget Office, US) 1996, *The economic and budget outlook: Fiscal years 1997–2006*, available at: www.cbo.gov/sites/default/files/104th-congress-1995-1996/reports/entirereport_7.pdf (accessed 20 January 2022).

Commonwealth of Australia 1998a, *Charter of Budget Honesty Act 1998*, available at: www.legislation.gov.au/Details/C2012C00230 (accessed 27 January 2022).

Commonwealth of Australia 1998b, *Productivity Commission Act 1998*, available at: www.legislation.gov.au/Details/C2018C00120 (accessed 21 February 2022).

Commonwealth of Australia 2002, *Intergenerational report 2002–03*, 2002–03 Budget Paper No. 5, Canberra, available at: treasury.gov.au/sites/default/files/ 2019-03/2002-IGR-report.pdf (accessed 19 January 2022).

Commonwealth of Australia 2010, *Australia to 2050: Future challenges*, Canberra, available at: treasury.gov.au/sites/default/files/2019-03/IGR_2010.pdf (accessed 19 January 2022).

Commonwealth of Australia 2015, *2015 intergenerational report: Australia in 2055*, Canberra, available at: treasury.gov.au/sites/default/files/2019-03/2015_IGR.pdf (accessed 19 January 2022).

Commonwealth of Australia 2021, *2021 intergenerational report: Australia over the next 40 years*, Canberra, available at: treasury.gov.au/sites/default/files/2021-06/p2021_182464.pdf (accessed 13 August 2021).

Dowrick, S and McDonald, P 2002. *Comments on intergenerational report, 2002–03*, Demography Program, The Australian National University, Canberra.

Edwards, M, Halligan, J, Horrigan, B, and Nicoll, G 2012, *Public Sector Governance in Australia*, ANU E Press, doi.org/10.22459/PSGA.07.2012.

European Commission 2021, *The 2021 ageing report: Economic and budgetary projections for the EU member states (2019–2070)*, available at: commission.europa.eu/system/files/2021-10/ip148_en.pdf (accessed 17 February 2023).

European Union 2022, *Working Group on Ageing Populations and Sustainability scope*, Economic Policy Committee, available at: europa.eu/epc/working-groups-epc/working-group-ageing-populations-and-sustainability_en#:~:text=The%20EPC's%20Working%20Group%20on,as%20to%20assist%20policy%20formation (accessed 1 February 2022).

Guillemette, Y, and Turner, D 2017, *The fiscal projection framework in long-term scenarios*, OECD Economics Department Working Papers No. 1440, OECD Publishing, available at: one.oecd.org/document/ECO/WKP(2017)72/En/pdf (accessed 1 February 2022).

International Monetary Fund 2007, *Manual on fiscal transparency revised (2007)*, Policy Paper 017, doi.org/10.5089/9781498333580.007.

Muhleisen, M and Towe, C 2004, *U.S. fiscal policies and priorities for long-run sustainability*, Occasional Paper 227, International Monetary Fund, doi.org/10.5089/9781589062955.084.

New South Wales Government 2012, *Fiscal Responsibility Act 2012*, available at: legislation.nsw.gov.au/view/html/inforce/current/act-2012-058#statusinformation (accessed 26 January 2022).

New Zealand Government 1994, *Fiscal Responsibility Act 1994*, available at: www.nzlii.org/nz/legis/hist_act/fra19941994n17270/ (accessed 26 January 2022).

New Zealand Government 2021, *Public Finance Act 1989* (as amended), available at: www.legislation.govt.nz/act/public/1989/0044/latest/DLM161685.html (accessed 13 September 2021).

New Zealand Treasury 2006, *New Zealand's long-term fiscal position*, available at: www.treasury.govt.nz/sites/default/files/2018-02/ltfp-06.pdf (accessed 27 January 2022).

New Zealand Treasury 2016, *He Tirohanga Mokopuna: 2016 statement on the long-term fiscal position*, available at: www.treasury.govt.nz/sites/default/files/2016-11/ltfs-16-htm.pdf (accessed 26 January 2022).

New Zealand Treasury 2021, *He Tirohanga Mokopuna 2021: The Treasury's combined statement on the long-term fiscal position and long-term insights briefing*, available at: www.treasury.govt.nz/system/files/2021-09/ltfs-2021.pdf (accessed 20 January 2022).

OECD (Organisation for Economic Cooperation and Development) 2015, *Recommendation of the Council on Budgetary Governance,* Public Governance & Territorial Development Directorate, 18 February, available at: www.oecd.org/gov/budgeting/Recommendation-of-the-Council-on-Budgetary-Governance.pdf (accessed 28 January 2022).

Parliament of Australia 2022, *Parliamentary budget office*, available at: www.aph.gov.au/About_Parliament/Parliamentary_Departments/Parliamentary_Budget_Office (accessed 1 February 2022).

Productivity Commission 2005, *Economic implications of an ageing Australia*, Productivity Commission Staff Working Paper, Canberra, doi.org/10.2139/ssrn.738063.

Productivity Commission 2023, *Productivity Commission*, available at: www.pc.gov.au/about/operate (accessed 20 February 2023).

United Nations 1982, *Report of the World Assembly on Aging,* August, available at: www.un.org/esa/socdev/ageing/documents/Resources/VIPEE-English.pdf (accessed 20 September 2021).

US Department of the Treasury 2021, *Financial report of the United States Government 2020*, available at: www.fiscal.treasury.gov/files/reports-statements/financial-report/2020/fr-03-25-2021-(final).pdf (accessed 26 January 2022).

Woods, M and Kendig, H 2015, 'Intergenerational report 2015: A limited and political view of our future', *Australasian Journal on Ageing* 34(4):217–19, doi.org/10.1111/ajag.12293.

3

The Intergenerational Report Should Be More Frank and Fearless about Fiscal Sustainability

Steven Hamilton

Key points

- The intergenerational report (IGR) should play an important role in disciplining decision-making in the short run to ensure it is more consistent with long-run fiscal sustainability.
- The outlook in the 2021 IGR has been negatively affected by the pandemic, mainly due to lower migration and the accumulation of debt; but, in the long run, it reflects a similar lack of fiscal sustainability to prior IGRs.
- Since the 2021 IGR was released, spending pressures in the National Disability Insurance Scheme and defence have intensified, interest rates have risen dramatically, and the government has downgraded the productivity assumption and dropped the previous cap on taxes.
- The IGR's framing around the 'three Ps' is not grounded in economics and distracts from the thing that really matters: productivity. And the economic assumptions raise the pervasive issue of there being insufficient flexibility in the scenarios considered.

- There are many measures of fiscal sustainability—regardless, while we are not in crisis, it is clear that current budget settings are unsustainable and need correction.

- The cornerstone of sound budget management is a quantifiable fiscal strategy, something eschewed in the recent budget; that needs to be rectified. Reform options on both tax and spending are needed, and have been widely discussed.

- To address the lack of innovation and influence of the IGR, and improve perceptions of its independence, it could be moved to another agency, such as the Parliamentary Budget Office or the Productivity Commission. And the same could be said of budget and economic forecasting generally.

Introduction

'How did you go bankrupt?'
'Two ways. Gradually, then suddenly.'
—Ernest Hemingway, *The Sun Also Rises*

After a long period of fiscal consolidation, the budget went into substantial deficit from 2008 during the global financial crisis, as was appropriate in the circumstances. Net debt—which at one point had in fact become net assets—rose sharply, albeit from a low level globally. It would take more than 10 years, until 2019, for the budget to return to balance. At which point the most significant global pandemic in a century struck, driving the budget even deeper into deficit than during the global financial crisis 12 years earlier, ratcheting up net debt even further.

Past periods of fiscal prudence and consolidation laid the bedrock upon which our effective economic response to major crises was built. But, over time, a series of decisions were made by governments of both major parties that were inconsistent with long-run fiscal balance. These include overly generous and unfunded superannuation tax concessions under the Howard government, the introduction of a near-unfunded National Disability Insurance Scheme (NDIS) under the Gillard government, and the unfunded Stage 3 tax cuts under the Turnbull and Morrison governments.

The intergenerational report (IGR) was introduced with the intention of it being a key economic institution to prevent the budget from drifting to a structurally unsustainable position. Yet the 2021 IGR reveals a significant structural gap that has emerged in the long run between spending and revenues. Many of the longer-run secular trends that have given rise to this unsustainability have been evident in successive IGRs since the first in 2002. But they appear to have had little impact given the budget has become less sustainable over time.

A detailed examination of the latest IGR is a worthwhile exercise for better understanding the long-run sustainability of the public finances in the wake of an acute crisis and amid building pressures. This is particularly important given the recent election of a new government, which has said it understands the budget challenges it faces and wishes to start a public conversation about budget sustainability. But it is also useful for understanding how the IGR functions as an economic institution and how it might be reframed to better fulfill its promise. This is particularly important given the government plans to release a new IGR during 2023, three years early. These are the two purposes of this chapter.

The role of the intergenerational report

Just as with the people they represent, it's common for governments not to 'intertemporally optimise'—that is, they systematically take decisions today that, were they still around in future, they would come to regret.

If it's unsurprising that each citizen might behave in ways they come to regret, it should be even less surprising for governments to do so, given it is often their successors who will suffer the consequences.

To combat myopia in individual decision-making, we typically encourage financial education, financial planning and advice, or rules of thumb for personal budgeting, and even legally mandate certain behaviours. But what do we prescribe for our policymakers? What institutions do we have to discipline politicians and public officials; to encourage them to take into account how their actions will affect their successors, to overcome short-term political incentives that are counter to maximising social welfare?

Some jurisdictions employ binding constraints on behaviour, such as deficit or debt limits, to prevent a government's decisions from imposing an unacceptable burden on future citizens. Indeed, Australia had such a debt ceiling, which periodically it had to seek parliamentary approval to raise, until it was abolished by the Abbott government in 2013 (*Commonwealth Inscribed Stock Amendment Act 2013*).

The IGR represents a softer constraint. It is a legislative requirement under the *Charter of Budget Honesty Act (1998)* (Cth) and appears now to be a permanent feature of Australian politics.

Separate from being a disciplining tool, the IGR provides an opportunity for politicians seeking to behave in a time-consistent manner. Where a government decision is needed today, which would generate benefits and costs unevenly across time, the IGR could serve as a communication tool for justifying such a decision—a tool that might help citizens overcome their own present bias.

The IGR is not about gazing into a crystal ball to predict the future. As a predictive exercise—'what will the future look like?'—it is certain to be wrong, likely wildly so. That is a futile exercise. Its purpose, rather, is to take a best guess of the sustainability of current policy settings, well before they become a serious problem. The object of interest is sustainability, not the level of GDP in 2060.

If at every point in time, current policy were adjusted so as to be sustainable according to our best guess of how it will translate into future outcomes, then we would simply rule out a set of very bad outcomes. If we were to do it often enough, there would be plenty of time to avoid bad outcomes at modest cost. If policy settings were not adjusted in response, then at least the unsustainability of current policy would be known publicly and inform debate.

The IGR should be viewed through this lens. Are current policy settings sustainable? Or do projected future outcomes indicate policy changes are required? Has the government configured the IGR to shift policy in the direction of greater time consistency? Are there changes one could make to the IGR's format to better achieve this purpose?

In practical terms, the IGR has two functions: to provide a coherent set of projections about how demographic and economic variables are currently expected to evolve over the next 40 years; and to illustrate the implications of those projections for the federal budget under current policy settings.

In annual budgets, governments typically forecast economic and budget conditions, and the budgetary impacts of policy decisions, over the coming four years (the 'forward estimates'). They also provide less sophisticated projections for policy and budget impacts over the coming decade (the 'medium term').

The IGR extends these medium-term projections to the long term. This requires modelling of the long-run evolution of demographics, based on current trends and expectations of future trends. It also requires assumptions about how policy will and will not change, based on current policy.

For example, migration is assumed to be capped in nominal rather than percentage terms (historical precedent tracking the latter), while the tax-to-GDP ratio is assumed to remain constant at 23.9 per cent (which would require explicit legislative change to achieve). So the IGR reflects a somewhat fuzzy relationship between current policy, future policy and future outcomes.

The 2021 IGR immediately justifies its existence by documenting a sharp fiscal deterioration just outside the 'medium term', around the mid-2030s (Commonwealth of Australia 2021:70); in contrast, according to the more recently released 2022 budget, current policy settings would appear sustainable (Commonwealth of Australia 2022). Only through the longer-term frame of the IGR does the unsustainability become apparent.

By generating a norm that the government of the day periodically considers the long-run impact of current policy settings, the hope is that the IGR generates sustainable policy. Permanent decisions, like structural spending or tax cuts, that are funded on the basis of temporary economic conditions may be politically tempting but are fiscally irresponsible—the IGR is intended to correct that time inconsistency.

Whether it actually does so depends on how clearly the issues are identified and necessary corrections explored. There have been some significant variations (and perceived levels of quality) across the five IGRs released by four separate governments across both political parties. The devil is in the detail, and the 2021 IGR is no exception.

Australia has the somewhat unusual practice of entirely non-independent economic and budget forecasting. The Treasury produces the economic and budget forecasts, but the document is ultimately authored by the treasurer and finance minister. If the treasurer wanted to be more optimistic about the economic outlook, and have that reflected in the budget forecasts, there would be nothing stopping them instructing the Treasury to that effect.

There is a degree of scrutiny of the process, via a number of channels. Some, but not all, documents are subject to Freedom of Information laws. Treasury and Finance department officials are required to attend Senate estimates and answer questions truthfully, including those pertaining to the budget process. The Treasury and Finance secretaries are required under the Charter of Budget Honesty to release a 'Pre-Election Economic and Fiscal Outlook' (PEFO) during election campaigns (*Charter of Budget Honesty Act 1998*, Part 7), within the caretaker period, when government is administered on a semi-independent basis.

But all of these constraints are imperfect and potentially subject to influence by the government of the day. The Treasury and Finance secretaries know what the political and institutional consequences would be of a major revision to the forecasts in PEFO relative to the most recent budget, and they can never be sure which side will win the election.

In turn, the government of the day can anticipate how public servants might respond to unreasonable requests. So the equilibrium we find ourselves in might avoid the most extreme distortions to independent forecasting but nevertheless afford substantial wiggle room. Whether that is exploited is known only to those involved—but the mere appearance of potential bias is sufficient to call the process into question.

It is in this context that the IGR is produced. The document is notionally written by Treasury officials, but it is a document formally authored and released by the treasurer of the day. So, ultimately, its contents are subject to their discretion.

That very fact—even the mere perception of it—undermines the role of the IGR as a disciplining instrument. If a government introduces policy that is unsustainable but generates a short-term political benefit, what prevents it from tweaking the IGR forecasts in order to conceal that fact? How, upon reading the IGR, would one know that had occurred?

As such, it is appropriate to view the IGR sceptically, and to study closely its assumptions, and in particular their internal consistency and coherency. Are each of the assumptions defensible and, as a whole, does the document's vision of the future make sense? Do the assumptions appear to be geared towards a predetermined outcome?

The 2021 IGR

Context

The 2021 IGR was delayed a year by the pandemic, and it is impossible to view the report without considering the impact of that once-in-a-century event on the economic and budgetary outlook.

The long-run economic and fiscal outlook presented in the 2021 IGR diverges from the prior 2015 IGR mainly for two reasons, both associated with the pandemic. The first is slower population growth due to lower migration during the pandemic and a lower fertility rate. The second is permanent deficits (and an associated substantial increase in net debt) following the deterioration in the short-term fiscal position during the pandemic and the accumulation of debt and its associated interest payments (in the prior IGR, which was based on the then government's proposed policies, not existing legislated policy, surpluses were predicted for the entire 40-year projection period).

Beyond these impacts, the 2021 IGR documents a fairly rapid return to pre-pandemic trends in a range of areas. But the economic and fiscal outlook has changed significantly in the year and a half since it was released. There has been a change of government, which has brought about a number of policy changes (e.g. child care), but also changes in key assumptions affecting the outlook (e.g. productivity, see Commonwealth of Australia 2022). There has also been a far sharper increase in inflation and interest rates than anticipated at the time the 2021 IGR was published. And key spending pressures have further intensified (e.g. the NDIS). An updated IGR, which would reflect these changes, is planned for 2023 (Wright 2022).

The key message from the 2021 IGR, only strengthened since, is that the public finances are unsustainable and major policy change will be required to make them so. The problem is far from a crisis, but reforms to correct it take time so the groundwork for them ideally would already have begun. The longer this is delayed, the greater the risks in the medium term—say, if we encounter another crisis of the order of the global financial crisis or COVID-19 pandemic.

Because the budget is in structural deficit, rather than falling as a share of the economy between crises, net debt has ratcheted up since 2008. Debt levels remain below the Organisation for Economic Cooperation and

Development (OECD) average (OECD 2023), and there is no sign of our running out of 'fiscal space'—but the brief fiscal crisis in the United Kingdom in late 2020 is a reminder of the potency of these medium-term risks (Hamilton 2022a). We should not take our ability to continue to introduce new and substantial unfunded government measures for granted.

Developments since the 2021 IGR

The two drivers of the unsustainability of the public finances in the long run, as presented in the 2021 IGR, are: (1) long-run cost pressures in areas such as health care and aged care, driven both by demographic factors (e.g. lower fertility and longer life expectancies) and non-demographic factors (e.g. cost increases); and (2) tax receipts being capped at 23.9 per cent of GDP, which prevents automatic growth in tax receipts via bracket creep to cover costs growing faster than the economy.

Long-run trends in these expenditures are covered elsewhere in this volume. But there are a number of areas in which recent (and likely future) trends suggest the outlook portrayed in the 2021 IGR is overly optimistic. In the October 2022–23 budget, while the budget position in the short term improved dramatically by virtue of higher commodity tax receipts and a more rapidly rebounding economy post-pandemic than expected, the longer-run fiscal outlook deteriorated dramatically (see Figure 3.1). Where the budget position steadily improved through the decade, it now flatlines. When these new forecasts are projected out 40 years in the 2023 IGR, the outlook can be expected to have deteriorated substantially.

This deterioration has several causes. In the budget, costs under the NDIS continue to grow at a seemingly unsustainable rate, in the order of 14 per cent per year for the federal component of NDIS costs (Commonwealth of Australia 2022). Major reform will be necessary to achieve NDIS cost growth even in line with cost growth in the broader health system. While health expenditures have grown faster in Australia than in the median OECD country, at around 5 per cent per year the rate is far below what is projected for the NDIS (Australian Institute of Health and Welfare 2019). If these faster NDIS growth projections were incorporated into the IGR, the long-run fiscal position would deteriorate dramatically.

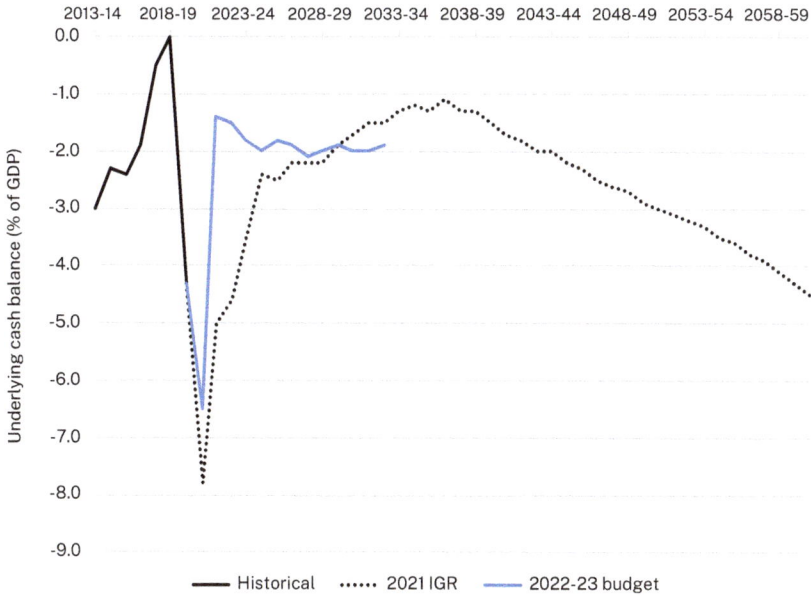

Figure 3.1: Underlying cash balance in the 2021 IGR vs 2022–23 budget.
Source: Commonwealth of Australia (2021, 2022).

In the IGR, defence spending is assumed to track the existing medium-term projections in the budget, and then to remain a constant share of nominal income. Defence spending has risen in recent years, but it seems likely to rise substantially in the years ahead, far outpacing growth in the economy (Stayner 2022). Defence spending is currently around 2 per cent of GDP and it seems conceivable that it may even grow beyond 3 per cent over the medium term. The nuclear submarine program, for example, could easily run into the many hundreds of billions of dollars.

The other major recent area of growth is in government borrowing costs. Short-term interest rates increased by around 3 percentage points during 2022 alone, compared to earlier guidance by the Reserve Bank of Australia that rates would not begin to rise until 2024. Consistent with this, the 2021 IGR did not project 10-year bond yields to begin to increase until 2025–26, and then only to converge to their long-run average rate of around 5 per cent over the subsequent 15 years. As of writing, the 10-year yield is at more than 3.5 per cent, and it's possible it could exceed 5 per cent in the next 12 months, nearly 20 years ahead of the IGR assumption (RBA 2023). This is faster even than the IGR's 'high-yield assumption', which itself would increase the deficit by 0.6 percentage points and gross debt by 14 percentage points by 2060. The 2023 IGR can be expected to incorporate an even worse outcome for government borrowing costs.

The tax cap of 23.9 per cent of GDP, assumed in the 2021 IGR, has since been dropped by the new government. Without the cap, tax receipts rise substantially over time, but likely not fast enough to offset rapid spending growth. It's important to understand that without the tax cap, average tax rates on personal income will rise considerably for those at all income levels. And the tax mix will skew towards personal income as it is the only major tax base that grows automatically as a share of the economy over time. It is difficult to conceive of this being allowed to proceed unabated over the coming 40 years. Whether the government incorporates such a constraint into the IGR projections without a tax cap remains to be seen.

Economic assumptions

The 2021 IGR promotes the 'three Ps' narrative, in which economic growth is said to be a function of growth in each of population, participation and productivity. This 'model' may be useful to politicians, but it is of dubious value in describing how the economy works.

In the IGR, population growth is modelled, as is common, such that it causes GDP but not GDP per capita to rise over time, other than due to compositional effects. For example, if population growth occurs disproportionately via immigration among younger, more productive workers, GDP per capita will rise—but this effect really ought to be seen as operating via the 'productivity' channel. Otherwise, population has no effect on GDP per capita in this kind of model.

In reality and over a long time span (such as the 40-year period considered in the IGR), the truth is that population growth *can* raise GDP per capita via agglomeration effects. Higher density, in and of itself, can make an economy more productive—raising rates of innovation and more easily overcoming the fixed costs that constrain low-population countries like Australia. This of course relies on the necessary public investments to facilitate that greater density. One could conceive of a more sophisticated, perhaps more speculative, modelling exercise considering such a possibility—but the IGR as it stands contains no such scenario. Population is substantively irrelevant.

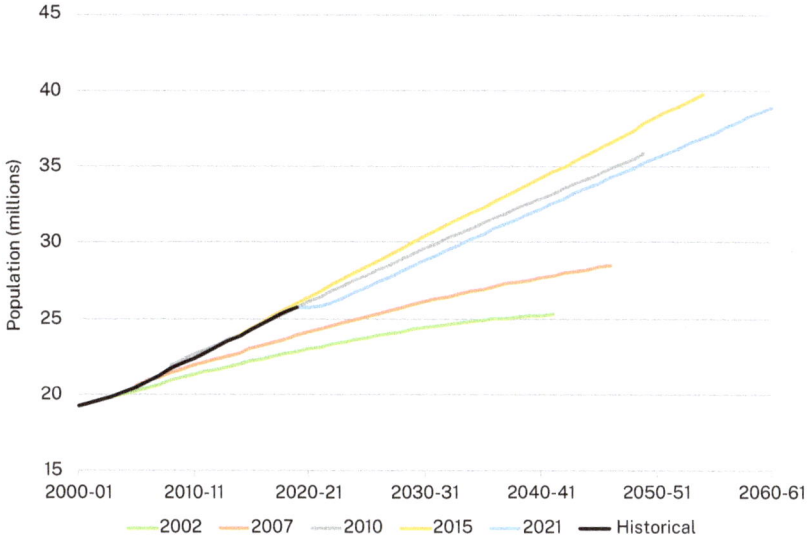

Figure 3.2: Population projections across IGRs.

Source: Commonwealth of Australia (2021).

Another major issue with the IGR is that, because the migration rate is fixed in absolute terms as a matter of policy, its central modelling scenario assumes that to be the case indefinitely, generating a reduction over time in both the migration rate and population growth rate. This is also a feature of past IGRs. The issue is that this policy is semi-regularly updated to keep the *rate* of migration at roughly a constant level over time, so past IGRs have systematically underestimated true migration and population growth rates (see Figure 3.2).

This raises a common issue applicable throughout the IGR: should it take a black-letter approach and assume the current policy or law is never changed, or should it model a more realistic scenario that reflects how policy is likely to be updated consistent with past practice? Each choice has its pros and cons; the trouble with the IGR as it stands is its inconsistency. As noted earlier, while not legislated, the 2021 IGR assumes the (former) government's 'policy' to cap tax receipts at 23.9 per cent of GDP will be implemented via unspecified future changes to legislation. Despite this policy, under the status quo tax receipts would in fact inexorably rise.

Broadly, this inconsistency in approaches in defining the status quo could be resolved simply with a richer examination of scenarios. It's worth noting that the IGR does consider an alternative scenario under which instead the migration *rate* is kept constant (implying future policy changes consistent with past practice), though this is an *alternative*. As such, it is not explored how this more realistic future population growth scenario would interact with other more realistic assumptions (such as the low-productivity scenario). So we are missing a single scenario that incorporates all of the most likely assumptions.

The second 'P', participation, is similarly unfit for purpose. Participation can indeed have a big effect on GDP growth, both in absolute terms and per capita, but most of this effect is spurious. Much economic activity that is of value to people is not measured in GDP. In particular, it does not measure the value of non-market goods. On the face of it, this production need not be any less valuable than that of market goods, and yet our measurement of GDP values it as zero. As such, an economy in which we act solely to maximise GDP growth, ignoring the change in non-market production, could well be one in which *lived* living standards go backwards.

The trouble with participation as a driver of economic growth is that it mostly just swaps the unmeasured for the measured and, in so doing, radically overstates the increase in true output (formal and informal) over time. Economists are, for convenience, fond of referring to non-work time as 'leisure'. Indeed, leisure is among the most valuable consumption goods— and yet it is tallied as economically worthless in the national accounts. Another missing category is home production. If you make dinner at home instead of eating out, the value of your time preparing the meal will not count towards GDP, though the value of the time of a professional chef who made dinner for you would have. Therefore, a trend towards eating out would raise GDP, but much of this effect would simply be an increase in what is measured.

What really matters, economically, is how productive you are at (and the enjoyment, or lack thereof, you derive from) cooking relative to the professional chef. Again, it's not 'participation' per se that matters for growing living standards, but rather improvements in productivity that greater participation might enable—a kind of rhyme with the story of population growth.

This issue is particularly acute regarding female labour force participation, the true gain in living standards from which is mechanically overstated by growth statistics that place a value of zero dollars on foregone home production. The lesson is not to maximise GDP as a matter of policy, because doing so would lead us to see greater 'participation' as desirable in and of itself without recognising that there is something given up in exchange.

We should remember that there is such a thing as too much participation. The IGR grapples not at all with this important issue. More participation is better, it readily assumes.

Which brings us to the only one of the 'three Ps' that actually matters. Notwithstanding all of the issues raised above, the IGR itself shows the other two Ps are, relatively speaking, just rounding errors in terms of measured economic growth over the next 40 years. Though it has become a bit of a cliché, we should heed Nobel laureate Paul Krugman's famous saying: 'Productivity isn't everything, but in the long run it is almost everything' (Krugman 1990). The 2021 IGR's sensitivity analysis makes clear that no assumption has a greater impact on the sustainability of the public finances than the assumed rate of productivity growth.

In the 2021 IGR, the government assumed productivity growth would return to its 30-year average of 1.5 per cent per year. This assumption was unchanged from the 2015 IGR, even though the 2010 and 2015 IGRs had both successively lowered the productivity assumption (see Figure 3.3). Critically, that period includes both the 1990s productivity boom and the 2000s mining boom. The average since the cooling of the mining boom has been a far lower 0.8 per cent per year.

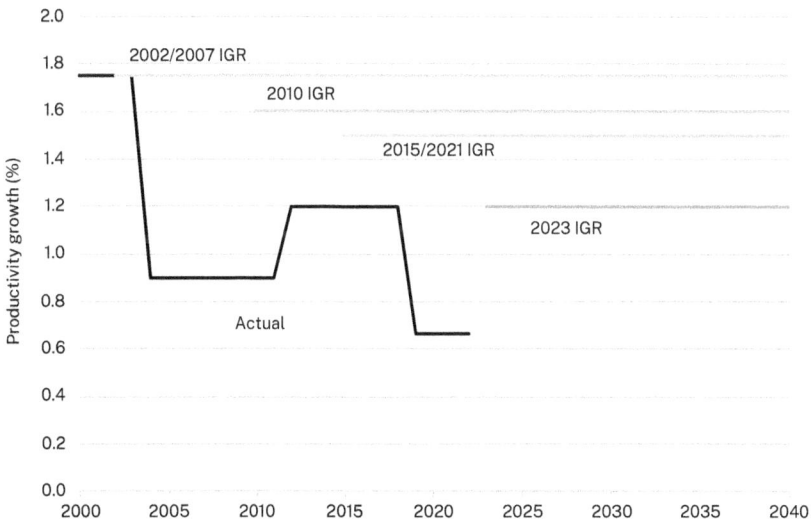

Figure 3.3: Actual vs projected productivity across IGRs.

Note: 'Actual' is the average labour productivity growth rate within productivity cycles defined by the Australian Bureau of Statistics.

Source: Australian Bureau of Statistics (2022); Commonwealth of Australia (2002, 2007, 2010, 2015, 2021).

The IGR's low-productivity scenario considered the average of the past 20 years of 1.2 per cent (similar to that assumed by foreign agencies like the US Congressional Budget Office), which still contains the mining boom and may thus be seen as optimistic. A 1.2 per cent productivity growth rate generates 9.5 per cent lower GDP, a 2.2 percentage-points-of-GDP higher deficit, and a 22.7 percentage-points-of-GDP higher net debt in 2060 (Commonwealth of Australia 2021:53). It matters a lot.

The central assumption was at the time clearly optimistic. The IGR itself notes most foreign-equivalent agencies had downgraded their long-run productivity assumption in light of recent history. There has been a secular decline in productivity across the world, and there is no reason to assume a reversal of that long-run trend. Indeed, an exercise such as the IGR should principally be about considering the implications of existing trends for the sustainability of the public finances. To assume, as the central scenario, an inexplicable return to the much faster growth of the past is inconsistent with this purpose. Considering a highly optimistic central scenario also precludes consideration of the implications of a future scenario significantly worse than the status quo, a critical risk management exercise.

The new government appears to concur with this judgement, as it lowered its productivity growth assumption to 1.2 per cent per year in the recent October 2022–23 budget (Commonwealth of Australia 2022). This assumption will presumably be incorporated into the 2023 IGR and enable consideration of an even-lower-productivity scenario, consistent with the pre-pandemic status quo, of 0.8 per cent per year. This would help communicate the risks to fiscal sustainability of continuing secular stagnation and highlight the importance of policy reforms that can help raise the rate of productivity growth.

Fiscal sustainability

There are a range of views among economists about what constitutes fiscal sustainability. In recent history, governments on both sides of politics have adopted a formal fiscal strategy, required under the charter, of achieving a budget surplus on average over the cycle. Such a goal would enable deficits during recessions due to countercyclical tax and fiscal policy offset by surpluses during periods of economic growth, and would see windfall gains returned to the bottom line (and unanticipated negative shocks, like a pandemic or natural disaster, detract from it).

Such a goal has nothing to say about the *level* of net debt, just that it must not be growing on average over time. There are also a range of views on the level of net debt that is sustainable. It is hard to argue with the trivial claim that there exists some maximum level of net debt that is sustainable; the only question that really matters is where does that point lie? Wherever it lies, prudent fiscal management that takes into account political constraints would prescribe stopping well short of it so as to maintain ample fiscal space for responding appropriately in a significant crisis. It's also clear a country like Australia faces a lower limit than the reserve-currency-issuing United States.

There is no suggestion Australia's current or projected level of net debt, which even in the latest, more pessimistic budget update is not forecast to exceed even one-third of GDP over the next decade, is anywhere near unsustainable. But where it was projected prior to the election to start falling over the next few years, it is now projected to continue to rise indefinitely— the very definition of unsustainable in the long run (Commonwealth of Australia 2022). At some point we will need to do something—if not now, when?

Moreover, after more than a decade since the global financial crisis, the budget only returned to balance in the year before the pandemic struck. So rather than generating surpluses in good times that draw down on net debt in order to generate capacity to finance a shortfall in the bad times, the budget position has led the level of net debt to ratchet up over time with each new crisis. This raises a legitimate question of how many additional crises we can withstand, given the strongly deteriorating fiscal position, before we run out of fiscal space—a possibility that recently brought the UK to the brink of financial crisis and beyond the brink of political crisis (Hamilton 2022a).

Prior to the recent federal election and in light of the budget pressures generated by the pandemic, the former government amended its fiscal strategy, reorienting away from an accounting-type balanced budget target to a commitment to stabilise and reduce net debt as a share of GDP over time. This reflects the fact that, as a matter of basic arithmetic, it is unnecessary to generate budget surpluses in order to shrink the level of net debt as a share of the economy over time; that is, the budget can become perfectly sustainable over time while never delivering an actual budget surplus.

This should be uncontroversial. It merely reflects a more modern conception of budget management in the economics literature focusing on the relationship between 'r', the real rate of interest on government borrowing, and 'g', the real rate of economic growth (Cochrane 2021). So long as $r < g$, then the economy is growing fast enough that net debt will shrink as a share of the economy over time. That is, the cost to service the debt is falling as a share of the economy, or our capacity to service our borrowing costs is improving over time.

This is a perfectly sound approach to budget management. There are some big downsides to the traditional 'balanced budget' approach—principally that governments may be constrained from responding appropriately in a crisis or might choose not to spend on or invest in things that would generate sufficient economic growth to at least partly 'pay for themselves'. Indeed, it is clear that when we were targeting balancing the budget on average over the cycle, we were 'leaving money on the table', choosing a smaller economy and lower living standards in future than was necessary to ensure fiscal sustainability.

But we must also keep in mind that the relationship between r and g, and thus the sustainability of the current level of net debt, depends on the choices we make. All other things equal, as net debt rises, the gap between r and g shrinks and eventually even flips. Poor public investments that fail to generate higher economic growth do the same. And, of course, unanticipated external shocks or emerging secular trends could well alter the relationship between r and g in ways that are beyond our control. We should not consider the current relationship to be immutable—it is no blank cheque with which to spend (or slash taxes) with abandon.

Another concern with such a benchmark is one of political economy. Perhaps the most important role of a fiscal strategy, and the targets and constraints it includes, is to discipline the government's internal decision-making. Relative to a balanced budget target, the stabilisation of net debt as a share of the economy is vaguer and more subject to forces beyond the government's control. There is something reassuringly concrete, as a means of anchoring government decision-making, about a balanced budget target. One alternative is to consider at any given time the deficit required (say, 2 per cent of GDP) to stabilise net debt as a share of the economy and enshrine that as the target instead of absolute balance.

Policy implications

The 2021 IGR tells a similar story to prior IGRs: the public finances are unsustainable. But the baseline has deteriorated considerably given the fiscal cost of the pandemic, which also worsens the long-run trajectory somewhat. And since the 2021 IGR, while things have improved in the immediate term, they have deteriorated considerably in the longer term, raising the urgency of correcting the long-run fiscal imbalance.

It seems clear the underlying cash balance needs to increase by roughly 2 percentage points of GDP on average over time—but this gap currently is expected to grow. That means the things chosen to fill that hole would need to grow too. The policy challenge is to execute a reasonably large structural fiscal consolidation in a reasonably short timeframe. That poses political risks, given that even revenue-neutral reforms have proved difficult to achieve in recent times. In this instance, we will need to take money away from people without giving them anything in return—other than a promise that the governments of their children and grandchildren more likely will be solvent.

This consolidation should begin with a clear, quantifiable fiscal strategy— a requirement under the Charter of Budget Honesty. The updated fiscal strategy in the recent 2022–23 budget was disappointing in this regard. Some of the task will be achieved via discrete policy changes, but much will be achieved gradually over time. The less disciplined is the growth in spending, the greater the discrete reform gains must be. Given the likely political cost, this doesn't seem the most sensible path forward.

The government should set a binding cap across government to keep real growth in spending to less than 2 per cent per year. And it should explicitly commit to offset any new spending with savings elsewhere. This exerts immediate pressure on growth in NDIS spending. Over time, governments of both sides at both federal and state levels have been successful in constraining the growth in health funding. That same discipline must be applied to NDIS funding in order for growth in spending overall to be contained.

Caps on real growth in spending can lead perversely to gaming of annual expenditures—seen most recently under the Gillard government. Movable spending items can be 'reprofiled' in order to sneak under the spending cap, with the budget numbers themselves becoming unmoored from reality.

Indeed, this being a mere reporting artefact is the best-case scenario—if real spending were to be gamed in response, that could involve real costs. This is unfortunately an unavoidable consequence of concrete budget rules—and not a good reason to eschew them entirely. But observers should keep this in mind when assessing outcomes against those rules.

One final point on spending, often overlooked in discussions of budget sustainability, is worth making. Over time, governments' uses of the balance sheet to pursue policy objectives have increased considerably. This has a straightforward, if cynical, explanation: it allows governments to claim a very big dollar spend to solve lots of problems at no cost to the budget bottom line. This trend is problematic for a range of reasons too extensive to discuss here. But the implication for the IGR, and fiscal sustainability broadly, is simple. The IGR should comprehensively consider the long-run impacts of and risks around these off-budget spending items, given they otherwise will fall through the cracks of the aforementioned budget rules.

While setting a spending cap, we should keep in mind that the scope for restraining (and reducing) government spending may be limited, both functionally and politically. A good share of the budget shortfall will need to be made up via increased revenue—perhaps 1.5 per cent of the required 2 per cent consolidation. Given the government has abandoned the former government's cap on tax receipts, if the new government does nothing then this part of the problem would automatically solve itself. The only federal revenue source that grows as a share of the economy, personal income tax, would close the gap via bracket creep.

But this is far from optimal. If an additional 1.5 per cent of GDP in tax revenues are to be collected, then the emphasis should be on doing so in the way that maximises social welfare. Personal income tax already accounts for a high share of federal revenues. There are alternative tax bases that collect the same amount of revenue without damaging economic output to the same degree. The need to make the budget sustainable should prompt a push to make the tax base more efficient. That means not relying on lazy bracket creep to do the budget repair job for us.

Part of the upcoming 'Stage 3' tax cuts, which flow from mid-2024, are about addressing bracket creep. The raising of the top tax threshold from $180,000 to $200,000, for example, doesn't come close to offsetting the wage growth experienced since 2008, the last time that threshold was adjusted. So scrapping Stage 3 entirely would be consistent with our relying entirely on bracket creep to solve our budget problem for us. One part of those tax cuts—eliminating the 37 per cent bracket—does not move the personal income tax system in the right direction, and could be scrapped. I estimate this would save the budget around $8 billion or 0.4 per cent of GDP a year.

Another obvious area in which both to raise revenue and improve the tax system is superannuation tax concessions. The tax treatment of superannuation is out of step with both what should be the intention of superannuation (to provide for an adequate retirement) and the tax treatment of other forms of saving. This is inefficient, inequitable and unsustainable. There are many options, but an obvious set of reforms would restore taxation of superannuation returns in the retirement phase and cap balances at $1.7 million. This would raise in the order of $5 billion to $10 billion or 0.25 per cent – 0.5 per cent of GDP a year (Hamilton 2022b). (A different approach to assessing superannuation tax concessions and to superannuation reform is explored in Chapter 5's detailed study of the 2021 IGR's examination of retirement incomes.)

Those two very significant and politically contentious policy changes would together barely raise half the required revenue to close the long-run structural budget shortfall. So a conversation must be had about more substantive reforms to the way we raise revenue. This should include a discussion of the rate and base of the GST, including federal–state financial relations broadly. It could also include a discussion of the appropriate taxation of natural resources. Ideally it would even include a discussion of estate taxation and the inclusion of the family home in the pension assets test. None of these is easy—but none of the more politically viable options would be sufficient to achieve fiscal sustainability.

There are many other areas of tax reform needed, but most would either be revenue neutral (as with a more uniform treatment of capital income taxation) or revenue negative (as with a lowering of corporate income tax rates and/or permanent expensing). So it would seem prudent, as many have called for, to get the ball rolling on a new tax reform discussion that would be all-encompassing, allowing us to both improve the tax system broadly and make the budget sustainable.

Concluding remarks

The IGR has never quite fulfilled its promise. Despite successive IGRs demonstrating the long-run unsustainability of the public finances, nothing has been done in response. Indeed, major unfunded spending decisions have been made, much to the detriment of long-run fiscal sustainability. The IGR needs to do a better job of encouraging long-run fiscal sustainability.

In the context of the new treasurer's stated intention of considering a broader range of budget outcomes (embodied in the 'wellbeing budget'), it is striking that the word 'inequality' does not appear anywhere in the 2021 IGR. Inequality is an important dimension of sustainability—just ask Marie Antoinette. There exists no systematic exercise by government in Australia to consider recent trends in inequality—which are a key outcome of and consideration for the setting of policy, including budget policy—and how current settings are expected to affect inequality going forward. Concerns about inequality have gained increasing prominence among the public in recent years, but also among economic scholars. The measurement of inequality is an exciting, burgeoning area of active research. This could be leveraged in upcoming IGRs to make the document more relevant and more useful.

One way to reinvigorate the IGR and better ensure its credibility would be to remove it from Treasury (and thus the treasurer and finance minister) and place it with an alternative, independent government agency, such as the Parliamentary Budget Office or Productivity Commission. A more dramatic step, in my view warranted, would be to spin off all budget forecasting functions from Treasury, embedding them in an arms-length agency that would also handle the IGR. This is the arrangement in the United Kingdom (and in the United States via the Congressional Budget Office), and it has a lot to recommend it, for reasons discussed earlier about the credibility or lack thereof of non-independent forecasting. This may enable more creativity and innovation.

Wherever the IGR lies, the document needs to be more useful. It needs to explore a greater variety of scenarios, those scenarios need to be more realistic and be better framed in terms of current policy or most likely future policy, and all the interactions between each of the scenarios across all the assumptions need to be communicated. One way to facilitate this would be to build an online tool connected to the various underlying modelling outputs, which would take user inputs of different assumptions and different policy options and return different results for fiscal sustainability under each of those assumptions. Ultimately, the IGR is simply a modelling exercise, but as it stands just a tiny, arbitrary fraction of the potential results from that exercise are revealed. It ought to be fully open source.

The ultimate goal is to better inform a public discussion about the sustainability of the public finances and in so doing overcome barriers to making difficult policy changes—policy changes that may involve trading off costs and benefits borne by different people at different points in time. Australia's current fiscal position is among the strongest in the world, and yet it is clearly unsustainable. And several significant, consequential policy decisions have been made in recent years that make it even worse in full knowledge of that unsustainability. An IGR that was fit for purpose would help us overcome these challenges.

References

ABS (Australian Bureau of Statistics) 2022, *Estimates of industry multifactor productivity*, Australian Bureau of Statistics, Canberra, available at: www.abs. gov.au/statistics/industry/industry-overview/estimates-industry-multifactor-productivity/latest-release (accessed 27 February 2023).

Australian Institute of Health and Welfare 2019, *Australia's health expenditure: An international comparison*, Australian Institute of Health and Welfare, Canberra.

Cochrane, J 2021, *r < g*, available at: static1.squarespace.com/static/5e6033a4ea 02d801f37e15bb/t/61021eb497ddc12e8106e3b6/1627528884849/rvsg.pdf (accessed 22 February 2023).

Commonwealth of Australia 2002, *Intergenerational report: 2002–03*, 2002–03 Budget Paper No. 5, Commonwealth of Australia, Canberra.

Commonwealth of Australia 2007, *Intergenerational report 2007*, Commonwealth of Australia, Canberra.

Commonwealth of Australia 2010, *Australia to 2050: Future challenges*, Commonwealth of Australia, Canberra.

Commonwealth of Australia 2015, *2015 intergenerational report: Australia in 2055*, Commonwealth of Australia, Canberra.

Commonwealth of Australia 2021, *2021 intergenerational report: Australia over the next 40 years*, Commonwealth of Australia, Canberra.

Commonwealth of Australia 2022, *Budget, October 2022–23—Budget paper no. 1—Budget strategy and outlook,* Commonwealth of Australia, Canberra.

Hamilton, S 2022a, 'UK is Australia's dark alternative future', *The Australian Financial Review,* 29 September.

Hamilton, S 2022b, 'Super tax breaks can end aged care crisis', *The Australian Financial Review,* 5 April.

Krugman, P 1990, *The age of diminished expectations,* MIT Press, Cambridge.

OECD (Organisation for Economic Cooperation and Development) 2023, *General government debt,* available at: data.oecd.org/gga/general-government-debt.htm (accessed 12 January 2023).

RBA (Reserve Bank of Australia) 2023, *Capital market yields—Government bonds,* Reserve Bank of Australia, available at: www.rba.gov.au/statistics/tables/xls/f02d.xls?v=2023-01-12-22-57-38 (accessed 12 January 2023).

Stayner, T 2020, '"Worst I have ever seen": Major review of Australia's defence force launched amid growing security threats', *SBS News,* 3 August, available at: www.sbs.com.au/news/article/worst-i-have-ever-seen-major-review-of-australias-defence-force-launched-amid-growing-security-threats/i7liw0m3a (accessed 12 January 2023).

Wright, S 2022, 'Chalmers enjoys beach break with family before policy tsunami in Canberra', *The Sydney Morning Herald,* 27 December.

4

The Demography of the Five Intergenerational Reports

Peter McDonald

Key points

- Relative to the first intergenerational report (IGR) (2002), rises in older-age labour force participation rates, driven mainly by favourable economic conditions and, to a lesser extent, changes in policy, have helped reduce the projected fiscal deficit in subsequent IGRs.

- The projected fiscal deficit has been reduced even more by increases in net overseas migration following the 2002 IGR.

- The projected trend of falling fertility in the 2002 IGR also led to enhancements of family support policy aimed partly at sustaining the level of fertility.

- The disturbing results of the 2002 IGR elevated population policy in Australia to a level reminiscent of the period of postwar reconstruction following the Second World War.

- As explained in the chapter, the rationale for the setting of the migration assumption for the 2021 IGR is flawed.

- Future IGRs should include more sensitivity analysis based on a wider range of assumptions about demography and labour force participation.

Introduction

The intergenerational report (IGR) is based upon a 'three Ps' model: productivity, participation and population. The IGR assumption about the growth rate of labour productivity is the most important of these three components regarding the future fiscal deficit. However, concern about the future ageing of the Australian population drove the decision to produce the first IGR. That the impact of population is significant is indicated by the observation that the first IGR in 2002 (IGR1) assumed that the growth rate of labour productivity would be 1.75 per cent per annum, a higher level than was assumed for the 2021 IGR (IGR5). Despite this, the fiscal deficit in IGR1 in 2041–42 was 5 per cent of GDP, a much larger deficit than that projected for the same year by IGR5, at 1.1 per cent. Clearly, between 2002 and 2021, the other inputs to the model must have changed substantially. As this is the demographic chapter, the focus here will be upon changes to the demographic inputs, but changes in labour force participation relative to the IGR1 projections are also important and are considered first. Then, the chapter examines changes in the assumptions across the five IGRs in relation to the three demographic components: fertility, mortality and international migration. The chapter shows that variations in these assumptions across the five IGRs have been substantial. This is partly because the results of previous IGRs, especially IGR1, led to changes in policy, especially policy relating to the level of international migration.

Changes in labour force participation rates

The projections of labour force participation rates that were used in IGR1 and the 2007 IGR (IGR2) were well below the levels that eventuated, especially at older ages. Dowrick and McDonald (2002) were critical of the pessimistic assumptions of future labour force participation rates that were made in IGR1. However, as late as 2005, the Productivity Commission was still projecting somewhat pessimistic labour force participation rates at older ages (McDonald 2012). As a striking example, IGR1 projected that the labour force participation rate for women aged 60–64 in 2021 would be 26 per cent and the Productivity Commission (2005) projected a rate of just under 40 per cent, both well below the level of 55 per cent that eventuated. These higher older-age labour force participation rates had a large impact on the fiscal position of the government (Temple et al. 2017).

Increased labour force participation at older ages is one of the major policy strategies to mitigate population ageing. From July 1995, the age for pension eligibility for women was increased by six months every two years from age 60 until it reached age 65, the level that had applied to men from 1909. An analysis by Ryan and Whelan (2013) concluded that the increase in the pension age for women from 60 to 65 increased the likelihood that a woman was working at age 62 by a significant 15 percentage points. The fact that this policy was in place from 1995 makes it even more surprising that IGR1 and IGR2 had relatively pessimistic assumptions about labour force participation for women aged 60–64 years.

Then, in 2009, the Labor government introduced measures to increase the pension age to 67 for both men and women through gradual increases during the period July 2017 to July 2023. Next, a proposal was made in the 2014–15 budget to continue to increase the pension age by six months every two years from 1 July 2025 until it reached 70 years, but this change was abandoned by the then coalition government in 2018. Changes were also made to superannuation to encourage longer labour force participation. This included the right to draw an income stream from superannuation while continuing to work—an incentive for part-time employment—as well as superannuation being tax free if accessed after age 60, no tax on lump sums and no tax on superannuation pensions. However, acting as an incentive to retire, the age pension in 1997 was fixed at 25 per cent of male average ordinary time weekly earnings. This was considered a level at which most people could live a comfortable life if they owned their own house (Swoboda 2014).

Despite all these changes, the rapid increases in labour force participation that applied during the first decade of the twenty-first century slowed considerably in the second decade (Chomik and Khan 2021). Analysing Australian Bureau of Statistics (ABS) Labour Force Survey data, McDonald and Moyle (2020) have shown that the historic increases in labour force participation at older ages were driven by favourable economic conditions, which saw people both re-enter work in mid-life (under age 55) and, in the following decades, delay their retirement with high retention rates. Entry to the labour force at ages 55 and over was very uncommon. This was particularly the case for women. Thus, policies for older people had little to no impact on labour force entry but may have had strong effects on labour force retention.

The methodology for the age- and sex-specific labour force projections used in IGR5 is based sensibly on an age and cohort econometric model (Gustaffson 2021). The results show only modest increases in labour force participation at older ages across the 40 years from 2020 to 2060, suggesting that the current policy regime has run its course in stimulating higher older-age participation.

Changes in the demographic assumptions, IGR1 to IGR5

Policy change

The most striking of the changes in the IGR assumptions across time are in the demography of the model. IGR1 projected that Australia's population would rise to 25.3 million by 2042. In fact, it took only 17 years, not 40 years, for Australia's population to reach 25.3 million. From IGR1 to IGR4, each successive IGR projected increasingly higher population numbers in the future (Figure 4.1). Assumed lower fertility and the short-term effects of COVID-19 on immigration produced a somewhat lower projection in IGR5. Changes in the trajectory of the demographic components in the IGR model were to a large extent the result of policy changes. Indeed, it could be said that the results of IGR1 elevated population policy in Australia to a level reminiscent of the period of postwar reconstruction following the Second World War.

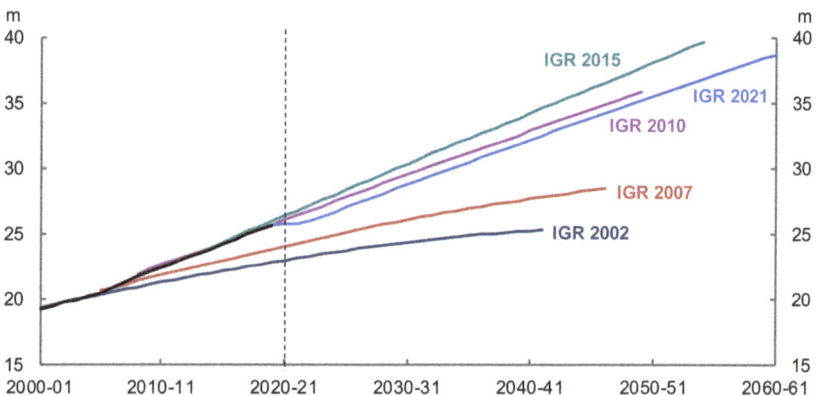

Figure 4.1: Population projections across IGRs.
Source: Reproduced from Commonwealth of Australia (2021:15).

IGR1 showed a large fiscal deficit by 2042 of 5 per cent of GDP, a result primarily of population ageing. The report suggested that this deficit could be addressed through control over expenditure, particularly the growth of government expenditure on health but also through increases in labour force participation and increased labour productivity. IGR1 did not recommend a population response. Even a careful reader of the first three IGRs would not draw the conclusion that the population P was important (McDonald 2012).

Despite this, starting slowly from 2000 but rapidly from 2004 following IGR1, the Howard government moved to moderate population ageing using demographic approaches. It substantially increased its migration program and introduced a family policy package aimed, at least partially, at increasing the birth rate. Enlargement of the migration program represented a major turning point in Howard's policy approach. Abul Rizvi (2020), who was the leading migration policy adviser in the Department of Immigration at that time, concluded that there were three main factors that led to the change in approach of the Howard government to immigration policy:

- Research highlighting the improved labour market performance of skill stream migrants, which was incorporated into the Liberal Party's 2001 election policy platform.
- Decline in fertility through the 1990s and the impact of this on population ageing that was highlighted in a number of articles and reports, including by Professor Peter McDonald and Dr Rebecca Kippen (1999, commissioned by the Department of Immigration), Withers (1999), and the Productivity Commission (1998), and picked up in then treasurer Peter Costello's first Intergenerational Report (2002).
- Ongoing complaints from industry and employer bodies about increasing skill shortages, including in regional Australia, and reinforced through criticism by the Australian Labor Party (Rizvi 2020:Chapter 5).

In 2004, the Howard government also introduced a comprehensive family policy package, which included a universal maternity allowance (later termed the Baby Bonus), a childcare tax rebate and substantial increases in the per child family allowance (Family Tax Benefit Part 1). This package had the dual policy objectives of supporting families with children while at the same time stimulating the birth rate (McDonald 2009).

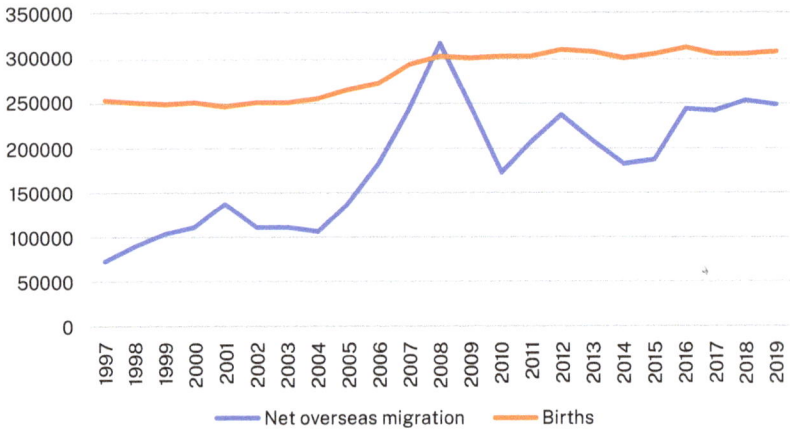

Figure 4.2: Births and net overseas migration (numbers), 1997–2019, Australia.

Source: Author, using published ABS data.

Subsequent to 2004, net overseas migration (NOM) more than doubled from 100,000 per annum to 220,000 per annum (2005–19 average) and the number of births increased from around 250,000 per annum to 300,000 per annum (Figure 4.2). Each successive IGR to IGR4 projected a larger and relatively younger population than the previous IGR and these demographic shifts were associated with a continual fall in the fiscal deficit as a proportion of GDP 40 years later (McDonald 2012, 2016). By IGR4, a fiscal surplus was projected 40 years out due to many factors, but primarily to the demographic mitigation of population ageing (the projection was based on the then government's proposed policies, not existing legislated policy).

IGR fertility assumptions

The number of births occurring in any one year is determined primarily by the number of women in the childbearing ages and the rate of birth that they experience. The appropriate rate of birth is the total fertility rate (TFR). TFR is the sum of the birth rates at each age in a given year. It is equivalent to the average number of births a woman would have if she were to experience these annual birth rates at every age across her lifetime. While it is a hypothetical measure in respect of the lifetimes of any real group of women, on an annual basis it does represent what might be called the force of fertility in that year.

The TFR, however, has one substantial problem. It is heavily affected by changes in the timing of births, especially changes in the timing of the first birth (McDonald and Kippen 2011). When births are delayed to some future point in time, the TFR falls in the short term but may rise in subsequent years when the delayed births take place.[1] This is exactly what happened in the years before and after IGR1. In the decade leading up to IGR1, first births were delayed year after year so that the TFR showed a continuous declining trend. The statistical modelling done by Treasury for IGR1 projected this decline to continue uniformly across the 40 years of the projection from 1.75 births per woman in 2002 to 1.6 births per woman in 2042 (see Figure 4.3). With the assistance of an economic boom in the first decade of the new century and the Howard government support package in 2004, those who had delayed their births were encouraged to have them. Instead of continuing to fall, the TFR rose to a 35-year high of 2.0 births per woman in 2007–08 (Figure 4.4).

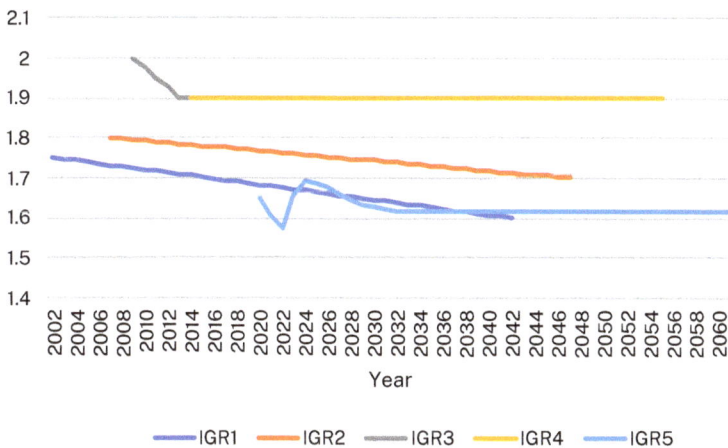

Figure 4.3: Total fertility rate assumptions in successive IGRs.
Source: Author, using information published in the five IGRs.

For IGR2 in 2007, consistent with the most recently observed value, Treasury moved the initial rate up to 1.8 but then assumed the continuous decline that had been assumed for IGR1. Just three years later in 2010, the initial fertility rate in IGR3 was taken as 2.0, again consistent with the most

---

1   Not all delayed births take place and so the delay of first births to older ages that has continued year after year in Australia since the mid-1970s has led to increasingly lower completed family sizes when women reach the end of their reproductive years (McDonald 2020).

recently observed value, but the rate was pushed down rapidly to a long-run constant level of 1.9. In 2015, IGR4 maintained the long-run assumption of 1.9 (Figure 4.3). However, instead of remaining constant at the high level of 1.9, the Australian TFR then fell rapidly, reaching 1.61 by 2019–20. This was not simply an Australian trend, as rapid declines between 2013 and 2019 were observed in all the English-speaking countries (Figure 4.5) and in most of the Nordic countries. Accordingly, IGR5 with its fertility assumption based on McDonald (2020), after some initial fluctuations related to COVID-19, projected a long run TFR of 1.62, ironically very similar to the level projected in IGR1.

In projecting the level of TFR in 40 years' time, we are projecting the fertility of women who are not yet born themselves, a very hypothetical exercise. It is also important to remember that the annual number of births is affected not just by the fertility rate; it is also affected by the number of women in the childbearing ages. This number is in turn affected by the level of NOM. Thus, in IGR5, while the TFR remains constant in the long run, the number of births rises year upon year to 2060. For perspective, the projected number of births in 2060 is 81 per cent higher using the IGR5 migration assumption compared with a projection assuming net zero migration between 2020 and 2060. This means that 45 per cent of all births in 2060 will be due to people who were not living in Australia in 2020.

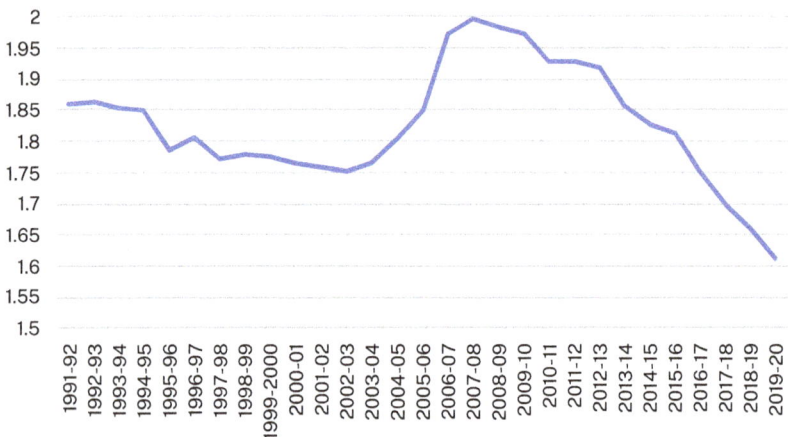

Figure 4.4: The TFR, Australia, 1991–92 to 2019–20.
Source: McDonald (2020) and ABS (2022a).

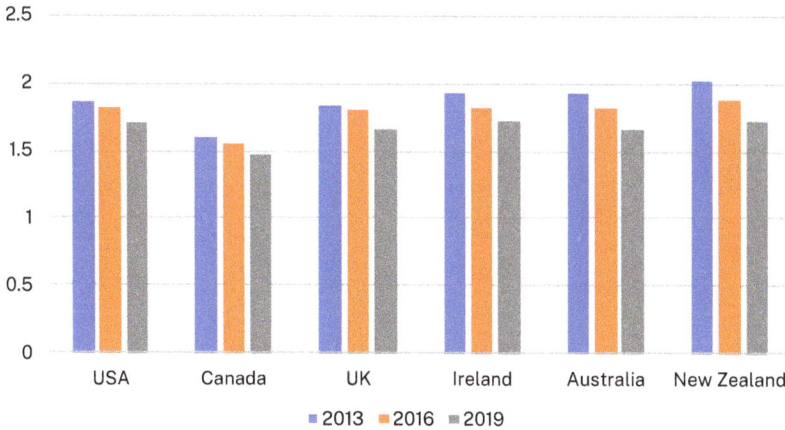

Figure 4.5: TFRs, English-speaking countries, 2013, 2016 and 2019.
Source: Author derived from reports of the statistical agencies of each country.

IGR mortality assumptions

Assumptions about future mortality rates in IGR5 are based on life tables produced by the ABS for 2017–19, to which the Australian Government Actuary's mortality improvement factors were applied.

Generally, it is considered that projections of future mortality are much more reliable than projections of future fertility. This is because almost all people who will die in the next 40 years are alive today and most are aged 40 and over at the commencement of the projection. Despite this, the IGR assumptions of future expectations of life at birth are quite variable across the IGRs, especially for men. For women, the assumed future expectations of life are quite similar for IGR2, IGR3 and IGR4. The IGR1 and IGR5 projections are also very similar but at a much lower level that the other three IGRs. Variations in male expectations of life were even greater (Figure 4.6).

These differences between the IGRs are important from a fiscal perspective because the highest government expenditures apply to persons aged 75 and over, now the ages at which most people die. In the 2018–20 life table for Australia (ABS 2022b), only 15 per cent of women die before their 75th birthday. Between 1971 and 2019, over five years of life on average was added to the expectation of life at age 75 for both men and women. This means an additional five years of government expenditure applying to an ever-growing older population. Furthermore, the Australian National

Transfer Accounts show that the average per person public expenditure on health for persons aged 75 years and over increased in real terms by a factor of six between 1981 and 2010 (Rice et al. 2016). The relatively low expectations of life projected in IGR5 imply lower levels of public expenditure than would be the case with the higher levels projected in IGR2, IGR3 and IGR4.

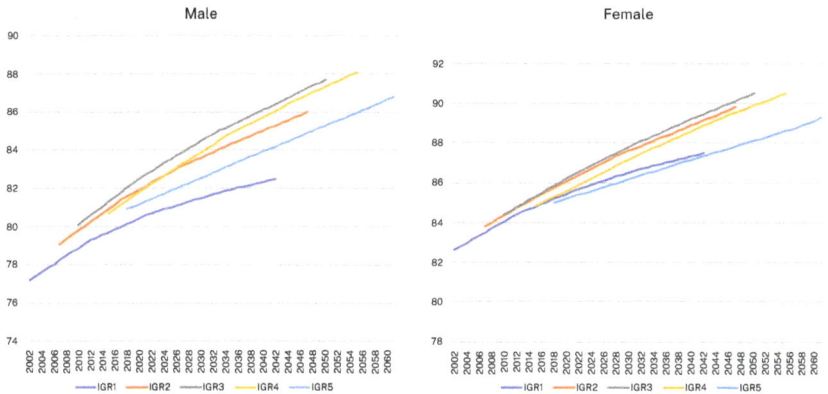

Figure 4.6: Expectation of life at birth assumptions in successive IGRs, males and females.

Source: Author, using information published in the five IGRs.

IGR migration assumptions

As described above, the Australian government has used overseas migration as a policy approach to mitigate population ageing since the early 2000s. As shown in Figure 4.7, each successive IGR has assumed a higher future level of NOM, rising from 90,000 in IGR1 to 235,000 in IGR5. The largest jump in assumed NOM occurs between IGR2 (2007) and IGR3 (2010), from 110,000 to 180,000. This increase, made initially by the Gillard government, was based upon reports made for the Department of Immigration in 2008 and 2010 (McDonald and Temple 2008, 2010). These reports concluded that the impact of immigration on GDP per capita (through mitigation of population ageing) was optimised if NOM was between 160,000 and 220,000. Since 2011, through several changes of government, the level of the government migration program has been set within this range and it is set to remain in this range until 2060 in the out years of IGR5.

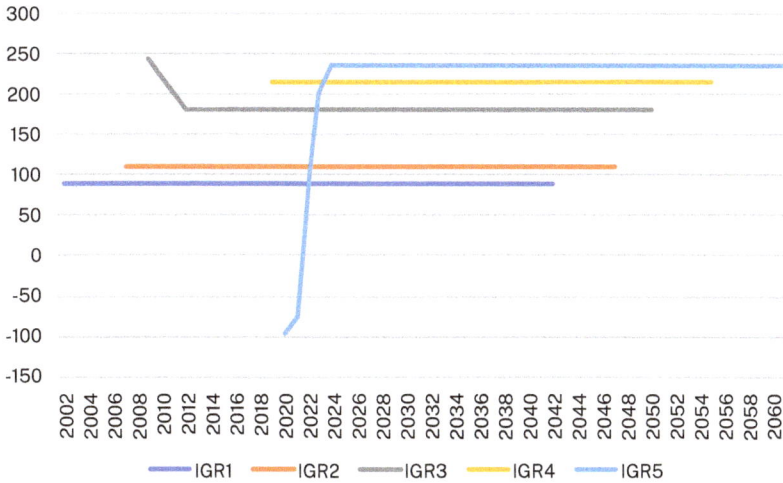

Figure 4.7: Net overseas migration assumptions in successive IGRs ('000s).
Source: Author, using information published in the five IGRs.

The annual migration program sets the indicative planning targets for grants of permanent residence in the skilled and family streams. In addition to these two streams, permanent residence grants are also made through the humanitarian stream (usually set around 13,500 per annum, but higher during periods of special need).

Population projections make assumptions about NOM, which is not the same as the number of grants of permanent residence that the government makes each year.[2] If the measured impact of migration on GDP per capita is based on the impact of NOM, how can this be reconciled with the setting of the annual permanent migration intake? The answer is that, although NOM fluctuates from year to year because of surges in temporary arrivals or departures, in the longer term, temporary migrants can only remain in Australia if they are granted permanent residence through the Permanent Migration Program. As the net impact of the combined movements of

2   NOM derives from the definition of the estimated residential population. A person is deemed to be a resident of Australia (as distinct from a visitor) if the person spends 12 months out of any given 16-month period in Australia. A NOM arrival is the arrival in Australia of a non-resident person who spends 12 out of the next 16 months living in Australia, while a NOM departure is the departure of a resident who spends 12 out of the next 16 months out of Australia. NOM is the excess of NOM arrivals over NOM departures. NOM is measured using passport movements. When a person leaves or enters Australia, the ABS applies a probability model that predicts whether the person will be a NOM departure or a NOM arrival after 16 months have elapsed. Sixteen months after the departure or arrival, ABS provides revised and final estimates of NOM.

Australian and New Zealand citizens is relatively small (less than 5 per cent of NOM from 2004–05 to 2015–16), in the long run, NOM and the migration planning levels (including the humanitarian stream) are very similar (McDonald 2018 and Figure 4.8). Nevertheless, temporary migration serves the very important purpose of providing a ready pool from which a majority of new permanent residents are selected.

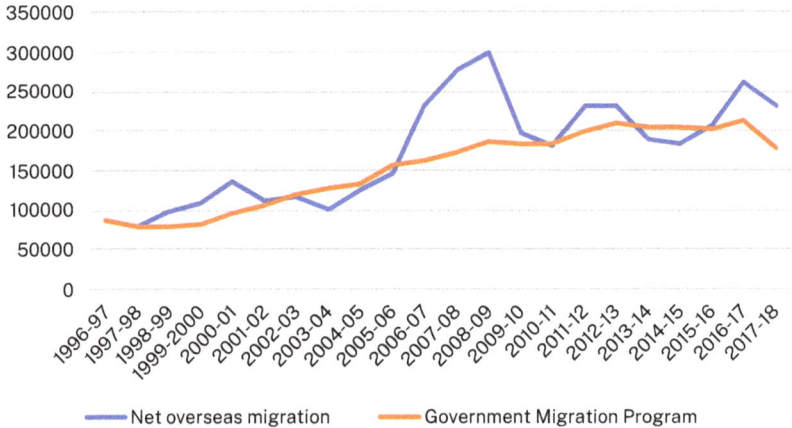

Figure 4.8: Annual net overseas migration (NOM) compared with the annual grants of permanent residence through the Permanent Migration Program, including the humanitarian stream, Australia, 1983–84 to 2016–17.

Source. Author, using ABS and Department of Home Affairs data.

For IGR5, Treasury provided the following explanation of its long-term NOM assumption as follows:

> The NOM assumption of 235,000 people per year over the long run reflects:
>
> **A.** the Permanent Migration Program (190,000 people per year from 2023–24)
>
> **B.** the Humanitarian Program (13,750 people per year)
>
> **C.** the flows of temporary migrants who reside in Australia for several years but do not transition to permanent residency (assumed to be a net inflow of 66,250 people per year, based on an historical average of the net inward flow of such migrants prior to the onset of the COVID-19 pandemic)

D. the flows of Australian citizens (assumed to be a net outflow of around 15,000 people per year, based on an historical average)

E. the number of permanent residents who subsequently emigrate (assumed to be a net outflow of around 20,000 people per year, based on an historical average) (adapted from Commonwealth of Australia 2021:157).

This explanation is clearly inconsistent with the argument made above that, in the long term, NOM will be equal to the sum of the Permanent Migration Program and the Humanitarian Program, that is A plus B, or 213,750 not 235,000. The Treasury explanation has two problems. First, it implies that the entire number of people granted permanent residence in a year (213,750 in the IGR5 assumption) are new arrivals to Australia. In fact, the majority of new permanent residence grants are made to persons already living in Australia on a temporary visa. The second problem is that the explanation implies that there will be an accumulation of 66,250 temporary residents every year for 40 years; that is, a total of 2.5 million temporary residents in 2060, most of whom would have lived in Australia for a very long time. If it is argued that some of these temporary residents would have become permanent residents, the permanent numbers in the Treasury explanation would have to be reduced accordingly.

For the past 75 years, Australian immigration policy has been based on permanent residence, with total opposition to people living in Australia on a temporary visa on a long-term basis. While this situation has applied to New Zealand citizens living in Australia, they have an agreed right to remain in Australia permanently, although they may not have formal permanent residence. However, a new trend has emerged in recent years that could lead to a long-term temporary population rather like that of the United States. A very large number of people, approaching 100,000, are in Australia at present having entered on a tourist or some other short-term visa and then claimed political asylum. Australia is required to provide temporary asylum to these people with full work rights until their case has been heard in the court. Because their number is so large, it takes a number of years before their cases are heard. For those for whom the case has been heard, the success rate is very low, well under 10 per cent. And those that have been unsuccessful in their legal argument have not been deported. Effectively, they are bogus asylum seekers for whom the aim, either their own or that of the organisers of the scam, is to work in Australia for as long as possible. Like workers in other countries in similar circumstances, they are highly vulnerable to exploitation.

Sensitivity analysis

IGR5 provides very limited sensitivity analysis. However, as far as production is concerned, the impact of variations of NOM and labour force participation upon GDP per capita are easily modelled using the method described in Appendix 4.1. Figure 4.9 shows the impact on GDP per capita in 2060 of varying levels of NOM relative to NOM equal to zero and of the further impact of applying the 2019 labour force participation rates of New Zealand replacing the rates projected for Australia in 2060. All other inputs are the same as those used in IGR5.

Compared with an assumption of zero NOM, GDP per capita in 2026 increases along the blue line in Figure 4.9 as NOM increases. The IGR5 assumption of NOM equal to 235,000 per annum would increase GDP per capita in 2060 by 9.1 per cent relative to a NOM of zero. NOM of 100,000 per annum would increase GDP per capita in 2060 by 4.8 per cent relative to NOM of zero. The blue curve indicates that there are diminishing returns to scale as the level of NOM is increased.

The orange line in Figure 4.9 mirrors the blue line but applies the labour force participation rates of New Zealand in 2019 in place of the IGR5 projected Australian rates of participation for 2060. New Zealand has near to the highest age-specific labour force participation rates of any OECD country.

Comparing the blue and orange curves, it can be concluded that the effect on GDP per capita in 2060 of an increase in participation to that of New Zealand (5.5 per cent with zero migration) would be equivalent to the effect of 125,000 NOM. Nevertheless, if Australia's labour force participation in 2060 was the same as that of New Zealand, increasing levels of NOM would further increase GDP per capita. With NOM equal to the IGR5 assumption and New Zealand labour force participation rates, GDP per capita in 2060 would be 15 per cent higher than it would be with zero migration and the projected 2060 Australian labour force participation rates.

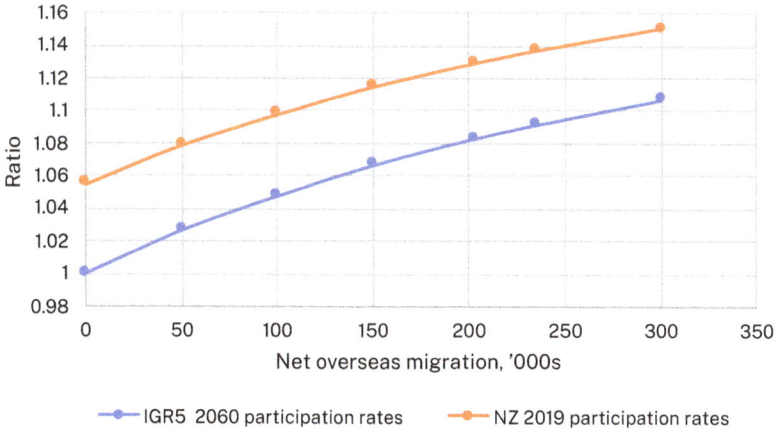

Figure 4.9: Sensitivity analysis of the impact of variations in migration and labour force participation on GDP per capita in 2060.

Blue: Ratio of GDP per capita in 2060 with varying levels of NOM to GDP per capita in 2060, compared with zero net migration.

Orange: Increase to GDP ratio in the blue curve if labour force participation rates for New Zealand in 2019 replace the Australian IGR 2060 projected rates.

Source: Author's calculations.

Concluding remarks

IGR5 includes a useful summary comparative table of the demographic assumptions that were made in the five IGRs to date, here reproduced as Table 4.1.

Table 4.1: Summary of IGR demographic assumptions.

Intergenerational report	Total fertility rate	Net overseas migration	Period life expectancy at birth in 2050 (years)		Population June 2050
	Babies per woman	People ('000)	Males	Females	People ('000,000)
2021	1.6	235	85.7	88.4	35.3
2015	1.9	215	87.5	90.1	37.8
2010	1.9	180	87.7	90.5	35.9
2007	1.7	110	87.6	90.2	28.5
2002	1.6	90	83.2	88.2	25.7

Source: Reproduced from Commonwealth of Australia (2021:158).

The first four IGRs projected the TFR on the basis of the most recent trends in that measure prior to the formulation of the report, meaning that they were heavily influenced by recent changes in the timing of births. This explains the fluctuations across the reports. IGR5 instead projects the cumulated cohort fertility by age of each successive birth cohort of women and then translates this back into annual fertility rates by age and, hence, the total fertility rate. This is a better approach, but it is only reliable for a decade or so into the future. Beyond that, any projection of fertility is highly speculative.

Trends in mortality are much more regular than fertility trends, and so it is surprising that the variations in projected expectations of life at birth are so large across IGRs. The IGR projections of mortality have been based on relatively simple statistical trend models. For future IGRs, it may be wise to model age-specific mortality rates at ages 75 and over, using variables such as education, health status, behaviours such as smoking, alcohol consumption, exercise and weight, and trends in causes of death.

Future levels of NOM are a matter of government policy. For this reason, future levels may not reflect the past. IGR5, in its explanation of the assumed long-term level of NOM, provided an indication of thinking about future policy. In particular, the level of the Permanent Migration Program, which had been lowered to 160,000 in 2019, was returned to its previous, longer-term level of 190,000. While the justification of the assumption of 235,000 for NOM in IGR5 was flawed, there are definite indications that, prior to its defeat, the Morrison coalition government was planning NOM in excess of 200,000 per annum, and the new Labor government has not changed this policy direction. Nevertheless, there is potential fluidity in migration policy. The two most recent premiers of New South Wales have advocated successively for a halving of migration and a doubling of migration; Julia Gillard in 2010 said that she was not in favour of a 'big Australia', but in her first budget as prime minister, the level of the Permanent Migration Program was increased.

In December 2018, the Council of Australian Governments (COAG) assigned responsibility for population policy (primarily, immigration policy) to a committee consisting of the treasurers of the nine Australian governments. This places an economic emphasis on migration policy, and this probably explains why the Treasury models OLGA and FIONA were used in IGR5 to demonstrate the economic effects of migration.[3] To support the new approach to population policy, in 2019, a Centre for Population was established in the Department of the Treasury in Canberra. The function of the centre is to assess, monitor and project changes to the size and distribution of Australia's population. The centre is the body that now has prime responsibility for the demographic assumptions used in the IGR and in all other Treasury modelling. Over time, this initiative should lead to a higher level of demographic expertise being applied to Treasury population projections, especially since the centre also consults broadly with academic demographers.

IGR1 generated considerable excitement and interest from the media because it was a novel approach. IGR5 did not have the same level of interest from the media and, one suspects, from Treasury itself. Perhaps a new approach is required. Given the uncertainty of projections as demonstrated by the variability across the IGRs and given the relatively arbitrary assumption of the future level of labour productivity, it may be preferable for the IGR to show the economic and fiscal implications of a much wider range of variation in the assumptions about future demography and labour force participation. This would better support consideration of alternative pathways.

References

ABS (Australian Bureau of Statistics) 2022a, *National, state and territory population*, Canberra, available at: www.abs.gov.au/statistics/people/population/national-state-and-territory-population/jun-2022 (accessed 20 February 2023).

ABS 2022b, *Life tables*, Canberra, available at: www.abs.gov.au/statistics/people/population/life-tables/2019-2021 (accessed 20 February 2023).

Chomik, R and Khan, F 2021, *Tapping into Australia's ageing workforce: Insights from recent research*, CEPAR Research Brief, available at: cepar.edu.au/sites/default/files/cepar-research-brief-ageing-workforce-australia.pdf (accessed 20 February 2023).

Commonwealth of Australia 2021, *2021 intergenerational report: Australia over the next 40 years*, Commonwealth of Australia, Canberra.

---

3   OLGA is the Overlapping Generations Model of the Australian economy, while FIONA is the Fiscal Impact of New Australians model.

Dowrick, S and McDonald, P 2002, *Comments on intergenerational report, 2002–03*, Demography Program, The Australian National University, Canberra.

Gustafsson, L 2021, *Australian labour force participation: Historical trends and future prospects*, Treasury working paper 2021–02, Department of the Treasury, Canberra, available at: treasury.gov.au/publication/p2021-164860 (accessed 20 February 2023).

McDonald, P 2009, 'Social policy principles applied to reform of gender egalitarianism in parenthood and employment', in J Gornick and M Meyers, *Gender equality: Transforming family divisions of labor (the Real Utopias Project)*, Verso Books, New York.

McDonald, P 2012, 'The population dimension in the intergenerational reports', *The Australian Economic Review* 45(3):335–43, doi.org/10.1111/j.1467-8462.2012.00695.x.

McDonald, P 2016, 'Ageing in Australia: Population changes and responses', in H Kendig, P McDonald and J Piggott (eds), *Population ageing and Australia's future*, ANU Press, Canberra, doi.org/10.22459/PAAF.11.2016.04.

McDonald, P 2018, 'Australia should continue its current comprehensive population policy—at least for the next decade', *Australian Population Studies* 2(2):3–11, available at: www.australianpopulationstudies.org/index.php/aps/article/view/35/18 (accessed 20 February 2023).

McDonald, P 2020, *A projection of Australia's future fertility rates*, Centre for Population Research Paper, Commonwealth of Australia, Canberra, available at: population.gov.au/research/research-fertility (accessed 16 February 2023).

McDonald, P and Kippen, R 1999, *Population futures for Australia: The policy alternatives*, Parliament of Australia, research paper 5, 12 October, available at: researchmgt.monash.edu/ws/portalfiles/portal/9389412/1999_McDonald_Kippen_parliamentarylibrary.pdf (accessed 20 February 2023).

McDonald, P and Kippen, R 2011, *Forecasting births*, ABS Catalogue Number 2051.0, Australian Bureau of Statistics, Canberra, available at: www.abs.gov.au/ausstats/abs@.nsf/featurearticlesbyCatalogue/E13B06B46B86F486CA2578D30013C44A?OpenDocument (accessed 20 February 2023).

McDonald, P and Moyle, H 2020, 'The cessation of rising employment rates at older ages in Australia, 2000–2019', *Australian Population Studies* 4(1):20–36, doi.org/10.37970/aps.v4i1.61.

McDonald, P and Temple, J 2008, *Demographic and labour supply futures for Australia*, Department of Immigration, available at: www.researchgate.net/publication/254945965_Demographic_and_Labour_Supply_Futures_for_Australia (accessed 20 February 2023).

McDonald, P and Temple, J 2010, *Immigration, labour supply and per capita gross domestic product: Australia 2010–2050*, available at: www.homeaffairs.gov.au/research-and-stats/files/labour-supply-gdp-2010-2050.pdf (accessed 16 February 2023).

Productivity Commission 2005, *Economic implications of an ageing Australia*, Productivity Commission, Canberra, doi.org/10.2139/ssrn.738063.

Rice, J, Temple, J and McDonald, P 2016, *A time series of Australian national transfer accounts: Detailed results of 1981–82, 1988–89, 1993–94, 1998–99, 2003–04 and 2009–10*, ARC Centre of Excellence in Population Ageing Research (CEPAR).

Rizvi, A 2020, *Using immigration as a tool of economic policy—The transformation of Australia's demography*, PhD thesis, University of Melbourne.

Ryan, C and Whelan, S 2013, *Age pension eligibility and female labour force participation*, School of Economics, University of Sydney.

Swoboda, K 2014, *Major superannuation and retirement income changes in Australia: A chronology*, Parliament of Australia, available at: www.aph.gov.au/About_Parliament/Parliamentary_Departments/Parliamentary_Library/pubs/rp/rp1314/SuperChron (accessed 20 February 2023).

Temple, J, Rice, J and McDonald, P 2017, 'Mature age labour force participation and the life cycle deficit in Australia: 1981–82 to 2009–10', *Journal of the Economics of Ageing* 10(2017):21–33, doi.org/10.1016/j.jeoa.2017.08.001.

Withers, G 1999, *A younger Australia*, ANU Public Policy Discussion Paper no. 63, March 1999, available at: openresearch-repository.anu.edu.au/bitstream/1885/41930/1/dp_63.html (accessed 20 February 2023).

Appendix 4.1. Decomposition of variations in GDP per capita

Suppose there are two 3P projections to time t from time 0, Projection A and Projection B.

If we assume that both projections have experienced the same rate of growth of labour productivity between 0 and t, and the two projections have the same patterns of unemployment and hours of work between 0 and t,

then:

Per Capita GDP(B)$_t$/Per Capita GDP (A)$_t$ = P$_t$(A)/ P$_t$(B)*L$_t$(B)/ L$_t$(A)

where:

P$_t$(A) = Total population of projection A at time t

P$_t$(B) = Total population of projection B at time t

L$_t$(A) = Total labour force at time t

L$_t$(B) = Total labour force at time t

Decomposing L into age- and sex-specific components:

L = $\sum_i$ P$_i$(M)*LFPR$_i$(M)+P$_i$(F)*LFPR$_i$(F)

where:

P$_i$(M) and P$_i$(F) are the populations of males and females at age I, and

LFPR$_i$(M) and LFPR$_i$(F) are the male and female labour force participation rates at age i.

Rewriting the first equation:

Per Capita GDP(B)$_t$/Per Capita GDP (A)$_t$ = $\sum_i$ p$_i$(M, A).LFPR$_i$(M, A)+p$_i$(F, A).LFPR$_i$(F, A)/ $\sum_i$ p$_i$(M, B).LFPR$_i$(M, B)+p$_i$(F, B).LFPR$_i$(F, B)

Where p$_i$(M, A) is the proportion that males aged i represent of the total population in Projection A

This decomposition enables us to see the impact of variations in age structure of the population and changes in age- and sex-specific labour force participation rates on GDP per capita.

5

Retirement Incomes: Increasing Inequity, Not Costs, across Generations Is the Intergenerational Problem

Andrew Podger, Robert Breunig and John Piggott[1]

Key points

- The 2021 Intergenerational Report (IGR), like its predecessors, tries to find reasons for concern about rising costs of retirement incomes as the population ages, but the evidence is striking about how well Australia has done to contain those costs even while greatly improving the incomes retirees will receive.

- Indeed, Australia's affluence-tested flat-rate pension, combined with pre-funded income replacement, generates projected retirement transfer outlays that decline over time as a percentage of GDP.

- There is little evidence that the IGRs have contributed much to improvements to retirement income policies: most of the improvements in both sustainability and effectiveness preceded the first IGR in 2002.

- Successive IGRs have switched the 40-year projections from a substantial increase in pension costs as a percentage of GDP to a substantial reduction.

---

1   The authors acknowledge the research assistance provided by Sophie Yan.

- The 2021 IGR suggests this will be offset by increasing superannuation tax expenditures, an assessment the authors consider to be highly deceptive.
- By focusing only on fiscal costs, the report fails to explore broader intergenerational policy issues including the likelihood of the deep inequality that exists within generations growing over time.
- To avoid this outcome, further reforms to the retirement income system are needed particularly to ensure superannuation savings are directed efficiently and effectively to deliver secure retirement incomes and to provide more adequate support to those with limited superannuation who do not own their own homes. Other possible measures include reviewing aged-care funding, exploring inheritance taxes and exploring land taxes.

Introduction

Increasing life expectancy and declining fertility throughout the developed world has generated widespread concern about the costs of retirement income provision, which in many countries is generated by a pay-as-you-go social security system. Australia is a fortunate exception as its affluence-tested flat-rate pension, combined with pre-funded income replacement, generates projected retirement transfer outlays that decline over time as a percentage of GDP.

In this chapter, we begin by documenting the history of retirement income policy in Australia, particularly in the light of an ageing population, and then discuss the projections reported in successive intergenerational reports (IGRs). We then highlight how projections of the costs of pensions have changed dramatically over the IGRs since 2002 from a substantial increase (as a percentage of GDP) to a substantial reduction.

We then review the 2021 IGR's attempts to downplay this change by projecting an increase in superannuation tax expenditures, suggesting that these more than offset the projected reduction in pension costs. We find this assessment highly deceptive, greatly exaggerating the level of tax expenditures and their projected growth and providing a misleading picture of their distributional impact.

The chapter then examines some intergenerational policy issues not explored by the 2021 IGR, which focuses only on fiscal costs. The fiscal perspective can help to draw attention to potential intergenerational inequality, but a broader review would identify the deeper and more pernicious inequality that exists within generations now and that is likely to grow over time.

The chapter ends with a discussion of a range of tax and transfer measures that would address this more serious policy concern, highlighting those that may be more politically feasible in the short and medium term. The latter include strengthening the efficiency and effectiveness of superannuation in delivering secure incomes in the retirement phase, addressing the complex interaction between superannuation and the pension means test and providing more adequate support for those with limited superannuation who do not own their own homes.

Retirement income policy and the ageing population: A brief history

While the Organisation for Economic Cooperation and Development (OECD) expressed concerns about the financing of the welfare state following the stagflation problems of the 1970s, it did not at that time draw attention to future demographic pressures (OECD 1981; Podger 1981). That only came later as Japan's rapid ageing became apparent and Europe's falling fertility rates suggested many other OECD countries were likely to follow suit. The United Nations held its first 'World Assembly on Aging' in 1982, mentioning the need to consider trends in population growth, age distribution and demographic structure, but not highlighting the budgetary pressures from ageing populations (United Nations 1982).

Despite Australia's relatively young age profile, questions began to be raised in Australia in the early 1980s that future dependency ratios might be adversely affected not only by the ageing 'baby boomer' generation but also by falling fertility rates and increasing life expectancy. Until then, Australian Bureau of Statistics projections had not factored in possible reductions in mortality rates among the aged (i.e. that those over 65 might live longer, as well as more people reaching age 65). This likelihood was raised by the Social Welfare Policy Secretariat (Myers 1980; Dixon and Foster 1980, 1982), which highlighted projected dependency ratios and the associated challenges for funding age pensions. Others questioned the seriousness of the concerns raised citing Australia's modest age pension arrangements (flat-rate and means-tested), the reduced financial costs of young dependants and the likelihood of increased capacity to pay with economic growth over the ensuing 30 years or more (e.g. Newton 1980). Nonetheless, the narrative of a major demographic challenge took hold in the 1980s (e.g. EPAC 1988), pursued also by the OECD, who worried in particular about the costs of the unfunded defined benefit superannuation schemes that most member countries operated (e.g. Hagemann and Nicoletti 1989; OECD 1998).

While the concerns in Australia were tempered by its more modest pension system, the ageing population did frame much of the discussion about how more adequate retirement incomes might be provided, preserving retirees' living standards as well as protecting them from poverty. Past attempts to introduce a social insurance-based national superannuation scheme such as that proposed by Hancock (1976) would no longer be advocated by either side of politics, but alternative ways developed that might not impose undue costs on future generations. Initially, these focused on reforms to occupational superannuation (promoting preservation, vesting and portability and constraining tax concessions), then steps were taken to widen superannuation coverage by defined contributions that employers were mandated to make in exchange for lower wage increases (in the 1986 National Wage Case). While the accumulating superannuation savings would in most cases supplement age pension entitlements, the additional retirement incomes would not rely upon future taxpayers; indeed, they would reduce future taxpayer support to some extent through the age pension means test.

This new model was set out in the Hawke government's 'Better Incomes: Retirement Income Policy into the Next Century' statement (Howe 1989). The subsequent shift from an industrial relations agreement to mandate the employer contributions to a statutory superannuation guarantee was explained in the Keating government's 'Security in Retirement: Planning for Tomorrow Today' statement (Dawkins 1992). The SG (superannuation guarantee) was then legislated to steadily increase to 9 per cent. It was around this time that Treasury began to model the impact over time of the emerging retirement incomes system (Gallagher and Preston 1993).

The emerging 'pillars' system involved a means-tested, general revenue-financed, flat-rate age pension as Pillar 1, aimed to alleviate poverty; a defined contribution, fully funded superannuation Pillar 2 to help maintain living standards in retirement; and other savings (essentially home ownership) as Pillar 3 providing added security. In 1994, the World Bank effectively endorsed the Australian approach as best practice in its publication, 'Policies to protect the old and promote growth' (World Bank 1994), noting how the second pillar would increase national savings and could fund additional investment while avoiding costs for future generations. The OECD also indicated support for the model emerging in Australia (OECD 1998). Australia had also drawn attention to the capacity of the second pillar to contribute to national savings (Fitzgerald 1993). (For a fuller description of the emerging Australian system compared to those in other countries, and a summary of debates over different 'pillar' arrangements, see Podger et al. 2014.)

In the meantime. the Hawke government had dropped (Commonwealth of Australia 1983) previous bipartisan support for universal age pensions, which had led to universal pensions for those over 70, and reintroduced (Commonwealth of Australia 1984) an assets test to complement the income test.

This action to contain age pension costs was extended in 1995 by the Keating government's decision to phase in an increase in the age pension age for women from 60 to 65 (to be the same as for men) and to phase out eligibility for wife's pension and Class B widows pensions (for 'widows' without dependants).

By the time the *Charter of Budget Honesty Act* was passed in 1998, projected Pillar 1 costs were already being wound back (notwithstanding the Howard government legislating the rate of the pension at 25 per cent of average weekly earnings) and the Pillar 2 contribution rate had increased to 6 per cent, promising significant improvements to most Australians' retirement incomes without burdening future taxpayers. By the time of the first IGR (Commonwealth of Australia 2002), the SG had increased to 9 per cent and the phasing out of pensions for women under 65 was well advanced; no new major measures had been taken to address the claimed costs of an ageing population.

By the time of the second IGR (Commonwealth of Australia 2007), two new measures had been taken, one addressing ageing pressures positively, the second exacerbating remaining pressures. In 2006, the Howard government established the Future Fund, drawing on revenues from the sale of Telstra and budget surpluses, to build a capital base to meet the costs of remaining unfunded public sector defined benefit superannuation schemes

(Costello 2006a). Associated with this was the closure of the largest such schemes to new members, replacing them with defined contribution schemes (the scheme for the military was not closed to new members until 2015, despite a report recommending closure in 2007 (Podger et al. 2007)).

The other measure involved removing remaining taxes on post-retirement benefits and earnings where tax had been paid on contributions (Costello 2006b) and relaxing caps on contributions. The caps were changed six times in the period from 2006 (Bateman 2018), the initial relaxation leading to a huge injection of funds into superannuation, almost certainly driven to avoid tax rather than for genuine retirement income purposes (Chomik and Piggott 2018). The ongoing costs of tax breaks for superannuation were significantly increased and it took another decade to effectively unwind this measure.

It was not until the 2010 IGR that further policy measures were taken to contain future costs, or at least to offset the costs of increasing the maximum rates of age pensions. These measures were not directly influenced by the IGR but by the Harmer Review, which questioned the adequacy of the single rate of pension particularly for those renting privately (Harmer 2009). The Rudd government announced a significant increase in both the single and married rate of pension in the 2010 budget, together with some tightening of the income test and the phased increase in age pension age from 65 to 67 for both men and women (Swan 2009).

The 2015 IGR was the first used directly to support proposals to limit the future costs of retirement incomes. The Abbott government, in its 2014 budget, proposed replacing wage-based indexation of age pensions with CPI indexation and phasing in further increases in the age pension age to 70 (Hockey 2014). The measures, advocated by a Commission of Audit (Shepherd et al. 2014), were not agreed by the parliament, but the 2015 IGR set out spending projections based on two main scenarios— the legislated policies and those the government had proposed. The first projections revealed significant increases in spending on pensions as a per cent of GDP, while the second revealed a slight reduction. The second, of course, involved a significant reduction in the value of the pension as a per cent of average earnings (though the projection assumed a return to wages indexation from 2028–29). In the event, the Abbott government did not pursue the measures, though it did substantially tighten the assets test instead in order to achieve the planned savings in the immediate four-year Forward Estimates (Morrison 2015).

In 2017, the Turnbull government amended the superannuation tax arrangements, effectively winding back the 2005 concessions and drawing on the 2010 Henry Report (O'Dwyer and Morrison 2016). The reforms introduced a progressive tax on contributions and firmly tightened contribution caps and limited the 15 per cent tax on fund earnings to those with accumulated savings below $1.6 million.

This brief history demonstrates that, while the IGRs and the Charter of Budget Honesty may have contributed to a general atmosphere of public concern about the costs of an ageing population, most of the measures taken concerning retirement incomes preceded the IGRs and were aimed at both enhancing retirement incomes and limiting the costs for future generations.

Changing IGR projections

The 40-year projections of pension costs as a percentage of GDP in the IGRs have steadily declined, with a remarkable turnaround overall from the 2002 IGR's finding of an increase from 2.9 per cent to 4.6 per cent to the 2021 IGR's finding of a decrease from 2.7 per cent to 2.1 per cent (Table 5.1).

Table 5.1: IGR 40-year projections of age and service pension costs.

	Starting cost (year) % of GDP	40-year projection % of GDP
2002 IGR	2.9 (2000–01)	4.6 (2041–42)
2007 IGR	2.5 (2006–07)	4.4 (2046–47)
2010 IGR	2.4 (2008–09)	3.9 (2049–50)
2015 IGR — current policy	2.9 (2014–15)	3.6 (2054–55)
2015 IGR — proposed policy	2.9 (2014–15)	2.7 (2054–55)
2021 IGR	2.7 (2020–21)	2.1 (2060–61)

Source: Commonwealth of Australia (2002, 2007, 2010, 2015, 2021).

The shift is related in part to changes in the denominator (GDP) including because of changes in population assumptions (particularly migration), workforce participation assumptions and terms of trade. More significant, however, have been revisions to the numerator because of changes to projected retirement income savings and their impact on pension entitlements via the means test. The key policy changes affecting the projections have been the legislated increase in the SG from 9 per cent to 12 per cent (2008), the increase in pension rates (2010), the phased increase in the age pension age from 65 to 67 (2010) and the tightening of the assets test (2017).

The shift is also demonstrated by the projected changes in the proportion of older Australians eligible for a full, part or no pension. The 2002 IGR did not refer to the proportions in 2001–02 nor those projected in 2041–42, but the main shift expected from increasing superannuation savings was from full-rate to part-rate pensions (the actual proportions of people over 65 receiving full, part or no pension in 2002 were 55 per cent/26 per cent/19 per cent (Chomik et al. 2018)). The 2010 Henry and 2009 Harmer Reports assumed around 80 per cent of those over 65 would continue to be eligible for some pension into the long-term future, albeit most on part-rate pensions. This seems to be the position implied by the 2010 IGR, which projected increased pension costs (albeit lower than previously). By 2015, however, the proportion of age pensioners (not including service, carer and disability pensioners over 65) had already fallen to 70 per cent, 42 per cent receiving the full pension and 28 per cent a part pension; adding in the other pensioners over 65 would raise the total to about 75 per cent, still well below the 81 per cent in 2002. The 2015 IGR projected a further reduction to 67 per cent (under existing policy) but did not mention how many of these would be full- or part-rate pensioners—presumably most would be part-rate. The 2021 IGR projected ratios of 25 per cent/35 per cent/40 per cent by 2060–61 from the existing 2020 ratios of 48 per cent/26 per cent/26 per cent.

These ratio changes reflect, of course, the improved retirement incomes that the majority of Australians can expect as a result of the expanding and maturing Pillar 2 superannuation scheme, which is essentially self-funded.

2021 IGR projections

Superannuation tax expenditures

The 2021 IGR questions this last point—that Pillar 2 is essentially self-funded—and any conclusion that the costs of the retirement income system to future generations of taxpayers will decline, despite the projected fall in age pension costs. Reference had been made in the 2015 IGR to the 'tax expenditures' involved in the tax treatment of superannuation, but it was not until the 2021 IGR that these were projected over the 40-year period. The 2021 IGR claims these 'tax expenditures' will rise from around 2 per cent of GDP to 2.9 per cent and that therefore the total cost of the retirement income system will increase from around 4.5 per cent to 5.0 per cent of GDP. The report of the Retirement Incomes Review similarly refers to an increasing level of tax expenditures (Callaghan 2020).

This assessment is highly deceptive, and contrasts with the more balanced discussion of the concept and level of superannuation 'tax expenditures' in the Treasury's 2017 Tax Expenditures Statement (Commonwealth of Australia 2017). This followed comments in a review of previous Statements by the House of Representatives Standing Committee on Tax and Revenue (2015:45) that the public misuses and misunderstands the estimates and suggesting that 'the warnings in the document are not sufficiently clear to inform enough of its users'. The criticisms were not new; in 1992 when mandatory superannuation was first introduced, Bateman and Piggott (1992:48) wrote that 'in the debate over appropriate tax treatment of superannuation saving, there is perhaps no issue which generates more confusion than that of revenue costs'. In its 2017 document, Treasury highlighted that identifying 'tax expenditures' is not a simple matter: it requires identifying a standard treatment that would or should apply were there no 'concessions' and considering likely behavioural impacts of the 'concessions' (e.g. on working or saving or the form of saving). It also directly cautioned against combining (adding or subtracting) the 'expenditures' from different 'concessions'.

Importantly, the 2017 document provided two sets of estimates of the superannuation 'tax expenditures' against two different possible standards: a Schanz-Haig-Simons comprehensive income tax standard (where contributions and fund earnings would be taxed at the individual's marginal rate of personal income tax, but benefits would be tax free—or TTE) and an expenditure tax standard (where contributions would be taxed but both fund earnings and benefits would be tax free—or TEE). It mentioned but did not provide estimates against an alternative expenditure tax standard (where benefits are fully taxed, but contributions and fund earnings are not—or EET), even though this is the more common approach internationally for taxing superannuation (OECD 2018). The two estimates provided were radically different: in particular, the 'tax expenditures' from exempting fund earnings switched from a positive $20 billion to a negative $10 billion! Almost certainly, using an EET regime as the standard would have revealed a further large negative 'expenditure' because contributions are currently taxed (at 15 per cent) and the negative 'expenditure' involved would be only partly offset by the failure currently to fully tax benefits.

Subsequent Tax Expenditure Statements (with varying titles) in 2018, 2020 and 2023 (Commonwealth of Australia 2018, 2020 and 2023) have not repeated the careful discussion in 2017 nor provided two sets of estimates: the only benchmark used is TTE, which is the one also used in the Callaghan Retirement Income Review Report (Callaghan 2020). Yet not only is TTE not applied to the majority of savings in Australia (including owner-occupied housing), but it has also repeatedly been criticised as inappropriate for any savings, most recently by the Henry Review (Henry 2010), and is certainly not used internationally for superannuation. The key reason why it is inappropriate is that it would greatly distort decisions about when to consume income that is earned, penalising the deferment of consumption when the whole purpose of the retirement income system is to facilitate the spreading of lifetime incomes. When deferment is compulsory, as is the case with the SG, TTE would amount to a hefty penalty against both current and deferred consumption.

Those advocating a more consistent tax treatment of savings (e.g. Varela et al. 2020) do not suggest a TTE regime but at most a TtE regime where the tax on fund earnings would be modest, well below most individuals' marginal tax rate (hence the use of lower case 't' for the tax applying to earnings), indeed somewhat lower than the 15 per cent currently applying to superannuation fund earnings for those in the accumulation phase. Against such a standard, the majority of the 'tax expenditures' identified in the 2021 IGR would disappear. Chomik and Piggott (2018), using a TEE expenditure benchmark, calculated that the total tax expenditures attributable to an average earner are about 6 per cent of the tax expenditures using the TTE standard; for a worker earning twice the average earnings, the figure is still just 11 per cent of the TTE regime figure. Against an EET regime, the tax expenditures would almost certainly disappear altogether. Gallagher (2016) suggests the current complex ttE regime (the lower case 't's referring to the application of lower tax rates to contributions and earnings than most taxpayers' marginal tax rate) is broadly equivalent to an EET standard at most income levels.

Precisely because Australia has a progressive personal income tax system, the Treasury TTE approach suggests the claimed tax expenditures are heavily skewed to those on high incomes. That also is misleading. As discussed further below, current arrangements do raise important equity issues not mentioned in the IGR. But if the claimed inequity of the current tax treatment of superannuation were to be addressed as implied by imposing a TTE regime, the whole of the retirement income system's Pillar 2 could well be destroyed.

Finally, the 2021 IGR ignores the caution in the 2017 Tax Expenditures Statement not to combine the different elements of 'tax expenditures'; indeed, it goes much further not only combining the (questionable) elements but adding them to pension expenditure estimates. All this seems designed to avoid drawing the most obvious conclusion that should be drawn from the IGR: that Australia's retirement income system does not face any serious cost pressures for future generations.

Other assumptions in the 2021 IGR

While the inclusion of dubious superannuation tax expenditures wrongly suggests a rising total cost of the retirement income system, the assumptions behind the projection of pension costs may have somewhat overstated the likely reduction in costs as a percentage of GDP. The assumptions are that income and assets test thresholds will increase by movements in the CPI. In fact, there is currently no automatic indexation of these thresholds, but past history suggests they are likely to be adjusted from time to time having regard not to price movements but movements in pension rates (which are tied to wage movements) and movements in the assets of average pensioners. There is no formal policy in this regard and the last change in 2017 was part of a broader change to the assets test. To the extent CPI indexation is below future adjustments to maintain relativities, the IGR projections will have slightly overstated future cost reductions, understating the likely number of full-rate pensioners and overstating the proportion not receiving any pension.

Intergenerational policy issues not explored in the 2021 IGR

The Intergenerational Report reveals some growth in the burden of government expenditures between generations, though as shown above this is not the case regarding retirement income costs and, as the report suggests, the increased burden projected is manageable and less than projected in previous IGRs. Inevitably, the overall picture presented has led to continued calls to address intergenerational inequality. But by focusing on fiscal costs and associated intergenerational inequality alone, it obscures the deeper and more pernicious inequality that exists within generations and that, because of government policy, is likely to grow over time. The IGR is completely silent on this key issue.

That older people are wealthier is the norm, not the problem. Society expects citizens to work hard, save and be financially comfortable in old age when they cannot or are not expected to work. A society that encourages savings and hard work is productive and innovative.

Young people who work hard should likewise be able to look forward to these same advantages of hard work and savings. It is likely that in the future, however, wealth at older ages will be determined less by hard work and thrift and more by birthright. If one's parents have assets, one will be well-off. If not, while hard work is likely to still pay off, certain assets may be out of reach for some even among the hard-working and thrifty. This appears at odds with the Australian principle of equality of opportunity for all.

Fundamentally, there are two policy areas that have created this problem. The first is counter-cyclical, macro-economic policy. The second is the broader area of tax and transfer policy. We will mostly discuss this second set of policies, but will briefly mention the first.

The standard mantra of responding to shocks is now 'go hard, go early and go [cash to] households'.[2] What this has meant in Australia, both in response to the global financial crisis and to the economic downturn induced by the COVID-19 pandemic, is injecting large amounts of money into all households, including those who are well-off. Breunig and Sainsbury (2023) show that the Australian government's COVID-19 response over-compensated people on average and document the odd outcome that average incomes actually increased in 2020. While this supported consumption and provided protection for those directly affected by public health restrictions and the less well-off, it may also have contributed to asset price booms for the wealthier. Surging asset prices driven mostly by low interest rates have grown much faster than wages, resulting in less well-off wage and salary

---

2   See Chris Uhlmann's interview with Ken Henry about lessons learned from past economic shocks and the Australian response to the Global Financial Crisis: www.youtube.com/watch?v=N5UHT2hBGdk.

earners falling increasingly further behind in their attempts to enter asset markets such as the housing market. The short- and long-term impacts of the government's COVID-19 stimulus policies are still being assessed and it will be some time before we fully know the costs and benefits and their distribution.

Inter vivos transfers have been contributing to inequality in younger generations during the COVID-19 period as cashed-up baby boomers transfer assets to their children to enter the housing market. Those without wealthy parents to provide low-interest loans or gifts are left behind. This will likely spill over into other areas beyond home ownership such as quality education and medical care. This is the inequality that we should be worried about, particularly as it is likely to increase over generations.

In supporting current consumption, macro-economic policy has also (of course) increased government debt. Whether or not the policy was 'over-done', the IGR projects deficits over the whole 40-year period, with net debt in 2060–61 still over 30 per cent of GDP. Accordingly, today's young will pay throughout their lives for the benefits citizens mostly older than them received. The burden of Australia's debt will rest heaviest on the non-wealthy, those whose income derives solely from salary and wages. This is driven by Australia's heavy reliance on income taxation—both corporate and personal—that fall particularly heavily on those who are economically active.

Australia's taxation system's reliance on income tax is in fact increasing and enabling wealth once accumulated to be held beyond the reach of taxation—principally by storing it in the family house and tax minimisation devices such as trusts. The disconnect between taxable income and wealth is growing: anyone earning more than $22,000 in 2022–23 (taking the Low Income Offset into account) is liable for income tax, while it is possible for Australians holding wealth valued in the tens of millions to have zero taxable income. Sainsbury and Breunig (2020) point out this possibility and discuss the difficulty in determining the degree to which this occurs in the Australian system.

More specifically, the tax and transfer system is exacerbating these problems in two ways: the retirement income system currently encourages inefficient risk management that tends to leave more savings to the next generation than retirees consciously plan, and the very uneven treatment of different savings vehicles tends to encourage investment in housing and its eventual transfer to the next generation.

Un-remedied, today's age–wealth disparity will augment societal inequality within age cohorts and in turn contribute to a larger age–wealth disparity in the next generation. And so on.

There are four key policy areas where government could consider addressing these inequalities: improving the efficiency of the retirement income system; aged-care funding; inheritance taxation; and land tax. In an ideal world, these changes would be part of a broad-based reform of the tax and transfer system.

Making the retirement incomes system more efficient and effective

While the retirement income system is successfully increasing the savings available to people at retirement so they can achieve adequate retirement incomes (broadly maintaining their pre-retirement standard of living), it does not yet encourage efficient management of the risks retirees face in the pensions phase. Those risks are real—how long they will live, inflation, investment risks, future healthcare requirements and sovereign risk (uncertainty about future government policies relating to the age pension, Medicare and aged care, in particular). The resulting precautionary behaviour is leading to people leaving more savings to the next generation than they consciously plan.

The government has foreshadowed reforms that would guide retirees towards purchasing retirement income products that more efficiently address most of these risks (APRA 2022). Funds would be mandated to offer the products the trustees consider would be in the retirees' best interests. Such products are likely to become the new default, replacing the current default of the minimum drawdown rules. In most cases, the products would include pooling of some savings to fund lifetime annuities instead of retirees inefficiently trying to address their longevity risk on their own.

But designing such products will require the funds to calculate their members' likely eligibility for the age pension. The pension means test needs to reinforce and complement the risk management approach built into the recommended product design, guiding funds and retirees towards the best approach to deliver secure and adequate total retirement incomes. A simpler, merged means test (combining the current separate income and assets tests) might improve the retirement income system's cohesion, balancing the core objective of concentrating assistance on those most in need with the objectives of retaining reasonable rewards for saving and working and encouraging sensible use of savings (Podger and Breunig 2021).

Greater coherence, and a reduction in distortions over how retirees manage their assets, would also be enhanced if owner-occupied housing was included in the assets test (or merged means test) with a suitably high threshold. This would also be one way to 'tax' currently untaxed assets. While illiquidity is sometimes cited as the reason to exclude the home from the test, the government's recently expanded reverse mortgage scheme provides a way for homeowners to draw on those assets, including if those assets were to limit access to the age pension. Commercial operators could supplement the income from the government's scheme for those with more substantial home assets (or compete if they can offer more attractive products).

Whether or not home assets are included in the means test, there is a strong case for increasing support for those who do not own their own homes. The Centre of Excellence for Population Ageing Research has reported repeatedly about the inadequacy of support for older Australian renters (e.g. Chomik et al. 2018; Chomik and Yan 2019). Its 2019 research paper refers to research showing that older Australian renters have among the highest relative poverty rates in the OECD (Chomik and Yan 2019:48).

Concern about sovereign risk is entirely legitimate, as the Abbott government's 2014 proposal to change pension indexation (from wage movements to prices) revealed. Retaining savings in case of future changes in entitlements, however, is adding to the problem of increasing transfers to the next generation. A better approach would be to lock-in the age pension parameters, including about indexation and the means test (see Podger and Breunig 2021) and to clarify the insurance offered by the aged-care system.

Aged-care funding

As aged-care reforms offer people more choice as well as higher quality care, there is a strong case for individuals to contribute more to the costs, particularly when they have substantial accumulated savings. Certainly, they should be expected to meet accommodation and living costs drawing on their retirement incomes and any housing assets. A capped contribution towards the costs of the care guaranteed by government would also seem to be entirely reasonable, the cap providing insurance against the possible need for expensive or extended care.

Knowledge of such a cap would also assist superannuation funds and retirees in designing retirement income products that efficiently manage the risk of aged-care requirements.

Inheritance taxes

If we want to keep a system that allows people to hold large amounts of assets and wealth free from taxation or inclusion in aged care or aged pension means tests (other than the tax on the income that originally funded the assets), then taxing that wealth at death might provide an alternative way to address growing inequality. One of the main drawbacks of addressing inequality through inheritance taxes, however, is that they can often be avoided through tax planning. Looking at other countries, such as the US or France, death duties raise only very small amounts of revenue. Given the extensive and very lightly regulated use of trusts in Australia, a death duty may be ineffective. It would also need to be combined with a gift tax on inter vivos transfers to be effective at dealing with the inequality issues raised earlier.

Land tax

Perhaps the simplest and most elegant reform to address wealth inequality would be a broad-based land tax. A tax based upon the unimproved value of land is highly economically efficient. It would also be progressive as the wealthiest individuals hold the most valuable land. By increasing the cost of holding land, it would reduce inefficient and speculative use of land. And it would also lower house prices and allow young people entry into the market. It is important to note, however, that a land tax does not necessarily make housing more affordable over the lifetime. But by shifting the costs of purchase into the future, it can relieve the credit constraint that many young people face and improve access to the housing market. In this respect, a land tax can be seen as a response to capital market imperfections.

Like inheritance taxes, land tax reform presents formidable political challenges. While the Australian Capital Territory and New South Wales governments have adopted reforms, looking to replace stamp duty with land tax, even this limited reform approach is proving to be difficult to achieve. The ACT has been successful as it combines the functions of a state government and a local authority. The NSW reform is more recent and more modest.

Conclusion

The IGR 2021 exaggerates the problems of future financing of the retirement income system and the risk of intergenerational inequity resulting. At the same time, by focusing only on fiscal costs, it ignores the more important issue of likely increasing inequity within future generations, as wealthy retirees leave more of their savings, often unintentionally, to the following generation. It also ignores the inequity caused by inadequate support for low-income retirees who do not own their own homes.

Future IGRs should address more meaningfully the challenges of rising inequality within future generations and highlight the policy directions needed to limit this risk including, in particular, in the area of retirement incomes.

While more consistent taxation of assets and savings could ameliorate this problem, the political challenges involved would be substantial. More feasible are measures to complete reforms to retirement incomes policies, particularly to guide retirees to more efficient and effective management of the risks they face, to improve cohesion between superannuation and the age pension (and also with the aged-care system) and to provide more adequate support for those who rely upon rental accommodation.

References

APRA (Australian Prudential Regulation Agency) 2022, 'APRA and ASIC release joint letter on the implementation of the retirement income covenant', press statement, 7 March, available at: www.apra.gov.au/news-and-publications/apra-and-asic-release-joint-letter-on-implementation-of-retirement-income (accessed on 21 February 2023).

Bateman, H 2018, 'Taxing pensions: The Australian approach', in R Holzmann and J Piggott (eds), *The taxation of pensions,* MIT Press.

Bateman, H and Piggott, J 1992, 'Superannuation guarantee charge—What do we know about its aggregate impact?', on Economic Planning Advisory Council (ed.), *Economic and social consequences of Australia's ageing population—Preparing for the 21st century*, Background paper no. 23, pp. 41–55. Australian Government Publishing Service, Canberra.

Breunig, R and Sainsbury, T 2023. 'Too much of a good thing? Australian cash transfer replacement rates during the pandemic', *Australian Economic Review* 56(1):70–90.

Callaghan, M 2020, *Report of the retirement incomes review*, Commonwealth Treasury, Commonwealth of Australia, Canberra.

Chomik, R, Bateman, H, Yan, S, Graham, S and Piggott, J 2018, *Retirement income in Australia: Part II—Public support*, CEPAR research brief, November 2018, UNSW.

Chomik, R and Piggott, J 2018, *Tax expenditures on pensions: Concepts, concerns and misconceptions*, Working Paper 11, Centre of Excellence in Population Ageing Research, UNSW, Sydney.

Chomik, R and Yan, S 2019, *Housing in an ageing Australia: Nest or nest egg?* CEPAR research brief, November 2019, UNSW.

Commonwealth of Australia 1983, *Budget 1983–84—Budget paper no. 1—Budget statement*, Commonwealth of Australia, Canberra.

Commonwealth of Australia 1984, *Budget 1984–85—Budget paper no. 1—Budget statement*, Commonwealth of Australia, Canberra.

Commonwealth of Australia 2002, *Intergenerational report 2002–03*, 2002–03 Budget Paper No. 5, Commonwealth of Australia, Canberra.

Commonwealth of Australia 2007, *Intergenerational report 2007*, Commonwealth of Australia, Canberra.

Commonwealth of Australia 2010, *Australia to 2050: Future challenges*, Commonwealth of Australia, Canberra.

Commonwealth of Australia 2015, *2015 intergenerational report: Australia in 2055*, Commonwealth of Australia, Canberra.

Commonwealth of Australia 2017, *Tax expenditures statement,* Commonwealth of Australia, Canberra.

Commonwealth of Australia 2018, *Tax benchmarks and variations statement,* Commonwealth of Australia, Canberra.

Commonwealth of Australia 2020, *Tax benchmarks and variations statement,* Commonwealth of Australia, Canberra.

Commonwealth of Australia 2021, *2021 Intergenerational report: Australia over the next 40 years*, Commonwealth of Australia, Canberra.

Commonwealth of Australia 2023, *2022–23 tax expenditures and insights statement*, Commonwealth of Australia, Canberra.

Costello, P 2006a, *Treasurer's budget speech 2006*, Parliament House, Canberra.

Costello, P 2006b, 'The launch of the Future Fund', Speech by the treasurer on 13 November.

Dawkins, J 1992, *Security in retirement: Planning for tomorrow today*, Statement by the treasurer, Parliament House, Canberra.

Dixon, D and Foster, C 1980, 'The social welfare implications of an ageing population', paper for the National Conference on the Ageing, ANU, April 1980, Social Welfare Policy Secretariat, Canberra.

Dixon, D and Foster, C 1982. 'Overall welfare financing: The future', paper for the conference on the Finance of Social Welfare, ANU Federal Financial Relations Centre. Social Welfare Policy Secretariat, Canberra.

EPAC (Economic Planning Advisory Council) 1988, *Economic effects of an ageing population*, Economic Planning Advisory Council Paper No. 29, Australian Government Publishing Service, Canberra.

Fitzgerald, V 1993, *National savings: A report to the treasurer*, Commonwealth Treasury, Canberra.

Gallagher, P 2016, 'Modelling alternative superannuation tax structures', paper prepared for the Committee on Sustainable Superannuation Incomes, Industry Super, Canberra.

Gallagher, P and Preston, A 1993, 'Retirement income modelling and policy development in Australia', Conference Paper 93/3, available at: treasury.gov.au/publication/retirement-income-modelling-and-policy-development-in-australia (accessed 22 February 2023).

Hagemann, R and Nicoletti, G 1989, 'Population ageing: Economic effects and some policy implications for financing public pensions', *OECD Economic Outlook* 2:51–96.

Hancock, K 1976, *A national superannuation scheme for Australia: Final report of the National Superannuation Committee*, Australian Government Publishing Service, Canberra.

Harmer, J 2009, *Pension review report*, Department of Families, Housing, Community Services and Indigenous Affairs, Commonwealth of Australia, Canberra.

Henry, K 2010, *Australia's future tax system: Final report*, Commonwealth of Australia, Canberra.

Hockey, J 2014, *Treasurer's budget speech 2014*, Parliament House, Canberra.

House of Representatives Standing Committee on Tax and Revenue 2015, *Review of the tax expenditures statement*, Parliament of Australia, Canberra.

Howe, B 1989, *Better incomes: Retirement income policy into the next century*, statement by the minister for social security, Australian Government Publishing Service, Canberra.

Morrison, S 2015, Media release by minister for social services, 6 May, Canberra.

Myers, GC 1980, *Population and public welfare policy in Australia: Report for the Social Welfare Policy Secretariat*, Social Welfare Public Secretariat, Canberra.

Newton, J 1980, *Population projections and social security*, Research paper no. 15, Research and Statistics Branch, Department of Social Security, Canberra.

O'Dwyer, K and Morrison, S 2016, 'Turnbull government delivers on fairer, more sustainable superannuation', Media release by Treasury portfolio ministers, 23 November, Canberra.

OECD (Organisation for Economic Cooperation and Development) 1981, *The welfare state in crisis: An account of the Conference on Social Policies in the 1980s, OECD, Paris, 20–23 October 1980*, OECD, Paris.

OECD 1998, *Maintaining prosperity in an ageing society*, OECD, Paris.

OECD 2018, *Financial incentives and retirement savings*, OECD, Paris.

Podger, A 1981, 'Social policies in the 1980s: Some observations from the OECD conference', *Social Security Journal*, Department of Social Security, Canberra.

Podger, A and Breunig, R 2021, *Completing Australia's retirement income system*, Tax and Transfer Policy Institute, Canberra, August 2021 (also published on the Academy of the Social Sciences in Australia website).

Podger, A, Knox, D and Roberts, L 2007, *Report of the review of military superannuation*, Department of Defence, Canberra.

Podger, A, Whiteford, P and Stanton, D 2014, 'Designing social security systems: Learning from Australia and other countries', *Public Administration and Development* 34(4):231–50, doi.org/10.1002/pad.1689.

Sainsbury, T and Breunig, R 2020, 'Tax planning in Australia's income tax system', *Agenda: A Journal of Policy Analysis and Reform* 27(1):59–83, doi.org/10.22459/AG.27.01.2020.03.

Shepherd, T, Boxall, P, Cole, T, Fisher, R and Vanstone, A 2014, *Towards responsible government: The report of the National Commission of Audit,* Commonwealth of Australia, Canberra.

Swan, W 2009, *Treasurer's budget speech 2009,* Parliament House, Canberra.

United Nations 1982, *Report of the World Assembly on Aging,* August, New York.

Varela, P, Breunig, R and Sobeck, K 2020, *The taxation of savings in Australia: Theory, current practice and future policy directions,* Tax and Transfer Policy Institute policy report No. 01-2020, available at: taxpolicy.crawford.anu.edu.au/sites/default/files/uploads/taxstudies_crawford_anu_edu_au/2020-07/20271_anu_-_ttpi_policy_report-ff2.pdf (accessed 18 February 2023).

World Bank 1994, *Averting the old age crisis: Policies to protect the old and promote growth,* Oxford University Press, Washington DC.

6

The Future of Social Security

Peter Whiteford

Key points

- The social security system is one of the largest and most significant areas of government spending in Australia and similar countries. Cash payments to individuals in 2022–23 were around $135 billion, or 20 per cent of the Commonwealth budget.

- Social security is also significant to individuals, with more than 5 million people receiving income support—either pensions or allowances—in 2022.

- The Australian system differs significantly from other countries' systems, apart from New Zealand's, in that payments are flat-rate and means-tested on current income and assets, and are financed from general taxation revenue rather than from social insurance contributions. As a result, benefits are more targeted to low-income households than in any other country in the Organisation for Economic Cooperation and Development (OECD).

- The continuation of current policies as assumed by the 2021 Intergenerational Report (IGR) implies that future generations of people of working age who receive income support will receive the same real payments as currently, even though wage earners are projected to be nearly 80 per cent better off in real terms in 40 years' time.

- The result would be much higher relative poverty among people of working age receiving benefits in the future, with a single unemployed person, for example, projected to receive a payment of around 10 per cent of the average male wage (compared to around 20 per cent in 2022). Child poverty would increase very substantially.
- If deep poverty among disadvantaged working-age adults and their children is to be avoided, then spending on social security payments needs to keep pace with general improvements in population living standards, with implications for future spending and budget deficits.
- Accordingly, the 2021 IGR should have included some sensitivity analysis about possible future adjustments to social security indexation arrangements.

Introduction

The 2021 Intergenerational Report (IGR) delivers a range of good news about the future of Australian living standards. Our children and grandchildren will be living longer than us and, *on average*, they will be much better off in material terms. However, the same assumptions imply that the poorest in the future Australian community will be much poorer in relative terms.

This chapter discusses the reasons why the IGR projections imply the ongoing impoverishment of the poorest groups in the Australian community. The remainder of the introduction summarises the main trends in social security spending projected in the latest IGR. The subsequent section outlines some of the main features of the Australian social security system. This is followed by a discussion of the policy assumptions leading to the projected ongoing fall in the relative position of working-age social security recipients. The chapter concludes with a discussion of the implications of these assumed trends for the sustainability of the system.

The 2021 IGR projects that a girl born in 2061 could expect to live for 89.3 years, compared to 85.4 years for a girl born in 2021. For boys, the corresponding increase in life expectancy at birth by 2061 is from 81.4 to 86.8 years.

Australia will be a much richer country than it is now. Productivity growth is assumed to be 1.5 per cent per year on average, which would lift real Gross National Income (GNI) per person by 1.3 per cent per year, from around $77,900 in 2020–21 to $128,900 in 2060–61.

Using the assumption specified in the report, real male total average weekly earnings (MTAWE)—the benchmark currently used to index age and disability pensions and some other payments—would rise from around $80,900 now to $144,600 in 2060–61. On average, Australians— particularly those employed—will be better off in real terms by close to 79 per cent, while income support for the unemployed and related payments will not increase at all in real terms.

Nevertheless, the 2021 IGR shows that Australia faces an extended period of difficult social policy choices. Even though the IGR projects continuing deficits over the entire 40-year projection period, some of the necessary assumptions used to generate these projections involve reductions in social security spending that have very unpleasant outcomes for many of the poor.

Table 6.1 shows the projections of the composition of government spending over time. Payments to individuals (not including age pensions) are projected to reduce from 3.9 per cent of GDP to 2.7 per cent.

Table 6.1: Composition of government spending over time.

	2021–22 (% of GDP)	2060–61 (% of GDP)
Health	4.6	6.2
Payments to individuals (excluding age pension)	3.9	2.7
Age and service pensions	2.5	2.1
Defence	2.1	2.3
Education	1.9	1.2
Aged care	1.2	2.1
NDIS	0.9	1.0
Infrastructure	0.5	0.4
Interest payments	0.8	1.9
Other payments (excl. NDIS state and GST)	5.3	4.0

Note: NDIS = National Disability Insurance Scheme.

Source: Commonwealth of Australia (2021:Chart 7.4).

Table 6.2 provides a disaggregated breakdown of projected changes in spending. Spending on Family Tax Benefit is projected to more than halve; JobSeeker Payment will fall by a similar level, while Youth Allowance and Austudy will fall by nearly two-thirds.

Table 6.2: Composition of payments to individuals, 2018–19 to 2060–61.

	2018–19 (% of GDP)	2019–20 (% of GDP)	2060–61 (% of GDP)
Family Tax Benefit	0.9	0.9	0.4
Disability Support Pension	0.9	0.9	0.8
JobSeeker Payment	0.5	0.9	0.4
Child Care Subsidy	0.4	0.4	0.3
Carer Payment	0.3	0.3	0.5
Parenting Payment Single	0.2	0.3	0.2
Youth Allowance and Austudy	0.2	0.3	0.1
Paid Parental Leave	0.1	0.1	0.1
Parenting Payment Partnered	0.0	0.1	0.0

Source: Commonwealth of Australia (2021:Chart 7.5.1).

Part of these projected changes in spending reflect the demographic assumptions made in the report, with children and young people falling as a share of the population. But a more important factor is that the level of payments will fall relative to wages and GDP per capita, because they are projected to remain the same in real terms.

The Australian social security system in context

'Social Security and Welfare' (Commonwealth of Australia 2022) is the largest single component of Commonwealth government spending. It is estimated to cost $221.7 billion in 2022–23, or 35.3 per cent of total budget expenses. Of that amount, around $135 billion or more than 20 per cent of the budget involves cash payments to individuals, including pensions, allowances, family payments and child care assistance, which, if separated out, would still be the largest single component of Commonwealth spending.

These income support payments (Department of Social Services 2022) are currently made to more than 5 million persons, just over 2.6 million people of working age and 2.5 million people of pension age. There are also 1.4 million families with 2.7 million children receiving Family Tax Benefit, of whom around 800,000 families are in work and not receiving income support payments. So, in total, there are currently more than 9 million adults and children in Australia receiving some form of financial support through the social security system.

And these are point-in-time figures; the Household Income and Labour Dynamics in Australia (HILDA) longitudinal survey (Melbourne Institute 2012) estimates that between 2001 and 2009 nearly two-thirds of Australian households of working age contained someone who had received an income support payment in this period—not including age pensions or family benefits. This reflects the fact that over the course of time, many people will experience unfavourable contingencies, including retrenchment from their job, personal illness or injury or illness and injury of a close family member, or the breakdown of a relationship, leading to a loss of income and the need to claim income support. Income support receipt was defined as having received payments for at least one week in the year, and on an individual basis this meant that about one-third of working-age individuals received income support in 2009. However, about 10 per cent of individuals received more than half of their income over the financial year from benefits, and 5 per cent received more than 90 per cent of their annual income from income support (Melbourne Institute 2012:40). Even smaller proportions were substantially reliant on income support for the full nine-year period, with only 1.2 per cent of the working-age population receiving 90 per cent or more of their income from benefits every year. What this emphasises is that the Australian social security system effectively provides insurance against risks for a much larger proportion of the population than is commonly understood, but at the same time it is essential for the long-term support of a much smaller, but extremely disadvantaged minority.

According to the Australian Bureau of Statistics Income Survey in 2017–18 (ABS 2019), more than 70 per cent of spending on social security benefits went to the poorest 40 per cent of households, accounting for roughly half of their disposable income. For the poorest 20 per cent of Australian households, social security payments provide more than 70 per cent of their income.

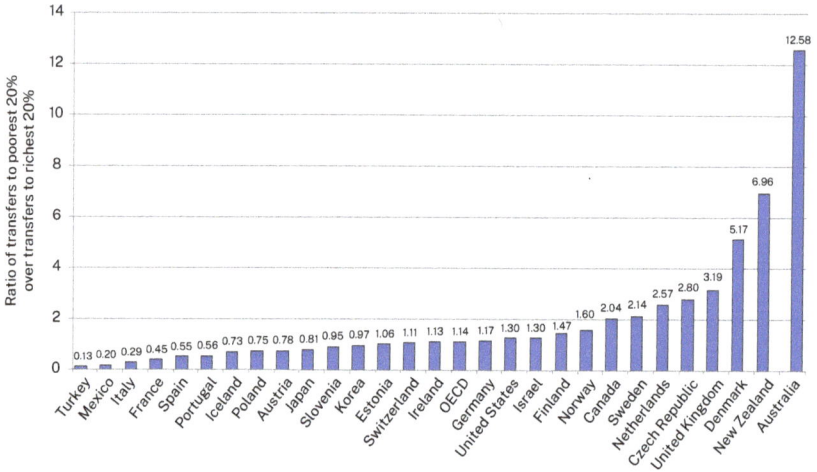

Figure 6.1: Australia's social-security system is more targeted to the poor than any other OECD country. Ratio of transfers received by poorest 20 per cent to those received by richest 20 per cent of households, 2012.

Source: Calculated from Causa et al. (2014).

Overall, the Australian social security system is more targeted to low-income groups than any other benefit system in the Organisation for Economic Cooperation and Development (OECD 2008, 2014). As shown in Figure 6.1, for most OECD countries, the poorest 20 per cent of the population receive about the same amount of social security cash payments as the richest 20 per cent.[1] In Australia, the poorest 20 per cent receive more than 12 times as much in social security benefits as the richest 20 per cent, reflecting the fact that we rely on income and asset-testing more than any other high-income country.

The high level of targeting of social security transfers also means that across-the-board cuts in social security spending in Australia would increase inequality and relative poverty to a greater extent than in any other OECD country (Causa et al. 2014).

This poses a real dilemma to any government considering 'budget repair'— it is difficult to cut the largest single component of Commonwealth spending without disadvantaging the poorest in the Australian community.

---

1   It should be noted that these systems are still redistributive to the poor, as the share of market income received by the lowest income group is much less than the share received by higher income groups.

Poverty will continue to increase if current policies are continued

The 2021 IGR, like most previous IGRs, assumes the continuation of existing policies for the indexation of working-age payments and family payments. But continuation of existing indexation policies means that people receiving many working-age payments will not receive any benefit from the increase in living standards projected in the report.

As noted above, pension payments—for the aged, people with disability and their carers—are indexed to the CPI and benchmarked to MTAWE. As shown in Figure 6.2 below, a single pensioner will see a slight reduction in the value of their total payments relative to MTAWE—from 31.1 per cent to 29.7 per cent—because the Energy Supplement of $14.10 per fortnight is not indexed. However, payments for the unemployed, low-income parents and people with barriers to work, as well as payments for children in low-income families, are indexed to the CPI.

What this means is that while the average worker is projected to be 79 per cent better off in real terms by the middle of the twenty-first century, the unemployed will be relatively worse off. A single person relying on JobSeeker would see their payment fall from just 20.7 per cent of MTAWE currently to around 11.4 per cent in 2060–61.

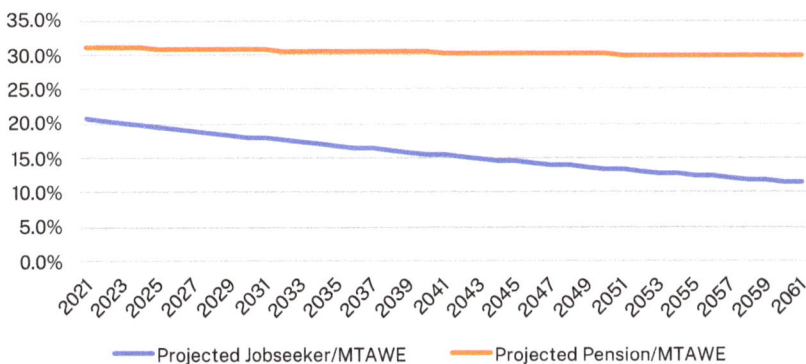

Figure 6.2: Projected pension and allowance payments for single adult as percentage of MTAWE, 2021 to 2061.
Source: Author's calculations.

The gap between allowances for the unemployed and pensions will continue to grow. Currently a person receiving JobSeeker Payment has a disposable income around two-thirds that of a full-rate pensioner. The IGR projections imply that by 2061 a job-seeker will receive less than 40 per cent of the pension level. Given that the current level of JobSeeker Payment is already recognised as inadequate (Whiteford 2012), we could ask whether these projected future levels of payments would be socially acceptable in the much richer country that Australia is likely to be.

It is also worth noting that the report assumes that the unemployment rate stays at around 4.5 per cent over most of the projection period, as did previous IGRs, but with the ongoing impoverishment of those who experience it and the potential halving of support for some of the most vulnerable unemployed.

The then Labor government's 2009–10 budget changed the indexation of Family Tax Benefits from wages to prices (Redmond et al. 2011). Under the same assumptions shown above, Family Tax Benefit Part A for the lowest-income families would also nearly halve relative to wages over the period up to the middle of the century. This might lead to an increase in the depth of child poverty (Whiteford 2014). The lower level of these payments will also reduce the share of families able to receive family payments, which have already fallen to little more than half of all families with children since the 1990s (Whiteford 2019), and disadvantages those with children in the tax transfer system relative to those without children.

Conclusions — What is sustainable?

If the implicit distributional outcomes of these spending trends are unacceptable in a society as rich as Australia—and in the even richer society we are projected to become—we need to recognise that these projected falls in expenditures may not happen. This means that the IGR may actually be underestimating the scale of the budgetary challenges ahead. Accordingly, the IGR should have included some sensitivity analysis about possible adjustments to existing social security indexation policies.

Is Australia's social security system sustainable over time?

The 2021 IGR defines sustainability as follows:

> Fiscal sustainability is important for maintaining macroeconomic stability, reducing economic vulnerabilities and improving economic performance. Fiscal sustainability is the government's ability to manage its finances so it can meet its spending commitments, now and in the future. It ensures future generations of taxpayers do not face an unmanageable bill for government services provided to the current generation. (Commonwealth of Australia 2021:xvi)

However, fiscal sustainability is only one part of the story. Glennerster (2010:689) argues:

> The challenges the world will face in the next half century are going to be partly the same but partly very different from the past five decades …

- Will their populations continue to vote the higher taxes required to support older and more demanding populations? This is a question of fiscal sustainability.
- Are their present bureaucratic structures capable of adapting to fast changing consumer expectations? Will other political priorities overtake social policy—climate change, population movement or responding to global economic crises? These are questions of political sustainability.
- In trying to respond to such concerns, will these institutions retain a commitment to the needs of the poorest and to enhancing social solidarity? This is a question of moral sustainability.

Moral or social sustainability is an essential part of the debate Australia needs to have about the future of spending and taxation. The projected deficits in the report also reflect the assumption that the projected Commonwealth tax-to-GDP ratio stays constant at 23.9 per cent of GDP from 2020–21 onwards.

In addition to having an open and serious public discussion of how to target Australia's social spending better, we need to look at the revenue requirements necessary to fund social and government spending more broadly. As Stewart (2015) has argued: 'Since federation, the Australian community has made broad choices about government expenditures, redistribution and taxes. It's time to do it again.'

References

ABS (Australian Bureau of Statistics) 2019, *Household income and wealth, Australia, 2017–18*, Canberra, available at: www.abs.gov.au/statistics/economy/finance/household-income-and-wealth-australia/2017-18#data-download (accessed 24 January 2023).

Causa, O, Araujo, S, Cavaciuti, A, Ruiz, N and Smidova, Z 2014, *Economic growth from the household perspective: GDP and income distribution developments across OECD countries*, OECD Economics Department working paper no. 1111, OECD Publishing, Paris, doi.org/10.1787/5jz5m89dh0nt-en.

Commonwealth of Australia 2021, *2021 intergenerational report: Australia over the next 40 years*, Commonwealth of Australia, Canberra, available at: treasury.gov.au/sites/default/files/2021-06/p2021_182464.pdf (accessed 24 January 2023).

Commonwealth of Australia 2022, *Budget 2022–23—Budget paper no. 1—Budget strategy and outlook*, Commonwealth of Australia, Canberra, available at: budget.gov.au/2022-23-october/content/bp1/index.htm (accessed 16 February 2023).

Department of Social Services 2022, DSS demographics—December 2021, data set, Canberra, available at: data.gov.au/data/dataset/dss-payment-demographic-data/resource/65515027-eb42-4257-9b32-6bfec21e00e8 (accessed 24 January 2023).

Glennerster, H 2010, 'The sustainability of Western welfare states', in FG Castles, S Leibfried, J Lewis, H Obinger and C Pierson (eds), *The Oxford handbook of the welfare state*, pp. 689–702, Oxford University Press, Oxford, doi.org/10.1093/oxfordhb/9780199579396.003.0047.

Melbourne Institute of Applied Economic and Social Research 2012, *Families, incomes and jobs: Volume 7—A statistical report on waves 1 to 9 of the Household, Income and Labour Dynamics in Australia survey*, University of Melbourne, Melbourne, available at: melbourneinstitute.unimelb.edu.au/__data/assets/pdf_file/0003/2155503/hilda-statreport-2012.pdf (accessed 24 January 2023).

OECD (Organisation for Economic Cooperation and Development) 2008, *Growing unequal: Income distribution and poverty in OECD countries*, OECD, Paris.

OECD 2014, *Social expenditure update*, OECD, Paris.

Redmond, G, Whiteford, P and Adamson, W 2011, 'Middle class welfare in Australia: How has the distribution of cash benefits changed since the 1980s?', *Australian Journal of Labour Economics*,14(2):81–102.

Stewart, M 2015, 'It's time to choose what kind of tax system we want', *The Conversation*, 2 March, available at: theconversation.com/its-time-to-choose-what-kind-of-tax-system-we-want-38050 (accessed 24 January 2023).

Whiteford, P 2012, 'Paltry Newstart Allowance is fast becoming a poverty trap', *The Conversation*, 20 April, available at: theconversation.com/paltry-newstart-allowance-is-fast-becoming-a-poverty-trap-6218 (accessed 24 January 2023).

Whiteford, P 2014, 'Australia bucks child poverty trend but the future looks a lot bleaker', *The Conversation*, 29 October, available at: theconversation.com/australia-bucks-child-poverty-trend-but-the-future-looks-bleak-33456 (accessed 24 January 2023).

Whiteford, P 2019, 'Social security since Henderson', in P Saunders (ed.), *Social security reform: Revisiting Henderson and basic income*, Melbourne University Press, Melbourne.

7

Australia's Housing System and Intergenerational Sustainability

Rachel Ong ViforJ

Key points

- In the context of housing, intergenerational sustainability is related to the ability to meet the housing needs of the current generation without compromising the ability of future generations to meet their needs.

- There are clear changes emerging that signal threats to intergenerational sustainability in the Australian housing system, thereby also impacting inter- and intra-generational equity as well as the retirement income system more generally.

- Most elderly retirees are likely to continue to be securely positioned in outright ownership, but younger generations face a much more precarious housing future.

- Today's young people are postponing their first home purchase, but the downward trend in home ownership rates among the young also reflects structural factors that hinder access to home ownership.

- Larger numbers of future retirees will spend their retirement as renters or mortgagors, calling into question the adequacy of the age pension for future retirees.

- The strategy of diverting superannuation wealth into housing at retirement may grow in popularity in the coming years, though this may exacerbate housing wealth inequality between those who are superannuation asset-rich versus those who are superannuation asset-poor.
- Policymakers will be confronted with soaring demand for rental assistance by future cohorts of low-income retirees, requiring reform to Commonwealth Rent Assistance to increase its adequacy and targeting, and growth to the supply of social housing.
- To prevent further polarisation in the housing system between the old and the young, between current and future retirees, and between the asset-rich and asset-poor, there is a clear need to widen the policy focus beyond home ownership to promoting housing security and affordability across all tenures and for all generations.

Introduction

Successive intergenerational reports have omitted any meaningful consideration of the housing system for intergenerational sustainability, despite the critical role that housing plays for the wellbeing of the Australian population and economy. This chapter addresses three questions in turn. First, why is housing an important intergenerational issue? Second, how is the current Australian housing system changing for both the young and old? Third, what policy implications might arise as a result of growing unsustainability in the housing system? This chapter highlights critical signs of growing intergenerational unsustainability across all housing tenures— from declining home ownership rates among young people, to concerns for tenure security and affordability in the expanding rental sector, and to a visible rise in homelessness for current and future retirees. The policy implications are wide-ranging, affecting the retirement income system and signalling an urgent need to improve housing security and affordability in both the ownership and rental tenures.

Why is housing an important intergenerational issue?

Housing in asset portfolios

Figure 7.1 highlights the enormous and growing importance of housing in household asset portfolios. In the figure, total assets are broadly divided into two categories: financial and non-financial assets. Residential dwellings and land make up a major portion of the latter. The figure shows that the aggregate real value of residential land and dwellings has risen significantly over time (as represented by the dotted line), from $1.6 trillion to $9.5 trillion between December 1988 and December 2021. On a per capita basis, the real value of residential land and dwellings rose from $97,000 to $369,200 per person over this period.[1] There was a 'take-off' in housing prices at the start of the housing market boom of the early 2000s. This surge in housing prices has been undeterred by two global crises—the 2008–09 global financial crisis and the COVID-19 health and economic crisis that began in early 2020.

These trends parallel a historical long-run decline in interest rates over several decades, reaching a trough during the COVID-19 pandemic before arguably normalising once more. This long-run decline in interest rates has led to large upward spirals in real housing asset prices and the upfront cost of home purchase, while easing the cost of servicing large mortgage loans.

Indeed, it is clear that real increases in residential land and dwelling values have largely driven the increase in the value of non-financial assets and exceeded the rate of growth in the value of financial assets. This is notwithstanding the growth in real per capita values of financial assets from $21,600 to $143,600 between 1988 and 2021 as the superannuation guarantee system matured. Housing assets have therefore made up a growing share of households' asset portfolios over time. Between 1988 and 2021, the contribution of residential land and dwellings to asset portfolios increased from 48 per cent to 55 per cent of total assets while the contribution of financial assets grew at a slower rate from 35 per cent to 39 per cent. In 1988, residential land and dwellings made up 74 per cent of the value of total non-financial assets held by the population; by 2021 this had risen to 90 per cent.

---

1   Real values are expressed at December 2021 price levels. See note under Figure 7.1.

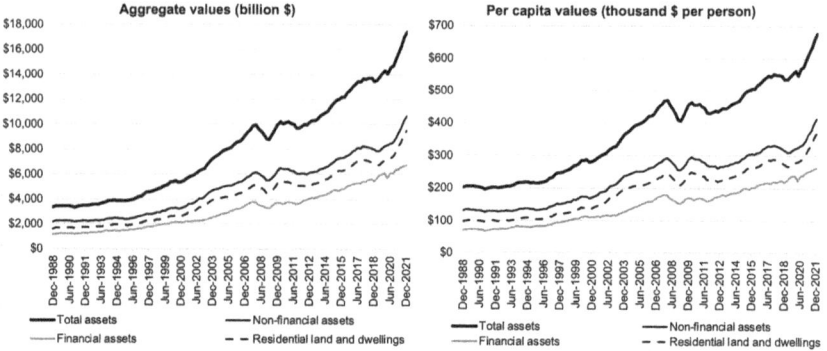

Figure 7.1: Real asset values, December 1988 to December 2021.

Notes: Asset values in current prices are converted into real values at December 2021 price levels using the 'all groups' Consumer Price Index from the ABS cat. no. 6401.0 (ABS 2022b). Asset per capita values are derived by dividing aggregate asset values in each quarter by the estimated resident population in the same quarter.

Source: Asset values from ABS cat. no. 5232.0 (2022a), population numbers from ABS cat. no. 3101.0 (2022c).

Housing and intergenerational policy planning

Because successive waves of house price appreciation since the 1970s have positioned the owner-occupied home as the centrepiece of households' wealth portfolios (and household debt), the family home's importance as a nest egg for retirees has grown, especially in the face of rising fiscal costs attributable to population ageing (Productivity Commission 2015). For young renters, these same cycles of house price increases have pushed home ownership further from their reach as growing numbers face a future with diminishing prospects of owning a home. This has naturally fuelled tensions and debates around growing intergenerational inequality (Rayner 2016). The dominance of housing among wealth portfolios therefore makes it an important consideration in any policy planning around intergenerational sustainability, especially where it pertains to wealth inequality.[2]

The concept of intergenerational sustainability in economic development originated in the United Nation's 1987 World Commission on Environmental Development (WCED) report, which relates it to development that seeks

---

2   Discussions around housing inequality have mostly focused on the contribution of housing to wealth inequality due to housing's dominant position within asset portfolios. However, there has been less attention on the links between housing and income inequality, where the influence of housing may be weaker. It should also be acknowledged that wealth inequality has always been more extreme than income inequality (Smith et al. 2022).

to 'meet the needs of the present generation without compromising the ability of future generations to meet their own needs' (WCED 1987:49). Padilla (2002) advocates for the sustainability requirement to be adopted in economic analysis of intergenerational problems, which represents 'an equity commitment to the future and implies the recognition that future generations have the right to non-deteriorated ecological and economic capacity' (2002:69). The concept is also tightly linked to fiscal sustainability, which reflects the government's ability to manage its finances to meet spending commitments to the present generation without creating an unmanageable financial burden for future generations of taxpayers (Commonwealth of Australia 2021a). In the context of housing then, intergenerational sustainability is related to the ability to meet the housing needs of the current generation without compromising the ability of future generations to meet their needs.

From a fiscal perspective, the 2021–22 federal budget papers reveal that housing and community amenities make up just 1 per cent of total expenditure (Commonwealth of Australia 2021b). This amounts to just $7 billion compared to $43 billion for education and $98 billion for health. Approximately another $5 billion is spent on Commonwealth Rent Assistance (CRA) under the social security heading. In comparison, the Productivity Commission (2022) reports that state and territory governments spent a total of $4 billion on recurrent expenditure for social housing and specialist homelessness services in 2020–21, excluding the federal government's contribution.[3] Additionally, state and territory governments spent $2.1 billion on capital (non-recurrent) expenditure on social housing in 2020–21.

What is missing from the federal budget papers are significant tax expenditures in the form of tax concessions and exemptions that are tied to housing assets. For instance, Grudnoff (2016) estimated capital gains tax exemption on the family home to cost $46 billion in 2015–16, and negative gearing has been estimated to cost $3 billion in 2013–14 prices (Duncan et al. 2018) and $3.7 billion in 2014–15 prices (Grudnoff 2015). Wood et al. (2017) costed the exemption of the family home from assets

---

3   According to the Productivity Commission (2022), total federal, state and territory government recurrent expenditure on social housing and specialist homelessness services was $5.7 billion in 2020–21, of which the federal government's contribution was $1.7 billion.

test for welfare payments at around $5.8 billion in 2011.[4] Other exemptions include the non-taxation of imputed rents derived from the family home, exemption of the family home from land tax and the capital gains tax discount on the sale of investment properties.

Studies also generally agree that the distribution of these housing tax expenditures is very unequal (see Duncan et al. 2018; Wood et al. 2017). They tend to favour those on higher incomes and/or who own property. These are typically older while those who rent are typically from younger generations. Assuming that current trends in housing tenure, fertility, life expectancy at birth and net overseas migration remain constant, Wood et al. (2017) projected that the aggregate value of homeowner tax subsidies would rise from $15 billion in 2011 to $22 billion in 2031, a 45 per cent real increase over the two decades. This far exceeds the 29 per cent real increase in CRA payments for renters projected over the same period. Thus, the balance of government support for housing weighs increasingly heavily in favour of older generations at the expense of younger generations.

The current housing system and intergenerational sustainability

Achievement of home ownership has long been held as a social ideal in Australia and other countries (Colic-Peisker et al. 2010). Colic-Peisker et al. (2015:168) note that 'home ownership remains a universal aspiration of Australians' that 'conveys a full socio-economic "adult status"'. On the other hand, renting has traditionally been viewed as an inferior tenure associated with poorer quality housing (Ronald 2008). Public renting in particular is a stigmatised tenure, typically reserved for marginalised people with complex needs (Jacobs et al. 2010). Thus, the Australian housing system has historically been dominated by owner-occupation with the private rental sector being a minority tenure and public rental a form of residual housing for the highly disadvantaged.

---

4   It should be pointed out that estimates of tax expenditures cannot be directly compared to actual outlays. As explained by Yates (2010), tax expenditures are usually estimated by deriving the tax that would be due from the concession beneficiaries if they were treated in the same way as those not receiving the concession. Thus, while these measures quantify the benefit to the taxpayer in receipt of the concession, they do not provide an estimate of the actual outlay to government of providing the concession, nor do they reveal how much revenue could be gained by its removal. Importantly, behavioural responses to the existence and removal of the concession are ignored in these estimations.

While this housing system structure has persisted over many decades, signs of a systemic change have emerged in recent years. This section describes how the Australian housing system has evolved over recent decades across the owner-occupation, private and public renting, and homelessness sectors. The implications of these trends for intergenerational sustainability in the Australian housing system are discussed.

Home ownership

Home ownership rates in Australia are usually calculated on a household basis (ABS 2016). This can be misleading as people who are living rent-free or boarding in their parents' homes are captured within the homeowner category when they are in fact non-owners living in dwellings owned by others. This issue has become especially pertinent in light of growing concerns regarding young people's home ownership prospects and clear evidence of delayed departures from the parental home. Among young people aged under 40 years old and living independently from their parents in 2001, the median age of departure from the parental home was 18 years old and the share who departed after they turned 21 years old was 23 per cent. By 2020, the median age of departure had risen to 20 years old and the share departing after turning 21 had risen to 38 per cent.[5]

Table 7.1 presents home ownership rates calculated from the Australian Bureau of Statistics (ABS) on a person basis from selected years between 1982 and 2017. Persons who are renting from, or living rent-free in, an owner-occupied household are classified as non-owners. This cross-sectional data is from the ABS Surveys of Income and Housing, which are repeated every few years, allowing us to track how home ownership shares have changed over the past 25 years.

The table shows that home ownership rates have been on a downward trend, falling from 71 per cent in 1982 to 63 per cent in 2017 among those aged 25 years and over. Importantly, there is a growing intergenerational housing wealth gap. It is clear that the decline in home ownership rates is steeper among younger age groups. Back in 1982, 56 per cent of those aged 25–34 years old were home owners, but by 2017 this share had dropped by an alarming 24 percentage points to just 31 per cent. Thus, less than one-third of young people aged 25–34 years are homeowners. It is also notable

---

5   These estimates have been calculated from the 2001 and 2020 Household, Income and Labour Dynamics in Australia (HILDA) survey using cross-sectional population weights.

that home ownership is on a decline among middle-aged cohorts; among Australians aged 35–44 years old, home ownership shares have dropped by 17 percentage points since 1982.

It is likely that the decline in home ownership rates among the young is driven by a combination of demographic and structural factors. Chomik and Yan (2019) argued that the rise in the median age of first homebuyers— from age 24 to 33 between 1981 and 2011—should be interpreted within a wider demographic context that has featured delays in all other major life events, including a delay in the median age of securing a first job, finishing education, having a child, getting married and death. Studies have shown that young people have been able to expand their rates of ownership as they age, but they never fully catch up to older birth cohorts. Longitudinal data analysis by Smith et al. (2022) showed that the home ownership rates of Australians aged 35–44 years in 2001 was around 75 per cent that year. In comparison, the home ownership rates among the birth cohort aged 35–44 years a decade later in 2011 were consistently lower at 69 per cent that year, rising to 72 per cent over the next three years, but never catching up to the earlier cohort. The study showed a similar depression of a few percentage points in home ownership rates as one birth cohort followed the next in the United States. Analysing census data from the ABS, the Australian Institute of Health and Welfare (2021) also showed that each birth cohort were able to expand their home ownership rates as they aged, but cohorts born in more recent years have not been able to catch up to the home ownership rates attained by cohorts born before them. Thus, structural factors have played a role in declining home ownership rates. In particular, rising real house prices and growing labour market precariousness, which are incompatible with long-term mortgage commitments, are pushing home ownership out of the reach of aspiring first homebuyers (Wood and Ong 2012).

Table 7.1: Home ownership rates, 1982 to 2017, by age band, per cent.

Age band (years)	1982	1990	2000	2009	2017	Percentage point change 1982 to 2017
25–34	55.5%	52.6%	45.1%	37.7%	31.1%	–24.4%
35–44	75.4%	76.4%	69.7%	62.1%	58.8%	–16.6%
45–54	78.3%	80.2%	79.2%	74.5%	69.5%	–8.8%
55–64	81.9%	82.0%	83.2%	80.9%	75.4%	–6.5%
65+	74.4%	79.1%	82.3%	81.8%	81.5%	7.1%
25+	71.3%	72.0%	70.1%	66.4%	62.7%	–8.6%

Note: The unit of analysis and measurement is the person.

Source: Author's own calculations from the ABS Surveys of Income and Housing.

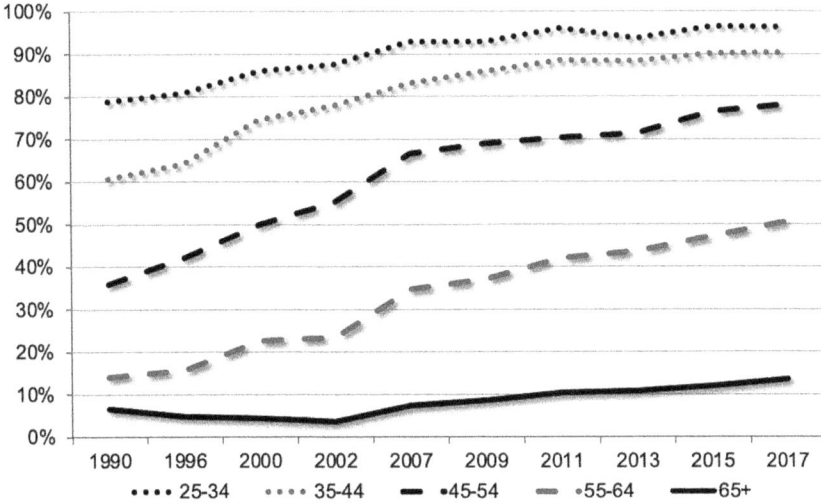

Figure 7.2: Share of homeowners who have a mortgage, by age band, 1990–2017, per cent.
Source: Author's own calculations from the ABS Surveys of Income and Housing.

While growing numbers in the population are experiencing 'lock out' from home ownership, those who make it into home ownership are taking on ever higher levels of debt. As shown in Figure 7.2, the share of homeowners who hold a mortgage has risen across all age groups. However, the rise in mortgage indebtedness is not restricted to younger age groups. Among owners aged 25–34 years, the share with a mortgage rose from 79 per cent to 96 per cent between 1990 and 2017. This increase has been even more dramatic among midlife owners, rising from 61 per cent to 90 per cent among the 35–44-year-olds, 36 per cent to 78 per cent among the 45–54-year-olds and 15 per cent to 51 per cent among the 55–64-year-olds.

Among mortgagors, loan-to-value ratios (LVRs) or the ratio of mortgage debt to house value has risen significantly across all stages of the life course (see Table 7.2). Among mortgagors aged 25–34 years, the LVR has climbed from 37 per cent to 61 per cent and among those aged 35–44 years, the LVR has nearly doubled from 28 per cent to 52 per cent. Thus, not only are growing proportions of homeowners taking on mortgage debt, but mortgagors are taking on growing levels of debt relative to house values. Furthermore, this rise in LVR is most obvious among younger age groups.

These trends reflect at least four underlying factors. First, as discussed above, a combination of demographic 'delays' and structural factors have contributed to delayed access to first home ownership (Chomik and Yan 2019; Smith et al. 2022). Second, real house prices have risen at a faster pace than household incomes, driving the need to borrow more to purchase housing. The ratio of housing prices to household disposable incomes climbed from around 2.5 in 1990 to nearly 6 by 2020 (RBA 2022). Third, until recently, borrowers enjoyed an extended period of historically low and declining interest rates (RBA 2022). This significantly reduced the cost of servicing home loans. Fourth, financial deregulation and innovations have increased in the mortgage market, so more homeowners have access to mortgage products that allow them to release housing equity for consumption without moving. Haffner et al. (2015) make a distinction between age-specific and non-age-specific in situ mortgage equity withdrawal products based on a review of six countries, including Australia. The authors found that, while the take-up of age-specific products such as reverse mortgages has been low, non-age-specific flexible mortgage products such as the current account mortgage have been more popular, with a take-up rate of around 20 per cent among owner-occupiers.

Overall, the growing incidence of mortgaged ownership and rising LVRs reflect an increase in the financial risk attached to owning a home. However, these measures are limited proxies for risk. As shown in Table 7.2, while mortgagors' mean LVRs rose across all age groups between 1990 and 2017, average net housing equity also increased significantly. Back in 1990, a typical mortgagor aged 25–34 years held net housing equity of $164,900. By 2017, this had increased to $239,387—a real increase of 45 per cent. Reflecting a widening intergenerational housing wealth gap, this increase is much larger in real terms among older age groups with those aged 65 years and over enjoying a 200 per cent increase in net housing equity in real terms. This rise in real housing equity makes an important contribution towards wellbeing in old age, from the perspective of financial security as well as housing security.

It may also be the case that because the superannuation guarantee system is maturing and working lives are extending later into the life course, current generations of homeowners may be more willing to carry debt into later life than before. Ong et al. (2021) find that mortgagors in metropolitan areas reduce their odds of exiting the labour force by around 17 per cent for every $10,000 increase in mortgage debt secured against the home. The study presents some evidence supporting the idea that those planning to retire later are more willing to borrow against their homes. However, the study also emphasises that those delaying their retirement will still be working when the risks of adverse life shocks are higher, for instance serious ill health, marital breakdown and redundancy. These risk exposures can negatively impact on a mortgagor's ability to reduce their mortgage debt in later life.

Table 7.2: Mean loan-to-value ratios and real net housing equity of mortgagors, by age band, 1990 and 2017.

Age band (years)	Loan-to-value ratio			Real net housing equity		
	1990	2017	Percentage change	1990	2017	Percentage change
25–34	37.1%	61.1%	24.0%	$164,912	$239,387	45.2%
35–44	27.7%	52.0%	24.3%	$237,084	$355,767	50.1%
45–54	23.9%	37.1%	13.2%	$277,077	$534,376	92.9%
55–64	17.0%	25.9%	8.9%	$267,565	$612,608	129.0%
65+	11.8%	23.0%	11.2%	$228,026	$695,776	205.1%

Note: The unit of analysis and measurement is the person. Net housing equity is derived by deducting the outstanding mortgage loan amount from the mortgagor's reported house value. The 1990 net housing equity estimates are converted into real values at 2017 price levels using the 'all groups' Consumer Price Index from the ABS cat. no. 6401.0 (ABS 2022b).

Source: Author's own calculations from the ABS Surveys of Income and Housing.

The private rental sector has typically been viewed as a transitional minority tenure in which young people reside temporarily while saving up for a deposit to purchase their first home. Thus, the assumption has been of a linear housing career in which a young person departing from the parental home passes through the rental tenure on the way to purchasing a first home. Once the home is bought, the mortgage debt is paid down gradually over time with outright ownership achieved by retirement (Wood and Ong 2012). However, this view of the private rental tenure is breaking down. Growing numbers of young Australians are renting long-term as they find themselves unable to overcome the deposit constraint to home purchase (Ong 2017). Recent work has also raised concerns around loss of home ownership due to adverse personal or family events among older Australians. Ong et al. (2015) showed that loss of home ownership due to divorce, separation, death of a partner or long-term ill health increases the risk of a return to private renting that is marked by long-term reliance on rental housing assistance (Ong et al. 2015).

Table 7.3: Percentage of low-income renter households in rental stress, by location, 2007–08 to 2017–18.

Year	Capital cities	Rest of state	All households
2007–08	38.5%	29.5%	35.0%
2009–10	47.0%	32.7%	40.9%
2011–12	44.9%	32.0%	39.7%
2013–14	49.8%	34.7%	43.7%
2015–16	48.7%	36.8%	44.3%
2017–18	47.8%	35.6%	43.1%

Notes: Low-income households in rental stress are defined as households in the bottom 40 per cent of the equivalised disposable household income (excluding CRA) distribution, calculated for greater capital city areas and rest of state, on a state-by-state basis, who are spending more than 30 per cent of gross household income on housing costs.

Source: Data from ABS (2019) as reported in AIHW (2021).

However, the expanding private rental sector is plagued by long-run housing affordability concerns. As shown in Table 7.3, the share of low-income rental households in rental stress has grown in both city and regional areas. Across Australia, the incidence of low-income rental stress has risen from 35 per cent to 43 per cent over 10 years. In capital cities, the increase largely occurred between 2007–08 and 2009–10. However, in regional areas, the rise in the incidence of low-income rental stress has been more even across the years. At the same time, the CRA system suffers from inadequacy and poor targeting. Ong et al. (2020) estimated that nearly two-thirds of low-income CRA recipients would be in rental stress without CRA. However, over one-third of low-income CRA recipients remain in rental stress after CRA is deducted from rents.

Furthermore, the public housing system is not well-positioned to support low-income renters in rental stress. While the public housing rental rebate formula sets rents at affordable levels by pegging them to 25 per cent of assessable income, Australia's public housing system has always been a small residual sector, unlike those in many developed Western European nations. As shown in Table 7.4, the number of tenantable public housing dwellings has been on a slow but steady decline over the last decade. At the same time, the number of waitlist applicants has hovered at around 150,000 with a reduction in the waitlist size from 166,500 to 140,600 between 2011 and 2018, showing unfortunate signs of reversal again in more recent years. The estimates in the table also indicate the severe rationing of the public housing stock. Indeed, the available stock would have to expand by around 50 per cent in order to accommodate everyone presently on the waitlist.

Table 7.4: Size of public housing stock and waitlist, 2011–20.

Year	Number of tenantable public housing dwellings ('000s)	Number of waitlist applicants ('000s)
2011	327.9	166.5
2012	327.6	164.3
2013	325.2	159.0
2014	321.2	154.6
2015	318.9	154.0
2016	316.9	147.9
2017	314.9	142.5
2018	310.0	140.6
2019	298.4	148.5
2020	296.4	155.1

Source: Productivity Commission (2016, 2021).

The ramifications of the system's inability to house a growing group of marginalised Australians is evident in the homelessness statistics. The homelessness rate has increased from 45 to 50 persons per 10,000 of the population. It has grown more rapidly among the young than the old. The homelessness rate is consistently highest among those aged 19–24 years old, and this has increased from 75 to 95 persons per 10,000 of the population between 2006 and 2016. On the other hand, the homelessness rate has consistently been the lowest among the oldest age groups and has remained more or less constant over time. Among those aged 65–74 years, the homelessness rate has hovered at around 25–27 persons per 10,000 of the population over time. Among those aged 75 years or over, the homelessness rate has remained at around 14–15 persons per 10,000 population.

However, homelessness rates do not provide a complete picture of how the homelessness sector has changed over time. The number of homeless persons in Australia has climbed from just under 90,000 in 2006 to over 116,000 in 2016. The largest increase has been detected among the older age groups, where the number of homeless rose by 54 per cent and 59 per cent among those aged 55–64 and 65–74 years, respectively. There was also a 53 per cent increase in the number of persons aged 25–34 who were homeless.

Table 7.5: Number of homeless persons and homelessness rate per 10,000 of the population, by age band, 2006–16.

Age band (years)	2006		2011		2016	
	N	Rate (per 10,000)	N	Rate (per 10,000)	N	Rate (per 10,000)
All	89,728	45.2	102,439	47.6	116,427	49.8
<12	15,715	50.5	17,767	53.6	15,872	44.8
12–18	9,788	51.1	10,718	54.9	9,955	51.0
19–24	12,155	75.4	14,479	83.1	17,725	95.3
25–34	15,848	59.2	18,411	62.1	24,224	71.9
35–44	13,180	44.9	14,225	46.4	15,745	50.1
45–54	10,581	38.3	12,247	41.5	14,278	46.0
55–64	6,950	31.7	8,478	33.9	10,682	38.8
65–74	3,560	25.9	4,097	25.2	5,651	27.2
75+	1,951	15.4	2,008	14.5	2,289	14.3

Source: 2006, 2011 and 2016 Census of Population and Housing.

A closer investigation by age and sex in Figure 7.3 reveals further differences. Between 2006 and 2011, the largest rise in the number of homeless persons was among female youths aged 19–24 years (34 per cent) and older men aged 65–74 years (26 per cent) and aged 55–64 years (28 per cent). However, between 2011 and 2016, the largest increase in the size of the homeless population was found among older women aged 65–74 years (51 per cent) and aged 55–64 years (27 per cent) and young men aged 25–34 years (30 per cent).

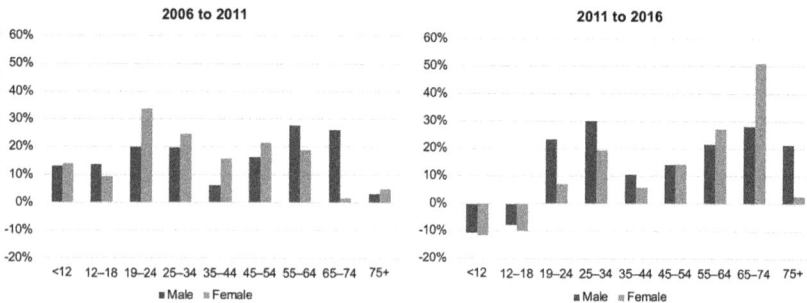

Figure 7.3: Percentage change in the number of homeless persons, by age band and sex, 2006–11 and 2011–16.

Source: 2006, 2011 and 2016 Census of Population and Housing.

Policy implications

There are clear changes emerging in the housing system that signal threats to intergenerational sustainability in the Australian housing system.

Most elderly retirees are likely to continue to be securely positioned in outright ownership, but younger generations face a much more precarious housing future, with growing numbers unable to access home ownership. It is of course possible that today's young people are postponing their first home purchase, but the scale of the downward shifts in home ownership rates across successive generations also reflect structural factors. The rise in mortgage indebtedness among young and middle-aged owners suggests an increase in financial risks attached to owning one's home. However, these risks may be mitigated by a growth in the amount of real housing equity held by mortgagors across all age groups, particularly among older mortgagors. Extensions to working lives as the population ages will also reduce the risk of holding debt over a longer period, as long as adverse life shocks such as serious ill health do not occur later in the life course.

The trends suggest that larger numbers from future generations will spend their retirement as renters. Low-income rental stress also shows no sign of abating and public housing remains highly rationed. Worryingly, homelessness rates have climbed across the wider population as the housing system fails more and more vulnerable Australians, both young and old. Indeed, the evidence suggests that some of the largest increases in the number of homeless persons have been among older Australians. In particular, the homeless population has grown by 51 per cent among older women aged 65–74 years between 2011 and 2016, albeit from a low base.

The policy ramifications for future retirees are potentially wide-ranging. As growing numbers enter retirement as renters or mortgagors rather than outright owners, the adequacy of the age pension may be called into question. Whether mortgage indebtedness in later life is a significant concern can depend on a number of factors. This includes the capacity to delay retirement, the ability to sustain good health for continuing employment, and the future trajectory of interest rates. Historically declining interest rates have made it more affordable to service mortgage loans despite higher upfront costs of home purchase, but interest rates have been on the rise as pandemic concerns have waned.

Of course, asset substitution strategies that shift wealth away from superannuation funds into property may be deployed by retired renters or low-equity owners to achieve outright ownership in retirement. While the evidence of this strategy is currently mixed, this may be because current retirees have not benefited fully from the superannuation guarantee system, which was only introduced in 1992. Future retirees are expected to have higher superannuation balances than previous generations of retirees due to the maturing superannuation system, increasing their capacity to pay off outstanding mortgage debt in retirement. Hence, this strategy of diverting superannuation wealth into housing may grow in popularity in the coming years. This asset substitution strategy is a rational move, given the obvious financial advantage under the age pension means test that is attached to storing wealth in the family home versus storing wealth in superannuation funds. Nonetheless, it will be important to monitor such asset substitution behaviour in future cohorts of retirees to assess its impacts on financial independence and age pension claims. Furthermore, to the extent that superannuation wealth expands households' capacity and willingness to borrow for home purchase, it potentially contributes to house price inflation and may fuel housing wealth inequality between those who are superannuation asset-rich versus those who are superannuation asset-poor.

For current and future retirees who retire as outright owners, their housing wealth will make important contributions to their financial security by limiting housing costs in old age and providing a resource that can be drawn upon to supplement income and meet old age costs such as health and aged-care expenditures. Enhancing elderly owners' capacity to draw down on their housing equity is a logical policy response to meeting the needs of an ageing population, given the significant amount of housing wealth held by older outright owners. In practice, however, some concerns have to be ameliorated to encourage housing equity withdrawal among those with sufficient levels of housing equity. There is, first, house price risk. Concerns regarding housing price fluctuations may discourage reliance on the use of housing equity withdrawals (Ong et al. 2013). Second, equity release may exacerbate repayment risk in later life if achieved through debt-based financial instruments such as flexible home loans. Schemes that include no negative equity guarantee, such as the Australian government's Home Equity Access Scheme, will go some way towards addressing these concerns.

In the rental sector, policymakers will be confronted with soaring demand for rental assistance by future cohorts of low-income retirees. The decline in home ownership rates among the young will likely lead to a significant expansion in the cohort of future retirees needing such assistance. According to Ong et al. (2019), the combination of tenure and demographic change is likely to increase demand for CRA among those aged 55 years or over by 60 per cent, from 414,000 in 2016 to 664,000 in 2031. The CRA budget cost for this age group is projected to rise steeply, from $972 million in 2016, to $1.55 billion in 2031 (at 2016 prices). At the same time, the unmet demand for public housing from private renters aged 55 and over is expected to grow by 78 per cent, from 200,000 households in 2016 to 440,000 households in 2031.

Unfortunately, the current CRA framework is riddled with problems of inadequacy and poor targeting. As reported earlier, over one-third of low-income CRA recipients remain in rental stress after CRA is deducted from rents. The real value of CRA has fallen well behind rent inflation over time, so there is a strong case for increasing CRA rates to improve affordability (Henry et al. 2010; Productivity Commission 2017; Callaghan 2019). For those without children, CRA is paid only as a supplement to pensions and allowances. Thus, some low-income earners without children may not qualify for CRA despite facing rental stress, due to the absence of a direct income test for CRA eligibility (Wood et al. 2005). On the other hand, the Henry Review report (Henry et al. 2010) notes that the design of CRA 'blurs the roles of income support and family payments' (p. 604). Private renters with children receive CRA as a supplement to Family Tax Benefit Part A (FTB(A)). The additional costs of raising children, including housing costs, are already recognised in the FTB(A) payment, which is paid at the same rate to all parents regardless of their housing tenure. Yet, the number of children is also taken into account when determining the maximum CRA rate, even though FTB(A) already makes allowance for the additional housing costs associated with children. Hence, there is a duplication of assistance with housing costs in CRA and family payments for private renters with children. This suggests a need to design reforms that reset CRA parameters to improve horizontal equity across all categories of low-income earners regardless of the number of children. A more significant reform would be to decouple CRA from the social security system and align CRA eligibility directly to housing stress indicators, though constitutional barriers may prevent this (Ong et al. 2020).

While reforms to CRA could improve low-income rental affordability and targeting, they will not address tenure insecurity concerns among low-income private renters. Public housing provides tenure security to vulnerable groups, but the public housing waitlist data clearly show that there is insufficient public housing stock to cater for the needs of those eligible for public housing. This is particularly concerning given the continued rise in homelessness among both young and old Australians. An obvious solution is to build more social housing, and indeed the current government intends to implement a Housing Australia Future Fund to build 30,000 new social and affordable housing properties in its first five years of government (Australian Labor Party 2022). However, this will only meet one-fifth of current unmet demand from public housing waitlist applicants. Other policy solutions will need to be added to the mix, including promoting business sector involvement in expanding social and affordable housing (SGS Economics and Planning 2022), incentivising landlords to offer longer-term secure leases to vulnerable households renting in the private rental sector (Wood et al. 2017), and reforming tenancy laws that exacerbate precariousness in housing conditions for renters such as provisions for 'no grounds' evictions (Ong ViforJ et al. 2022). More generally, system-wide increases to housing supply and relaxation of planning policies where they are restrictive can improve affordability and tenure security outcomes of vulnerable population groups.

Conclusion

The trends highlighted in this chapter signal an urgent need to realign housing policies to directly address long-run changes in the housing system. Successive Australian governments have implemented and maintained policies that promote home ownership, including first home purchase assistance schemes and tax expenditures that preference owners over renters. The majority of current elderly retirees own their home outright and therefore have access to a store of wealth in the family home to cushion their financial wellbeing in older age. On the other hand, home ownership prospects have diminished for significant numbers of young people and the proportion of Australians renting into old age is set to grow. Homelessness is rising among both the young and old—a clear sign that the housing system is failing the most vulnerable in our society. To prevent further polarisation in the housing system, there is a clear need to widen the policy focus beyond home ownership to promoting housing security and affordability across all tenures and for all generations. Finally, there is no single short-term solution that can address the scale and complexity of the nation's intergenerational housing affordability challenges. Instead, a long-term commitment to multi-pronged reform strategies will be required.

Acknowledgement

Rachel Ong ViforJ is the recipient of an Australian Research Council (ARC) Future Fellowship (FT200100422) funded by the Australian government. This research is also partly supported by an ARC Discovery Project (DP190101461). This chapter uses unit record data from the Household, Income and Labour Dynamics in Australia (HILDA) Survey. HILDA was initiated and is funded by the Australian Government Department of Social Services (DSS) and is managed by the Melbourne Institute of Applied Economic and Social Research (Melbourne Institute). The views expressed herein are those of the author and should not be attributed to the Australian government, DSS or the Melbourne Institute.

References

ABS (Australian Bureau of Statistics) 2016, *Housing tenure data in the census, 2013–2014*, Australian Bureau of Statistics, Canberra.

ABS 2019, *Housing occupancy and costs, 2017–18*, cat. no. 4130.0, Australian Bureau of Statistics, Canberra.

ABS 2022a, *Australian national accounts: Finance and wealth*, Time series workbook, cat. no. 5232.0, Australian Bureau of Statistics, Canberra.

ABS 2022b, *Consumer price index*, Time series workbook, cat. no. 6401.0, Australian Bureau of Statistics, Canberra.

ABS 2022c, *National, state and territory population*, Time series workbook, cat. no. 3101.0, Australian Bureau of Statistics, Canberra.

AIHW (Australian Institute of Health and Welfare) 2021, *Australia's welfare 2021*, available at: www.aihw.gov.au/reports-data/australias-welfare (accessed 1 July 2022).

Australian Labor Party 2022, *Safer and more affordable housing: Labor's housing Australia future fund*, available at: web.archive.org/web/20220522020614/https://www.alp.org.au/policies/safer-and-more-affordable-housing (accessed 16 February 2023).

Callaghan, M 2019, *Report of the Retirement Incomes Review*, Commonwealth Treasury, Canberra.

Chomik, R and Yan, S 2019, *Housing in an ageing Australia: Nest and nest egg?* ARC Centre of Excellence in Population Ageing Research, Research Brief, November, available at: cepar.edu.au/sites/default/files/cepar-research-brief-housing-ageing-australia.pdf (accessed 1 July 2022).

Colic-Peisker, V, Johnson, G, and Smith, SJ 2010, '"Pots of gold": Housing wealth and economic wellbeing in Australia', in SJ Smith and B Searle (eds), *The Blackwell companion to the economics of housing: The housing wealth of nations*, pp. 316–38, Wiley-Blackwell, Oxford, doi.org/10.1002/9781444317978.ch14.

Colic-Peisker, V, Ong, R and Wood, G 2015, 'Asset poverty, precarious housing and ontological security in older age: An Australian case study', *International Journal of Housing Policy* 15(2):167–86, doi.org/10.1080/14616718.2014.984827.

Commonwealth of Australia 2021a, *2021 intergenerational report: Australia over the next 40 years*, Commonwealth of Australia, Canberra.

Commonwealth of Australia 2021b, *Budget 2021–22—Budget paper no. 1—Budget strategy and outlook*, available at: archive.budget.gov.au/2021-22/bp1/download/bp1_2021-22.pdf (accessed 16 February 2023).

Duncan, A, Hodgson, H, Minas, J, Ong, R and Seymour, R 2018, *The income tax treatment of housing assets: An assessment of proposed reform arrangements*, final report no. 294, Australian Housing and Urban Research Institute, Melbourne, doi.org/10.18408/ahuri-8111101.

Grudnoff, M 2015, *Top gears: How negative gearing and the capital gains tax discount benefit the top 10 per cent and drive up house prices*, The Australia Institute policy brief, April, available at: australiainstitute.org.au/wp-content/uploads/2020/12/Top-Gears-How-Negative-Gearing-and-CGT-benefits-top-10-per-cent.pdf (accessed 10 January 2022).

Grudnoff, M 2016, *CGT Main Residence Exemption: Why removing the tax concession for homes over $2 million is good for the budget, the economy and fairness*, The Australia Institute Policy Brief, January, available at: australiainstitute.org.au/wp-content/uploads/2020/12/TAI-Capital-Gains-Tax-on-the-Primary-Residence.pdf (accessed 1 July 2022).

Haffner, M, Ong, R and Wood, G 2015, 'Mortgage equity withdrawal and institutional settings: An exploratory analysis of six countries', *International Journal of Housing Policy* 15(3):235–59, doi.org/10.1080/14616718.2015.1048091.

Henry, K, Harmer, J, Piggott, J, Ridout, H and Smith, G 2010, *The Australia's future tax system review*, report to the treasurer, available at: treasury.gov.au/review/the-australias-future-tax-system-review (accessed 16 February 2023).

Jacobs, K, Atkinson, R, Colic-Peisker, V, Berry, M and Dalton, T 2010, *What future for public housing? A critical analysis*, final report no. 151, Australian Housing and Urban Research Institute, Melbourne.

Ong, R 2017, 'Housing futures in Australia: An intergenerational perspective', in Committee for Economic Development of Australia (ed.), *Housing Australia*, pp. 79–94, Committee for Economic Development of Australia, Melbourne.

Ong, R, Jefferson, T, Wood, G, Haffner, M and Austen, S 2013, *Housing equity withdrawal: Uses, risks, and barriers to alternative mechanisms in later life*, final report no. 217, Australian Housing and Urban Research Institute, Melbourne.

Ong, R, Wood, GA and Cigdem, M 2021, 'Housing wealth, mortgages and Australians' labour force participation in later life', *Urban Studies* 59(4):810–33, doi.org/10.1177/00420980211026578.

Ong, R, Wood, G, Cigdem-Bayram, M and Salazar, S 2019, *Mortgage stress and precarious home ownership: Implications for older Australians*, final report no. 319, Australian Housing and Urban Research Institute, Melbourne, doi.org/10.18408/ahuri-8118901.

Ong, R, Wood, G and Colic-Peisker, V 2015, 'Housing older Australians: Loss of homeownership and pathways into housing assistance', *Urban Studies* 52(16): 2979–3000, doi.org/10.1177/0042098014550955.

Ong ViforJ, R, Hewton, J, Bawa, S and Singh, R 2022, 'Forced housing mobility and mental wellbeing: Evidence from Australia', *International Journal of Housing Policy* 23(1):138–62, doi.org/10.1080/19491247.2022.2059845.

Ong ViforJ, R, Pawson, H, Singh, R and Martin, C 2020, *Demand-side assistance in Australia's rental housing market: Exploring reform options*, final report no. 342, Australian Housing and Urban Research Institute Limited, Melbourne, doi.org/10.18408/ahuri8120801.

Padilla, E 2002, 'Intergenerational equity and sustainability', *Ecological Economics* 41(1):69–83, doi.org/10.1016/S0921-8009(02)00026-5.

Productivity Commission 2015, *Housing decisions of older Australians*, Productivity Commission, Canberra.

Productivity Commission 2016, *Report on government services 2016*, Productivity Commission, Canberra.

Productivity Commission 2017, *Introducing competition and informed user choice into human services: Reforms to human services*, Productivity Commission, Canberra.

Productivity Commission 2021, *Report on government services 2021*, Productivity Commission, Canberra.

Productivity Commission 2022, *Report on government services 2022*, Productivity Commission, Canberra.

Rayner, J 2016, *Generation less: How Australia is cheating the young*, Redback Quarterly, Carlton.

RBA (Reserve Bank of Australia) 2022, *The Australian economy and financial markets: Chart pack*, July, available at: www.rba.gov.au/chart-pack/pdf/chart-pack.pdf? v=2022-07-09-15-00-23 (accessed 1 July 2022).

Ronald, R 2008, *The ideology of home ownership: Homeowner societies and the role of housing*, Palgrave Macmillan, Basingstoke, doi.org/10.1057/9780230582286.

SGS Economics and Planning 2022, *Give me shelter: The long-term costs of underproviding public, social and affordable housing*, Report for Housing All Australians, available at: housingallaustralians.org.au/whatwedo/give-me-shelter/ (accessed 1 July 2022).

Smith, SJ, Clark, WAV, Ong ViforJ, R, Wood, GA, Lisowski W and Truong NTK 2022, 'Housing and economic inequality in the long run: The retreat of owner occupation', *Economy and Society* 51(2):161–86, doi.org/10.1080/03085147.2 021.2003086.

WCED (World Commission on Environment and Development) 1987, *Our common future*, Oxford University Press, Oxford.

Wood, G and Ong, R 2012, *Sustaining home ownership in the 21st century: Emerging policy concerns*, final report no. 187, Australian Housing and Urban Research Institute, Melbourne.

Wood, G, Cigdem-Bayram, M and Ong, R 2017, *Australian demographic trends and implications for housing assistance programs*, final report no. 286, Australian Housing and Urban Research Institute, Melbourne, doi.org/10.18408/ ahuri-5303901.

Wood, G, Forbes, M and Gibb, K 2005, 'Direct subsidies and housing affordability in Australian private rental markets', *Environment and Planning C: Politics and Space* 23(5):759–83, doi.org/10.1068/c0445.

Yates, J 2010, 'Tax expenditures in housing', in M Stewart (ed.), *Housing and tax policy*, pp. 39–91, Australian Tax Research Foundation, Melbourne.

8

Situating Social Developments within Intergenerational Reports

John McCallum, Lindy Orthia and Diane Hosking

Key points

- The 2021 Intergenerational Report says little about social developments, consistent with most previous reports. This is a problem because social developments inherently impact economics and demographics, yet the report's projections view economic and demographic trends as if they occur in isolation.

- The one social development the 2021 report touches on is workforce gender inequality, but its exploration of the economic consequences of this remains limited, it offers few solutions and it does not attempt to project future outcomes of different policy pathways on this issue.

- Population ageing is another key issue in the 2021 report, but it is framed solely as a fiscal burden on society. Alternative framings, such as emphasising older people's social contributions as workers, carers and volunteers, could lead to different conclusions about the social meaning of ageing and its costs.

- The 2010 Intergenerational Report is the only one to have engaged with social sustainability issues separately from an economic agenda. Uniquely, it recognised two forms of intergenerational inequity requiring redress: the problem of overburdening one generation with the costs of maintaining wellbeing for another, and the inherited disadvantage some groups of Australians face that has harmed generation after generation. The report recognised the role of social capital in effective solutions.

- This chapter recommends future intergenerational reports take inspiration from the 2010 report and the concept of social capital to meaningfully incorporate attention to social developments. Aotearoa New Zealand's 2021 Living Standards Framework may also provide an inspirational model for Australia to follow.

Introduction

A chapter on social developments in the 2021 Intergenerational Report (Commonwealth of Australia 2021) could be very brief, given the report is almost entirely focused on demographic and economic projections and their future budgetary consequences for the Commonwealth. However, those projections incorporate trends in workforce participation, migration, birth rates, population age distribution and other inherently social phenomena that could equally be discussed within frameworks beyond economics and demographics. This chapter argues that intergenerational reports should place greater emphasis on social developments, examining the consequences of current social policies and likely future social issues for Australia. It suggests the value of social capital should be meaningfully reincorporated into future reports to facilitate this.

Most chapters in this volume assess the accuracy and sustainability of current policies through future projections. It is necessary to take a step back from that approach in this chapter, and return to first principles, because of the limited treatment of social developments in the 2021 and previous reports.

In addition, other ways to measure sustainability are needed beyond future projections. While the projected costs of an ageing population prompted the first Intergenerational Report, in 2002, because of an ideological concern about intergenerational inequity—specifically, the perceived problem of younger generations 'footing the bill' for older generations—the distribution of costs across generations is not the only form of inequity. This chapter argues that future reports should attend to another form too: the perpetuation of disadvantage for some groups of Australians from one generation to the next because more advantaged groups do not adequately 'foot the bill' for them.

To elaborate these arguments the chapter is divided into three parts. Section 1 assesses the 2021 report's treatment of social phenomena, identifying some shortcomings of its reductive approach. Section 2 delves into recent social research about aged care and ageing to illustrate important angles future reports might attend to in these domains, respecting the foundational importance of ageing costs to the intergenerational report program. Section 3 discusses alternative models that future intergenerational reports could adopt to highlight and project social issues. This last section analyses the strengths and limitations of the 2010 Intergenerational Report because it remains the only one to tackle social issues in any depth.

1. Social issues in the 2021 Intergenerational Report

The place of social developments over 20 years

To understand the place of social developments in the 2021 report, we must first review how the themes of intergenerational reports have changed across the years. Social developments rated little attention in any of the five produced thus far except for the 2010 report. The 2002 report was framed explicitly as a budget document about the long-term sustainability of government finances. It included attention to fertility, migration, employment, health, aged care, welfare, education and environment, but solely as contributors to demographic-driven economic change and projected spending and revenue. The 2007 report was little different in its low attention to social developments. The 2010 report explicitly changed the emphasis to include 'a comprehensive discussion on environmental challenges and social sustainability' (Commonwealth of Australia 2010:iii), with its final chapter entitled 'A sustainable society'. The 2015 report reverted to the earlier model of discussing any social phenomena in fiscal terms and the 2021 report largely followed suit, including in its limited discussion of major developments such as the climate crisis, COVID-19 and the Royal Commission into Aged Care Quality and Safety.

The 2010 report was the only one produced by a Labor government. It demonstrated the fact that there are few statutory rules for structuring an intergenerational report, so the government of the day can decide what the priority themes are (see Chapters 1 and 2, this volume). The *Charter of Budget Honesty Act 1988* (Cth), which governs the contents of intergenerational reports, specifies only that the report must 'assess the long term sustainability of current Government policies … including by taking account of the financial implications of demographic change' (Commonwealth of Australia 1998:Clause 21). We thus have licence to imagine future intergenerational reports will look quite different. The deserved attention to the implications of a longer living baby boom generation diminishes through the first half of the next 40 years, leaving space for broader views on social sustainability as Australia moves towards a more stable population age profile, albeit older overall than at present. The issue is whether sufficient attention is being given to current policy issues that have strong social dimensions with longer-term implications, and if there are social issues that are only now emerging or are foreseeable in the future.

The limitations of an economic frame

The 2021 report does not devote any concerted attention to social sustainability despite incorporating phenomena of social import within its economic and demographic modelling. Even the social impact investment principles released in 2017 under the Turnbull prime ministership (Caneva 2017) are not mentioned in the report despite their relevance to both economic and social sustainability. On some economic measures, especially those related to workforce participation, the report does discuss gender inequality, and in its chapter on government spending it discusses several budget items with social implications such as aged care, health, education and welfare. But all are framed with an economic–demographic lens. Migration and birth rates receive more attention throughout the report but are also framed in these narrow terms. No consideration is given to sociocultural factors that may influence migration and birth rates, of which there are many.

By discussing these social factors in purely economic terms, the Morrison government missed the opportunity to address the high likelihood that there will be profound social and cultural change over the next 40 years. They did not evaluate their own policies in the light of social change trajectories to identify problems that may emerge if prevailing policies continue, or the possibility that change will bring new, imaginative solutions to the problems they identify. The report lacks vision for different ways of organising and thinking about our lives.

The government also missed opportunities to discuss how different social policies might enhance the economic outlook that was its primary concern. For example, resolving pay inequality between haves and have-nots would increase the retirement income of many Australians and reduce dependence on pensions and funded aged care. A greater focus on preventative health that considers people's social and cultural realities, including improvements to cultural safety in health care, could also reduce health spending in the future (Goris et al. 2013). And Australians are more likely to be comfortable paying for aged care through taxes or individual savings if they are satisfied with its quality, safety and value for money (Woods et al. 2022). It would make sense to monitor these and other social factors when trying to project the future implications of today's policies, because all may have an impact on sustainability, including fiscal and economic sustainability.

The one social development addressed: Gender and workforce participation

As far as questions of social change and social inequality go, the 2021 report only addresses one in any depth: gender inequality in the workforce.[1] The developments documented by the report include:

- Women's participation in paid work has increased since 1978, the increases in recent decades being more profound at older ages. Overall participation rates are expected to increase with more participation by older women in particular, influenced in part by legislated increases to age pension eligibility age.

- Primary unpaid caring responsibilities fall disproportionately to women. Mothers do more than fathers and are much more likely to reduce paid work after having a child. The report does not project future trends for these measures.

- Caring responsibilities are the reason women most commonly cite for working part-time, whereas for men it is studying. Women on average work fewer paid hours per week than men. Almost half of employed women are working part-time compared to about 20 per cent of men, though the rates for both have increased since 1978. The report does not project future trends for these.

---

1   Note this refers only to a gender binary that compares women to men and does not acknowledge non-binary people and other gender minorities or their contributions and barriers to participation.

- Women's average hourly earnings remain significantly lower than men's, including in industries where women are overrepresented. Again, the report does not project future trends for this, perhaps because there is no clear trend, with the gap rising slightly between 2011 and 2014, falling between 2014 and 2019 and plateauing during the COVID-19 pandemic (Workplace Gender Equality Agency 2022a, 2022b).

The gender pay gap also impacts women's retirement savings. Women live longer, spend more time in aged care and are more likely to need the age pension, funded aged care and other income support because of these lower earnings and savings. Therefore, increasing women's average wages would have wide benefits. But despite this obvious connection, the report does not explore the potential economic benefits that firmer action to shrink the gender wage gap could have for Australia over the next 40 years, nor the 40-year economic costs of inaction.

The report includes few policies to address gender inequality in work. It notes the link between equality-promoting policies and economic growth, stating that 20–40 per cent of the per person economic growth in the United States between 1960 and 2010 was attributable to reducing barriers to paid work faced by women and minority groups. But it does not apply the lessons from this historical trend by projecting outcomes of current workplace trends on economic growth. On page 38 it notes only that 'continued policy support could further encourage female participation' (Commonwealth of Australia 2021). On page 40 it mentions recent policy reforms to make childcare more available and affordable and reduce disincentives for second income earners. But it gives no details and does not project any changes based on these.

Another social development deserving greater attention is population ageing. While this is a central issue in the 2021 report, it is not adequately addressed or recognised as a broad social development. The next section discusses some problems with the way ageing is framed in the 2021 report and potential alternative frames that could be considered for future reports.

2. Contextualising social developments related to ageing

Overdue attention to policy implications of an ageing population

A serious focus on population ageing has been a public issue since the 1970s, but policy action has lagged the demographic changes. As early as the 1970s, John Goldthorpe of the University of Oxford flagged ageing as the next 'big thing'. International experts such as demographer George Myers of Duke University came to The Australian National University's Research School of Social Sciences in the 1970s and '80s and advised the Australian Bureau of Statistics (ABS) on modelling the future ageing of the baby boom, as well as the impact of longer life expectancies.

There have been (and continue to be) identifiable social structural changes due to population ageing that directly challenge existing policy settings. Trends have included:

- The increasing proportion of the population with complex health needs, frailty and dementia.
- The breakdown of retirement as a fixed life stage, with increased longevity and the need for income to cover more years of life.
- A reset of the 'retirement' lifestyle with the maturing of the superannuation guarantee.
- Increasing interest in work in later life both as a financial necessity and to provide purpose to the individual.
- Not spending saved money and assets, particularly tax advantaged super funds, in large part because older Australians expect they will have to cover substantial out-of-pocket health costs (Hosking et al. 2022; see also Chapter 5, this volume).
- A major move from family and domestic to formal and residential aged care, though in practice supplemented by family members' unpaid care (particularly by women).
- Resistance to paying for care services because of traditional expectations that ageing will be supported by public welfare.
- Growing expressions of the political power of older people.

With the vision of hindsight, many of these social trends have not been addressed effectively and this has left policy development lagging behind the needs and aspirations of older Australians. Obvious exceptions are the superannuation guarantee and the formalisation of home care services. On other issues, neglect or inadequate policy changes have created greater complexity by 'band-aiding' rather than developing new policies to replace those outdated by social change. For example, the 2021 Intergenerational Report notes: 'In 2018–19, the Australian Government funded around 80 per cent of total aged care spending, with user contributions largely making up the remaining 20 per cent' (Commonwealth of Australia 2021:103). However, it does not acknowledge the significant family and volunteer contributions to care nor the extent to which this expenditure pattern is the consequence of slow policy development.

While considerable additional expenditure on aged care and ageing is needed, the broader context shows there is more to this picture. The prevailing discourse about a societal burden of aged-care costs has dominated the arena and that is a problem for several reasons. In the following sections, we examine the issue from different perspectives that show how alternative framings and models can lead to different kinds of conclusion about the social meaning of ageing and aged-care costs.

Framing aged-care costs versus healthcare costs

Aged-care quality is one of the most urgent social issues requiring major reform in Australia. The Morrison government's response to the final report of the Royal Commission into Aged Care Quality and Safety accepted (or accepted in principle) 126 of the 148 recommendations, and it supported an alternative approach to implementing another four (Royal Commission into Aged Care Quality and Safety 2021; Department of Health 2021). Yet the main comment about the Royal Commission in the 2021 Intergenerational Report is:

> The response to the findings and recommendations of the Royal Commission has significantly increased Australian Government spending on aged care and will continue to do so in the medium and long term. (Commonwealth of Australia 2021:105, Box 7.2.1)

There is no reference to the significant benefits from cleaning up poor-quality and degrading services, the social benefits of improving the quality of later life, or the fundamental human rights principle of honouring our social contract to ensure all citizens are properly cared for. Nor was there discussion of the relationship between quality and user pays incentives, with recent evidence suggesting resentment towards paying and planning for aged care is likely to diminish if the system changes sufficiently to become an attractive option for later life care (Woods et al. 2022). The omission of these social and cultural aspects of aged-care policies from the intergenerational report is disappointing, especially at the beginning of an era of rapid sectoral change in the Royal Commission's wake.

By contrast, health costs are consistently covered by intergenerational reports and their projected growth vastly outweighs that of aged care, but this is not presented as being as significant a problem as aged care. The 2021 report agrees that health cost growth is not driven primarily by ageing, a fact evidenced since 1990 (Barer et al. 1990). Health costs are managed by solidarity between all generations and, in support of this, health costs increase across all ages not just among older groups. This example of intergenerational solidarity is not considered an important focal point in the reports compared to the lesser cost of aged care.

In-built factors that offset the rising cost of aged care have received less attention too. For example, investing in preventative health can reduce aged-care costs and long-term health costs. The maturation of the superannuation system may also reduce reliance on the age pension by retirees, because future retirees can expect a much larger average superannuation balance compared to current figures. And while demand for health services and aged care will increase in the short term, other areas of government spending such as payments to families and education will see a reduction in growth as the population ages (see Chapter 2, this volume). The 2021 report does mention this with a light discussion (Commonwealth of Australia 2021:92) but does not emphasise it.

Older people as contributors to the economy

The notion that aged-care costs are ballooning communicates the stereotype that older people are dependent on taxpayers because they lack agency and the ability to contribute to society. Once again, incorporating a broader social perspective on this point can shed new light. Analyses of ABS data by researchers at the Centre of Excellence in Population Ageing Research showed that nearly 80 per cent of people aged in their early 60s had good or excellent health, which was equivalent to people in their 40s thirty years ago. They also highlighted that a quarter of people aged 55–64 hold a degree, more than double the rate of people aged 45–54 thirty years ago (Chomik and Khan 2021). These findings show that the current capacity and resources of people entering old age may limit their future dependency on younger taxpayers.

An important point to note is that 15 per cent of older Australians engage in paid work after the age of pension eligibility, thus contributing taxes and other benefits to the community (OECD 2021). Other retirees would like to return to paid work but face numerous barriers to doing so including ageism, restrictions on pensioners earning income and a lack of appropriate job opportunities (Orthia et al. 2022). Incorporating projections of measures related to these issues would give context to older Australians' dependence on the state, and policy responses could be developed that change net pension expenditure projections. Supporting later life work for the willing and able increases individuals' ability to pay for services, enhances their social engagement, can maintain their health and can overall improve individuals' ability to avoid becoming dependent in later life, provided work conditions are appropriate and financial necessity is not the primary motivation (Nemoto et al. 2020).

In addition, many older Australians engage in volunteer work, making a multi-billion-dollar contribution to the economy. They also engage extensively in unpaid caring labour for parents, partners, grandchildren, other family and friends. This can come at a significant personal cost, yet their contribution remains unrecognised in intergenerational reports because of the reports' blinkered focus on the government's aged-care budget. If unpaid caring labour were factored into aged-care cost calculations, the proportion contributed by 'users' would be much greater than the 20 per cent quoted in the 2021 report (Commonwealth of Australia 2021:103).

Finally, supporting individuals to incorporate aged-care costs into their financial plans for later life could reduce government expenditure on aged care. Planning for aged-care costs can also provide more choice and thus better outcomes if care is required in the future. Projections in future intergenerational reports might fruitfully incorporate planning-related metrics such as the growth of care navigation and advocacy systems, public trust in aged-care quality and safety, and willingness among wealthier Australians to pay for their care, for example through the body of assets they never spend in retirement (Woods et al. 2022).

Intergenerational solidarity trumps inflammatory ageism

The repeated emphasis on ageing costs regularly inflames ageist public discourse, pitting generations against one another in ways that do not reflect the realities of family relationships over generations or of disadvantage in Australia. This has led some social observers to allege discriminatory attention on the elderly (McCallum and Rees 2018). This ageism takes focus away from the serious risk of growing social inequality in oncoming cohorts. For example, in 20 years, when the baby boom bulge has flattened, the windfall gains from housing will have passed onto privileged sections of the next generations as inheritances (see Chapter 7, this volume). Those who have not had access to this 'unearned' wealth will predictably have lower home ownership rates, and probably more unstable employment and poorer living environments. This points to the need for future intergenerational reports to become more emphatically reports for *all* generations. They should not continue to effectively pit young against old when the more important concern is haves versus have-nots, with the gap widening between them.

In contrast to public expressions of intergenerational conflict there is a strong prevailing sentiment within Australia of intergenerational solidarity that does not get reported as widely. In a 2019 survey, 2,794 older Australians predominantly aged 60+ wrote free text comments on issues affecting younger people today that they were particularly concerned about (Ee et al. 2021). The issue respondents mentioned most frequently was jobs, with almost one-third (31 per cent) mentioning concern about issues such as unemployment rates, job security, pay, conditions and JobSeeker income support. Three other issues were each mentioned by over one-fifth of respondents: housing affordability and costs of living (27 per cent), drug and alcohol use (23 per cent), and education access and standards (20 per cent). In addition, around 10 per cent mentioned climate change and the state of the planet they would leave behind; an issue that 77 per cent of older Australians want action on (National Seniors Australia 2021). Generally, respondents sought government support to ameliorate or resolve these issues; clear evidence of intergenerational solidarity. They also held a widely expressed view that younger people live in more demanding and competitive environments than those of yesteryear.

Older Australians displayed considerable empathy towards the situation of younger people through their comments. A few respondents specifically declined to list issues of concern, instead asserting their desire for younger and older people to work together to address societal problems. Survey respondents generally did not express the expectation that younger people should prioritise supporting the ageing population. These older Australians were more concerned about the welfare of younger people.

On this evidence, addressing the needs of both younger and older groups should be the future direction for intergenerational reports. With few exceptions, all Australians will grow old and have a common interest in comfort and care at that stage. A critical question for intergenerational reports in the 2020s and beyond is whether the demographic focus on age will decrease in relevance with a flattening baby boom bulge, albeit accompanied by an older profile than today (see Chapter 4, this volume). Consequently, future intergenerational reports can and should take a broader view of ageing in their 40-year projections; a view that meaningfully encompasses social and cultural matters, deepening the Australian intergenerational compact.

3. Looking back to look forward: Learning from the 2010 report

The 2010 report's unique approach to social issues

The 2021 Intergenerational Report's engagement with social developments is inadequate, but the same cannot be said for every intergenerational report. The 2010 report's approach to social topics differed from all the others. Understanding its approach can inform how governments prepare their reports in future years.

The 2010 report distinguished itself in at least three ways. The first difference is philosophical, in that the 2010 report made room to consider social sustainability issues distinct from an economic agenda. This was positioned as promoting social inclusion to redress entrenched disadvantage in income, education, employment, health, community resources and political voice. This difference may have been partly inspired by an influential 2009 report by the French Commission on the Measurement of Economic Performance and Social Progress, which challenged the usefulness of the GDP as a measure of social progress. Known as the Stiglitz-Sen-Fitoussi report

(2009), the document was referenced in the 2010 Intergenerational Report (Commonwealth of Australia 2010:84), with the commission's thinking on the dimensions of wellbeing given as an example that might be followed in Australia.

The 2010 report also differed from the others methodologically. It used several methods to assess social outcomes. More than that, following the Stiglitz-Sen-Fitoussi report recommendations, it discussed the problems with using a single measure such as GDP to quantify wellbeing, the affordances of various alternatives, the lack of consensus on appropriate measures, and the crucial insight that a lack of easy measures may lead to undervaluing factors that contribute to wellbeing. It also relied more heavily than other reports on quality external sources. Its 12-page reference section dwarfed the three- to four-page reference sections of the 2002, 2007 and 2015 reports. The 'Sustainable society' chapter alone ran to over six pages of references, including numerous papers from more than 20 peer-reviewed journals in diverse fields. In contrast, the 2021 report has no reference section, only footnotes, across which there are just five references to peer-reviewed journal papers, all economic.

The third distinct trait of the 2010 report was its interpretation of 'intergenerational'. The term is usually interpreted as referring to the allocation of resources between people of different ages, and how a changing society will affect the life course of different generations of people. This definition treats all 15–19-year-olds as a cohort, all those over 85 years as a cohort, and so on, applying little differentiation within those cohorts except sometimes by gender. By contrast, the 2010 report recognised the structural disadvantage faced by some groups of Australians irrespective of their age—for example, First Nations people and people from low socio-economic groups—for whom the disadvantage experienced by one generation is usually passed on to the next. The 2010 report noted that children of parents who achieved low educational attainment tend to perform more poorly in school (Commonwealth of Australia 2010:99), and children of parents who relied heavily on government income support are themselves more likely to rely on income support in adulthood (2010:102). It also noted that disadvantage compounds, so geographic locations facing one kind of disadvantage also tend to be disadvantaged in other ways, and abuse and neglect have rolling consequences for children in terms of educational and employment outcomes (2010:102–3).

In these cases, the intergenerational issue of interest is not just whether a prosperous status quo can be sustained and improved in future generations with a fair distribution of costs between generations, but how governments can halt inherited disadvantage by breaking the self-perpetuating status quo cycle that has harmed generation after generation and, unchecked, is likely to exacerbate inequality. This entails a social compact between different classes, communities and cultures within Australian society, not just between generations.

Measuring social inclusion to inspire action

Consistent with its recognition of two kinds of intergenerational inequity, the 2010 report finished with a statement that the government was 'seeking new ways to overcome disadvantage in the Australian population' (2010:103). It outlined eight principles for social inclusion (2010:104, Box 6.4), which can be summarised briefly as:

1. Building on individual and community strengths.
2. Building partnerships with key stakeholders.
3. Developing tailored services.
4. Giving a high priority to early intervention and prevention.
5. Building joined-up services and whole-of-government(s) solutions.
6. Using evidence and integrated data to inform policy.
7. Using locational (socio-geographic) approaches.
8. Planning for sustainability.

The presence of these principles affirms the need for greater vision within intergenerational reports. It emphasises the importance of improving quality of life values for more marginalised people as well as sustaining high quality of life values for less marginalised people. The approach shows why a sole focus on projections is inadequate for a genuine sense of social sustainability, considering the 1987 United Nations Brundtland Commission definition of sustainability: 'meeting the needs of the present without compromising the ability of future generations to meet their own needs' (United Nations n.d.). Social inclusion measures are needed to enable all members of current generations—not just future generations and not just select members—to meet their own needs.

Developing ways to assess the implementation of social inclusion principles would be useful for future reports because it would allow them to be incorporated into projections in addition to tracking current progress. We know that 'what gets measured gets done' in the policy sphere, so finding ways to measure complex social phenomena will enable governments to focus on them.

Methods already exist for assessing the principles' implementation, and methodological experts can no doubt devise and refine appropriate strategies for assessing relevant arenas if the political will is there. For example, First Nations scholars have developed measures for assessing self-determination and tailoring within services (Principles 1 and 3) (e.g. Davis 2013). Network analysis could be useful for assessing community partnerships and interagency cooperation (Principles 2 and 5) (e.g. Cunningham et al. 2021). International and historical comparisons can assess whether problems have been prevented early (Principle 4) (e.g. Tran et al. 2020). Bibliometric studies can analyse the evidentiary basis of policies (Principle 6) (e.g. Vilkins and Grant 2017). Mapping disadvantage against service provision and grounding impacts with social research could facilitate evaluation of locational approaches (Principle 7) (e.g. Pineda-Pinto et al. 2021). As with all these methods, researchers continue to debate appropriate methods of planning for social sustainability (Principle 8), but there are existing methods for evaluating this too (e.g. Landorf 2011).

These are only examples of what is possible; again, future researchers can work with governments to devise rigorous but realistic methodologies for this evaluative purpose. The complexity of social developments should not be an excuse for excluding them from future intergenerational reports.

Reincorporating the 2010 report's more easily measurable social indicators is also sensible, provided they remain valid and relevant. It did not project all measures forward but did track historical changes indicative of current trends. For example, it tracked private household income by quintiles over 20 years, showing changes in inequality. It tracked the two lowest quintiles' amounts of disposable income over 20 years as an indicator of poverty relief provided by the tax and transfer system. It reported the percentage of Australians who experienced relative income poverty (earned less than half median income) in the past six years and the number of years they experienced it for. It gave a snapshot of disease rates for six non-communicable diseases, comparing the highest and lowest income quintiles as a measure of the impact income disadvantage has on health.

The report also included comparative statistics showing the entrenched disadvantage faced by First Nations people on multiple measures, including unemployment, post-secondary attainment, key health indicators, life expectancy, hospitalisation rates, household income and the proportion of children under state care and protection orders. The federal government's Closing the Gap initiative was designed to redress all of these and the 2017 Uluru Statement from the Heart highlights some of them, so reporting on them and projecting them seems critical to include in future intergenerational reports. As it stands, the 2021 report did not discuss the situation of First Nations people at all for any measure. There can be no excuse for this glaring omission.

New indicators for a better future

At their core, intergenerational reports should be about societal sustainability and, by implication, the wellbeing of society's members. Assessing sustainability and wellbeing entails more than indicators of the government's fiscal balance. The fundamental contribution of the 2010 report was its argument that wellbeing should be measured 'through the prism of the stock of economic, environmental, human and social resources' (Commonwealth of Australia 2010:83). This is a principle missing from the 2021 report that should be reinstated in future reports.

The key unifying concept here is social capital. The 2010 report stated that 'Human and social capital are key components of the "stock" of resources passed to future generations', and it defined social capital as 'the social relationships, networks and norms within society and the institutions that underpin these, such as the justice system, governance and representative democracy' (Commonwealth of Australia 2010:93).

World Bank comparisons of the 'true wealth' of nations showed that social capital indicators of trust, civic engagement and institutional effectiveness were linked to cross-country differences in economic wellbeing and economic growth (Scrivens and Smith 2013). Government policies have a profound effect on social capital through their influence on institutional quality, income inequality, poverty, housing mobility and ownership rates, family wellbeing, the construction of the built environment and educational outcomes. The most common approach to measurement is through indicators. The World Social Capital Monitor was developed in the context of the UN's 2030 Agenda and its associated Sustainable Development Goals. Stakeholders provide country and location information and score eight characteristics of social capital on a 10-point scale (Verbeek and Dill 2017):

1. The local social climate.
2. The trust among people.
3. The willingness to co-finance public goods by austerity measures.
4. The willingness to co-finance public goods by taxes and contributions.
5. The willingness to invest in local economy self-managed enterprises.
6. The helpfulness among people.
7. The friendliness among people.
8. The hospitality among people.

In Australia there were attempts to develop a social capital measurement framework in the early to mid-2000s by the Australian Institute of Family Studies (Stone 2001) and the ABS (Edwards 2004). However, except for the 2010 Intergenerational Report, social capital has not featured prominently in major Australian studies of economic sustainability or economic performance.

The 2010 model may not be the appropriate model for applying the social capital concept in all future circumstances. The report itself noted that the 'different perspectives people and societies have on wellbeing will result in different assessments as to whether wellbeing has improved over time' (Commonwealth of Australia 2010:86). Taking inspiration from other key documents will be important, such as the Stiglitz-Sen-Fitoussi report, which has since been foundational in developing the OECD's 11 measures of wellbeing (OECD n.d.). That document was also foundational to Aotearoa New Zealand's intergenerational report equivalent, the Living Standards Framework (The Treasury (NZ) 2018). The revised Living Standards Framework released in 2021 incorporates the concept of social capital and offers a highly sophisticated take on the multiple dimensions of sustainability, organised into three tiers: 'Our individual and collective wellbeing', 'Our institutions and governance' and 'The wealth of Aotearoa New Zealand' (Te Tai Ōhanga/The Treasury 2022). Under these headings it incorporates unique adaptations to reflect that nation's current values, for example the concept of 'collective wellbeing' includes indicators for cultural capability and belonging, political engagement and voice, social support and love from family and friends, and sufficient leisure time. Social cohesion—including the ability to express identity, a sense of belonging, trust held in others and freedom from discrimination—is one of four measures under the 'Wealth of Aotearoa New Zealand' tier, alongside financial and physical capital, human capability and the natural environment. These social phenomena are not easy to measure, yet Aotearoa New Zealand has committed to them as its indicators of wellbeing and sustainability. As in many things, Australia would do well to emulate its neighbour's example in future reports.

While adopting and adapting Aotearoa New Zealand's model is desirable, the 2010 model nonetheless offers some useful starting points for future intergenerational reports. Pragmatically, building on Australia's own past practice may be the way to get traction on this matter. Perhaps the most important starting point is the 2010 report's insistence that some factors contributing to wellbeing and sustainability are not quantifiable. These include the enjoyment we get from the environment, the quality of life we gain from education beyond its work applications, the inherent benefits of good health and freedom from violence, and the important role of communities in co-designing tailored responses to problems. Finding ways to project our progress in cultivating these values might make the difference between having a future to plan for and not having one at all.

References

Barer, M, Nicoll, M, Diesendorf, M and Harvey, R 1990, 'From Medibank to Medicare: Trends in Australian medical care costs and use from 1976 to 1986', *Community Health Studies* 14(1):8–17, doi.org/10.1111/j.1753-6405.1990.tb00015.x.

Caneva, L 2017, 'Govt releases social impact investment principles', *Pro Bono Australia*, 9 August, available at: probonoaustralia.com.au/news/2017/08/govt-releases-social-impact-investment-principles (accessed 14 June 2022).

Chomik, R and Khan, F 2021, *Tapping into Australia's ageing workforce: Insights from recent research*, ARC Centre of Excellence in Population Ageing.

Commonwealth of Australia 1998, *Charter of Budget Honesty Act 1998*, available at: www.legislation.gov.au/Details/C2012C00230 (accessed 14 June 2022).

Commonwealth of Australia 2010, *Intergenerational report: Australia to 2050: Future challenges*, Canberra, available at: treasury.gov.au/sites/default/files/2019-03/IGR_2010.pdf (accessed 17 February 2023).

Commonwealth of Australia 2021, *2021 intergenerational report: Australia over the next 40 years*, Commonwealth of Australia, Canberra, available at: treasury.gov. au/sites/default/files/2021-06/p2021_182464.pdf (accessed 17 February 2023).

Cunningham, R, Jacobs, B and Measham, TG 2021, 'Uncovering engagement networks for adaptation in three regional communities: Empirical examples from New South Wales, Australia', *Climate* 9(2):21, doi.org/10.3390/cli9020021.

Davis, M 2013, 'Community control and the work of the National Aboriginal Community Controlled Health Organisation: Putting meat on the bones of the UNDRIP', *Indigenous Law Bulletin* 8(7):11–14.

Department of Health 2021, *Australian Government response to the final report of the Royal Commission into Aged Care Quality and Safety, Commonwealth of Australia as represented by the Department of Health*, Commonwealth of Australia, Canberra.

Edwards, R 2004, *Measuring social capital: An Australian framework and indicators*, Australian Bureau of Statistics, Canberra.

Ee, N, Orthia, L, Hosking, D and McCallum, J 2021, *Worry about the younger generation: Older Australians' intergenerational solidarity*. National Seniors Australia, Canberra.

Goris, J, Komaric, N, Guandalini, A, Francis, D and Hawes, E 2013, 'Effectiveness of multicultural health workers in chronic disease prevention and self-management in culturally and linguistically diverse populations: A systematic literature review', *Australian Journal of Primary Health* 19(1):14–37, doi.org/10.1071/PY11130.

Hosking, D, Minney, A and McCallum, J 2022, *The evolution of retirement income: A 2022 snapshot*. National Seniors Australia and Challenger, Canberra.

Landorf, C 2011, 'Evaluating social sustainability in historic urban environments', *International Journal of Heritage Studies* 17(5):463–77, doi.org/10.1080/1352 7258.2011.563788.

McCallum, J and Rees, K 2018, *Respect for age: Going, going or gone? Views of Older Australians*, National Seniors Australia, Brisbane.

National Seniors Australia 2021, *Older Australians and climate change 2021*, National Seniors Australia, Canberra, available at: nationalseniors.com.au/uploads/03202 13485PAR-InfographicDevelopment-FINAL_1.pdf (accessed 17 June 2022).

Nemoto, Y, Takahashi, T, Nonaka, K, Hasebe, M, Koike, T, Minami, U, Murayama, H, Matsunaga, H, Kobayashi, E and Fujiwara, Y 2020, 'Working for only financial reasons attenuates the health effects of working beyond retirement age: A 2-year longitudinal study', *Geriatrics & Gerontology International* 20(8): 745–51, doi.org/10.1111/ggi.13941.

OECD (Organisation for Economic Cooperation and Development) n.d., 'Measuring well-being and progress: Well-being research', *OECD* [website], available at: www. oecd.org/wise/measuring-well-being-and-progress.htm (accessed 23 May 2022).

OECD 2021, 'Labour force participation rate', *OECD Data* [website], available at: data.oecd.org/emp/labour-force-participation-rate.htm#indicator-chart (accessed 25 August 2022).

Orthia, L, Hosking, D and McCallum, J 2022, *'If people want to work they should be able to': Older Australians' perspectives on working after retirement*, National Seniors Australia, Canberra.

Pineda-Pinto, M, Nygaard, CA, Chandrabose, M and Frantzeskaki, N 2021, 'Mapping social-ecological injustice in Melbourne, Australia: An innovative systematic methodology for planning just cities', *Land Use Policy* 104:105361, doi.org/10.1016/j.landusepol.2021.105361.

Royal Commission into Aged Care Quality and Safety 2021, *Final report: Care, dignity and respect, Volume 1: Summary and recommendations*, Commonwealth of Australia, Canberra.

Scrivens, K and Smith, C 2013, *Four interpretations of social capital: An agenda for measurement*, OECD Statistics working papers, no. 2013/06, OECD Publishing, Paris, doi.org/10.1787/5jzbcx010wmt-en.

Stiglitz, J, Sen, A and Fitoussi, J-P 2009, *Final report by the Commission on the Measurement of Economic Performance and Social Progress*, Paris.

Stone, W 2001, *Measuring social capital: Towards a theoretically informed measurement framework for researching social capital in family and community life*, Australian Institute of Family Studies.

Te Tai Ōhanga/The Treasury (NZ) 2022, *The living standards framework dashboard*, Te Kāwanatanga o Aotearoa/New Zealand Government, available at: www. treasury.govt.nz/publications/tp/living-standards-framework-dashboard-april-2022 (accessed 23 May 2022).

Tran, VC, Guo, F and Huang, TJ 2020, 'The integration paradox: Asian immigrants in Australia and the United States', *Annals of the American Academy of Political and Social Science* 690(1):36–60, doi.org/10.1177/0002716220926974.

The Treasury (NZ) 2018, *Our people our country our future living standards framework: Background and future work*, New Zealand Government, available at: www. treasury.govt.nz/sites/default/files/2018-12/lsf-background-future-work.pdf (accessed 23 May 2022).

United Nations n.d., 'Sustainable development goals: sustainability', *United Nations Academic Impact* [website], available at: www.un.org/en/academic-impact/sustainability (accessed 14 June 2022).

Verbeek, J and Dill, A 2017, 'The forgotten dimension of the SDG indicators—Social capital', *World Bank Blogs: Voices* [blog post], available at: blogs.worldbank.org/voices/forgotten-dimension-sdg-indicators-social-capital (accessed 25 August 2022).

Vilkins, S and Grant, WJ 2017, 'Types of evidence cited in Australian Government publications', *Scientometrics* 113:1681–95, doi.org/10.1007/s11192-017-2544-2.

Woods, M, Sutton, N, McAllister, G, Brown, D and Parker, D 2022, *Sustainability of the aged care sector: Discussion paper*, University of Technology Sydney, Sydney.

Workplace Gender Equality Agency 2022a, *Australia's gender pay gap statistics*, available at: www.wgea.gov.au/publications/australias-gender-pay-gap-statistics (accessed 17 June 2022; site now updated/discontinued).

Workplace Gender Equality Agency 2022b, *Gender pay gap data*, available at: www.wgea.gov.au/pay-and-gender/gender-pay-gap-data (accessed 17 February 2023).

9

Health and Aged Care in the Intergenerational Report

Diane Gibson, John Goss and Jane Hall

Key points

- The five successive intergenerational report (IGR) projections for Commonwealth health and aged-care expenditure have varied substantially and over relatively short timeframes (10–20 years) have not been accurate.

- Projections can be improved if there is a more detailed understanding of the past drivers of health expenditure. This requires decomposition into the different drivers of ageing, population growth, disease rate changes, health inflation and extra volume of services delivered per case of disease.

- Changing patterns of disease have major implications for expenditure relating to both health and aged-care services. The dramatic reduction in circulatory disease from the 1970s has had consequences for life expectancy and health expenditure that were not even imagined in the 1950s; more accurate forecasts for diseases such as dementia, diabetes and kidney disease, mental illness and cardiovascular disease are needed for the future.

- Population growth and the volume of health services delivered per case of disease were major drivers of health expenditure in the last decade.

- Ageing is a driver of health expenditure growth, but accounted for only 0.9 per cent out of an annual real growth of 3.6 per cent per year in admitted patient and out-of-hospital medical services. Yet this factor gets excessive attention in public debate.

- Two years after our aged-care system was described as 'cruel and harmful' by the Royal Commission, the IGR has produced only the most basic of projections for the future of aged-care expenditure in Australia, taking little account of the expenditure that would be necessary to implement the Royal Commission's recommendations.

- The higher increases in National Disability Insurance Scheme (NDIS) expenditure estimated in the October 2022–23 budget illustrates the benefits scenario analysis would have provided in areas such as aged and disability services where existing policy is volatile and the impact uncertain.

- The focus of the IGR on expenditure inevitably emphasises costs without acknowledging the benefits provided by those expenditures. This is particularly relevant for expenditure on health, aged-care and disability services.

- The IGR takes a very narrow focus by considering Commonwealth expenditure only. The other main sources of financing, state/territory governments and individuals, need to be considered as some state governments and the Productivity Commission have done, at least in part.

Introduction

To the extent that Australians have followed the 'story' in the intergenerational reports (IGRs), they see the future of health care as becoming increasingly costly due to population ageing. Yet that story is overstated, partly due to the increase in participation among older workers noted by Peter McDonald in Chapter 4, and partly because of a failure to analyse the actual drivers of health expenditure. Factors such as the higher volumes of services being used per case of disease and population growth are more important considerations in driving growth in health expenditure, and, looking forward, potential changes in patterns of disease are also an important consideration.

The chapter begins with a brief review of the policy background of health, aged-care and disability services delivery systems in Australia. This is followed by a critical analysis of the health expenditure projections presented in the 2021 IGR (Commonwealth of Australia 2021a), including a decomposition analysis that demonstrates the importance of a more disaggregated understanding of the drivers of health expenditure. The next sections critically examine the IGR projections on aged-care expenditure and the National Disability Insurance Scheme (NDIS). The chapter then examines the implications of the IGR's heavy reliance on population growth, age structure changes and historical service trends, and argues that a more nuanced analysis would incorporate several important factors such as changing disease patterns and increasing volume of services, relying less on historical trends and more on how recent and emerging trends are likely to affect morbidity, service use, patterns of care and prices in the future. We conclude that population ageing has been overstated as a driver of increasing expenditure.

In this chapter, we focus on the health and aged-care components of the 2021 IGR. Health and aged care were identified in the first IGR as imposing the greatest demand for increasing government spending; and this has continued in the 2021 projections. The validity of these projections are, therefore, key to the IGR conclusions. Healthcare projections are based on an analysis of recent trends in growth within various components of the health sector and key assumptions about the drivers of future growth, disaggregated into demographic and non-demographic factors. Non-demographic factors, in particular the prevalence of chronic conditions but also rising incomes and technological advances, account for over half the increase in projected real per capita health spending. Aged-care expenditure projections are much less disaggregated, with growth simply described as due to demographic and non-demographic factors.

The headline figures are presented as a percentage of GDP. While this gives a sense of the size of the Commonwealth government–financed health sector, it does rely on a number of assumptions about the size and composition of the population and improvements in productivity in general, as well as the projections of health and aged-care service use and expenditure.

The impact of COVID-19 on the health system has been, and continues to be, immense. Not least of this is a new level of uncertainty. The IGR projections show a small but discernible increase in Commonwealth health expenditure in 2020 and 2021, then a return to the pre-existing trajectory. For aged care, the Royal Commission report has highlighted wide-ranging, longstanding systemic failures. The IGR projects an increase in aged-care expenditure over two to three years then a plateauing of expenditure (as a percentage of GDP) until 2040–41. Both these system shocks warrant careful analysis of the ongoing impact. In the following sections, we look at the comprehensiveness of the analysis provided, and the robustness of the assumptions underpinning it.

The first IGR to include projections on the NDIS based on full operation of the scheme was the 2021 report. Growth projections are modest, although higher than the initial 2015 IGR analysis (Commonwealth of Australia 2015). Little underlying information is available; and this sector remains subject to high levels of uncertainty. In estimates released by Treasury in October as part of the 2022–23 budget, there was already a major increase in the projected NDIS spend over the medium (2022–23 to 2032–33) term (Commonwealth of Australia 2022).

Background

The first IGR was published in 2002 with the aim of planning to meet the challenges of an ageing population (Commonwealth of Australia 2002). This was not the first attempt to assess the implications of population ageing. The International Year of Older Persons in 1999 had served to focus attention on a range of issues including the combined effects of increasing life expectancy, the ageing of the baby boom population and reducing fertility, which meant shrinking tax revenues to support the more generous social support programs (Productivity Commission and Melbourne Institute of Applied Economic and Social Research 1999). Even earlier, the Economic Planning and Advisory Council had produced a paper addressing similar issues (Clare and Tulpelé 1994). The first IGR, produced in the early years of the new century, was a clear message not to expect increasing generosity in public benefits, with a strong emphasis on the need to live within our means and to keep government spending in check.

The focus on the problem of ageing for government health expenditure was encouraged by concerns from the United States, with a similar ageing profile to Australia. In 2000, the 65 and over age group in the United States was projected to grow from 12.5 per cent of the total population to 16.6 per cent by 2020, with the comparable figures for Australia being 12.1 per cent and 16.8 per cent (Anderson and Hussey 2000). However, the United States had not achieved universal coverage for health insurance and as a large population cohort turned 65 years, they were newly eligible for Medicare. This was clearly a looming problem for the United States

(Weiner and Tilly 2002). However, universal coverage had been achieved in Australia in 1984, so there would be no new cohort eligible for government health benefits. Many European nations had much older populations and had not been crippled by health or aged-care expenditures. It is worth noting here that 'government' for the purposes of the first and successive IGRs is the Commonwealth government; expenditure by state and territory governments is excluded from consideration. This gives a very partial and misleading view of health, aged care and disability services expenditure as state and territory governments are, or have been, major funders of such services.

Structural and policy changes have led to the Commonwealth share of government funding for health falling from 65.5 per cent in 2001–02 to 60.5 per cent in 2020–21 (AIHW n.d.). When calculated as a proportion of total health expenditure, Commonwealth funding has fallen from 44.0 per cent in 2001–02 to 42.7 per cent in 2020–21. State funding has increased from 23.2 per cent to 27.9 per cent, while the private share of funding has decreased from 32.8 per cent to 29.4 per cent. So funding share changes are one of the biggest drivers of Commonwealth health expenditure, yet this redistribution is obscured by excluding state funding (and private funding) from the analysis.

This partial analysis focused attention on the Commonwealth support for Medicare and its sustainability in terms of the federal budget rather than the national economy. The first IGR was produced by the Howard Liberal-National government, which, in 2002, had held power for six years, after 13 years of a Labor government which had re-established universal tax-financed health coverage (Hall et al. 2020). The Liberal Party for most of its time in opposition had maintained opposition to Medicare. This changed in 1996, with a commitment to 'maintain Medicare in its entirety', although also with more support for private insurance (Hall and Savage 2005; Hall and Maynard 2005). Focusing on only Commonwealth expenditure meant the changes to private health insurance and Commonwealth/state funding arrangements were not explicit.

Meanwhile, aged care in Australia has been under almost continuous reform since the 1980s, with successive waves of major policy shifts toward expanding the community care sector (a joint Commonwealth- and state-funded suite of programs) and reducing reliance on residential care (a Commonwealth responsibility). The *Aged Care Act 1997* (Cth) and later the *Aged Care (Living Longer Living Better) Act 2013* (Cth) also modified means-testing arrangements to increase the proportion of overall costs paid by service users and reduce that paid by the government. By 2011 agreement was reached to transfer financial and administrative responsibility for the jointly Commonwealth- and state-funded Home and Community Care program to the Australian government, a change that once fully implemented in 2018 meant the Australian government was, for the first time, responsible for planning, funding and administering all aged-care services. Over time, then, the balance of aged-care funding between public and private expenditure and between state and territory governments and the Australian government has been subject to change.

This is the first IGR to include analysis of the NDIS which is jointly governed and funded by the Commonwealth and state and territory governments. Prior to the progressive implementation of the NDIS from 2016, states and territories were responsible for specialist disability services under the Commonwealth/state National Disability Agreement. The implementation of the NDIS was a major change to the model of disability services in Australia, enhancing access for people with disability via a non-means tested, demand-driven system.

Health projections

Australian government spending on health is projected in the 2021 IGR to grow from 4.1 per cent of GDP in 2018–19 to 4.7 per cent in 2021–22 (mostly because of COVID-19) and then to decline to 4.4 per cent in 2022–23. It is then projected to remain largely stable until 2032–33 and then to rise steadily to reach 6.2 per cent by 2060–61. These estimates are substantially lower than the estimates of previous IGRs at all times, with two notable exceptions.

First, the 2015 IGR showed a flattening or decline of expenditure growth from 2014–15 until 2036–37 (Commonwealth of Australia 2015). Second, the 2021 IGR includes an expenditure spike in 2020–21 and 2021–22 due to the COVID-19 pandemic (discussed further below). Even over relatively short timeframes (10–20 years), the projections have not been accurate. Of course, the aim of the IGR is not to provide necessarily accurate forecasts but to demonstrate the effect into the future of existing policy settings. But this does make it important to understand the past experience that is the basis for the projections, and to understand when it is likely that the future will be different to the past.

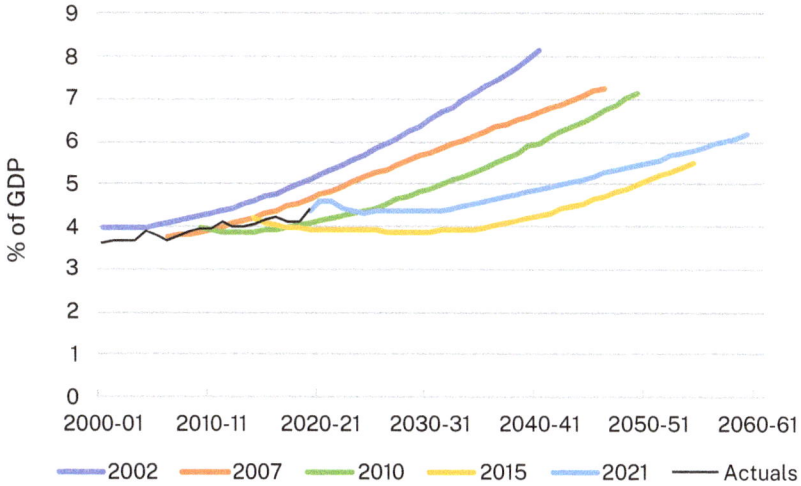

Figure 9.1: Australian government health expenditure as a percentage of GDP: Successive IGR projections.

Source: Commonwealth of Australia (2021b:Chart 7.1.3.).

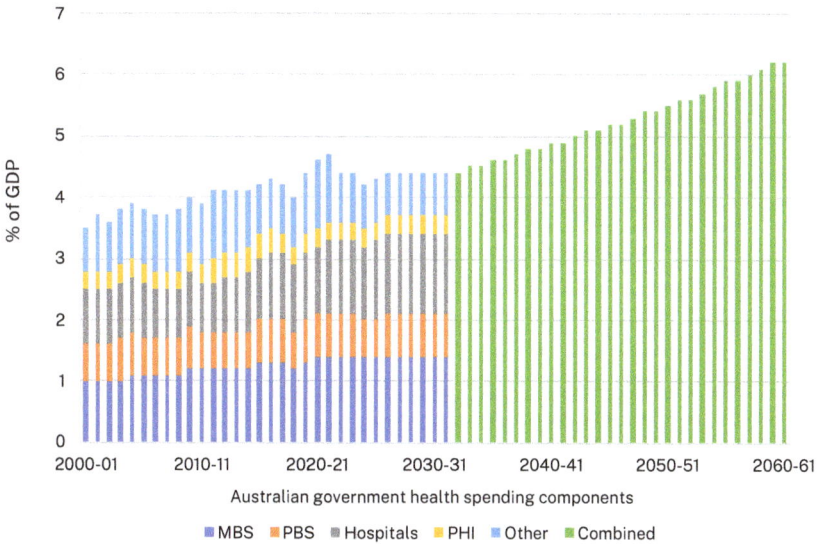

Figure 9.2: Australian government health expenditure actuals (2000–01 to 2020–21) and projections (2021–22 to 2060–61).

Source: Commonwealth of Australia (2021b:Chart 7.1.6).

Commonwealth health expenditure in the 2021 IGR is divided into MBS (Medicare Benefits Schedule), PBS (Pharmaceutical Benefits Schedule), public hospitals and private health insurance support, all by age, and 'other'. Projections are made for each component separately until 2032–33, and thereafter the projections are made for health as a whole. That the total share of GDP looks constant over the coming decade is due to health expenditure growing at the same rate as GDP. After that point, Australian government expenditure rises as a per cent of GDP at a steady rate. This shows how important it is to understand what lies behind the estimates.

Drivers of growth are divided into demographic and non-demographic factors (Commonwealth of Australia 2021b:Chart 7.1.5). Out of projected real health expenditure growth of 3.3 per cent per year in the period 2019–20 to 2060–61, the demographic factors account for 1.4 per cent per year of the growth, and the non-demographic factors account for 1.9 per cent of the growth. But there is no further decomposition of the drivers of growth. The IGR should have divided the demographic factor into ageing and overall population growth factors, and it should have divided non-demographic factors at least into volume of services per person and excess health inflation (non-demographic factors should ideally be divided into the three factors of growth in expenditure: per prevalent case of disease, excess health inflation and disability/disease rate changes). There should also be analyses of the impact of income growth and technological changes on health expenditure growth (the technology impact likely to affect both expenditure per prevalent case of disease and disability/disease rate changes).

Decomposition analysis of health expenditure projections

The decomposition analysis presented below demonstrates the importance of a more disaggregated understanding of the drivers of health expenditure. The analysis undertaken for the period 2011–12 to 2018–19 shows more detail as to the drivers of growth in health expenditure in the last decade. As indicated in Table 9.1, the overall total real (gross national expenditure, or GNE, deflated) expenditure on admitted patient services and out-of-hospital medical services in this period grew at 3.63 per cent per year. This is quite similar to the IGR's projected real Commonwealth health expenditure growth of 3.3 per cent per year for the period 2019–20 to 2060–61.

Table 9.1: Decomposition of total real health expenditure growth, 2011–12 to 2018–19, annual average growth rates.

		Admitted and out-of-hospital medical services	Admitted patient services	Out-of-hospital medical services
Total real expenditure growth		3.6%	3.7%	2.7%
Demographic	**Total demographic**	2.4%	2.3%	2.3%
	Population growth	1.5%	1.4%	1.6%
	Ageing	0.9%	0.9%	0.7%
Non-demographic	**Total non-demographic**	1.2%	1.4%	0.4%
	Disease rate changes	0.1%	0.1%	0.1%
	Excess health price inflation	0.4%	0.7%	-0.5%
	Volume of services per case of disease growth	0.7%	0.6%	0.7%

Source: Original analysis undertaken by Goss using data from Australian Institute of Health and Welfare (AIHW) health and disease expenditure databases, and burden of disease databases for disease rate changes (AIHW n.d.). Expenditure is deflated by the gross national expenditure (GNE) deflator.

The demographic component for total expenditure on admitted patient services and out-of-hospital medical services grew by 2.42 per cent per year in this period and the non-demographic component grew by 1.18 per cent per year.

In this analysis, the demographic growth is split further into the population growth component of 1.53 per cent per year and the ageing component of 0.88 per cent per year. This split is important, as it shows that in Australia the population growth factor—which is largely driven by net immigration—is more important than the ageing factor. This is in contrast to most European countries where the ageing factor is more important than the population growth factor.

The non-demographic growth rate of 1.18 per cent per year can be split into an increase in expenditure because of disease rate changes of 0.01 per cent per year, an increase because of excess health price inflation of 0.4 per cent per year, and an increase in the volume of services delivered per case of disease of 0.67 per cent per year.

The disease rate changes of 0.01 per cent per year reflect the net effect of disease prevalence rate changes. Some diseases such as diabetes, kidney disease, musculoskeletal and injuries have added to expenditure because of their increases in prevalence in this period, whereas diseases such as cardiovascular disease, respiratory and gastrointestinal diseases have reduced expenditure because their prevalence decreased. Overall, in the period 2011–12 to 2018–19, disease rate changes led to a slight increase in health expenditure, whereas in the period 1994 to 2003 (Goss 2008) and 2000–01 to 2011–12 (Goss 2022), disease rate changes led to a slight decrease in health expenditure.

Excess health inflation showed a growth rate of 0.4 per cent per year as the excess health inflation for admitted patient services of 0.69 per cent per year was moderated by the negative excess health inflation for medical services of –0.5 per cent per year. The negative excess health inflation for medical services is most unusual and reflects government constraints on growth in Medicare medical benefits. It is not expected that the government will be able to continue to exercise the same extent of control on growth in Medicare benefits over coming decades. The volume of services per case of disease factor grew by 0.7 per cent per year in this period. This split is informative, as it shows the very small role played by the net disease prevalence rate changes over this period in contrast to the more significant role played by excess health inflation and volume of services per case of disease. In this period, while specific disease prevalence rates changed, the net effect is small, as increases in some disease groups were offset by decreases in others.

Pharmaceutical expenditure

The growth in pharmaceutical expenditure varied significantly in the period 2000–01 to 2019–20. In the period 2000–01 to 2004–05, the average growth in real expenditure was 6.9 per cent per year, but in the period 2009–10 to 2014–15 there was an average fall in real expenditure of 1.6 per cent per year. Overall in the 2000–01 to 2019–20 period, the average growth was 2.9 per cent per year. The fluctuations were due to different factors at different times. In the early period, a number of high-cost pharmaceuticals were added to the PBS. A major factor in the decline from 2009–10 to 2014–15 was drugs, such as the statins, going off patent, so the price of these drugs reduced significantly. The increase in pharmaceutical expenditure of 20 per cent from 2015–16 to 2017–18 was almost entirely due to increases in volume associated with the listing on the PBS of new Hepatitis C treatment drugs (see Figure 9.3).

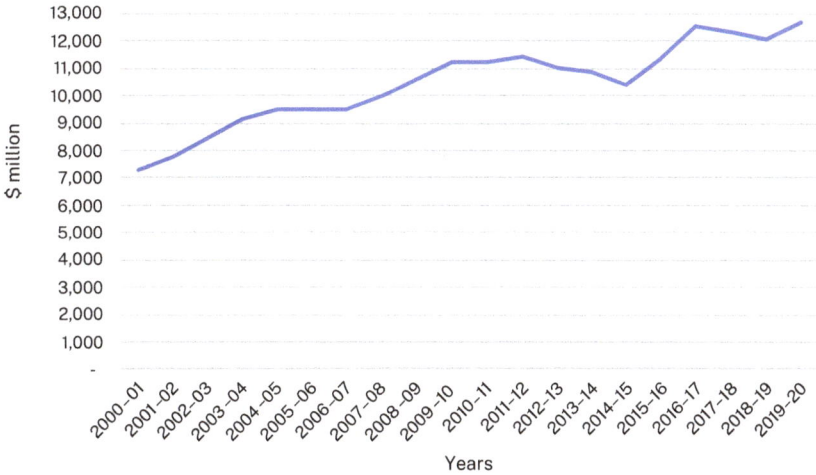

Figure 9.3: Real pharmaceutical expenditure 2000–01 to 2019–20, 2018–19 prices.

Note: Expenditure is total expenditure on benefit paid pharmaceuticals deflated by the GNE deflator.

Source: AIHW (n.d.: analysis of data on pharmaceutical benefits).

When there are such major fluctuations in the growth of expenditure due to policy or circumstance or other factors, as has been the case with pharmaceutical expenditure, using past growth as a guide to expenditure growth in the future will produce unreliable projection numbers. This is not a reason to avoid making expenditure projections, but it does show the importance of sensitivity analyses to allow for the intrinsic uncertainty of projections based on what has happened in the past.

Aged-care projections

In the 2021 IGR, Australian government spending on aged care is projected to grow from 1.2 per cent of GDP in 2020–21 to 2.1 per cent of GDP in 2060–61 (equivalent to $113 billion in 2020–21 dollars). This is an input-based projection based on historic patterns of expenditure and demographic drivers, with the inclusion of an additional $4.5 billion in annual expenditure by 2023–24 in line with projected budget changes announced by the federal government in response to the Royal Commission into Aged Care Quality and Safety in 2021 (see Figure 9.4). The 2021 IGR notes that this is on average 0.2 percentage points higher than the 2015 IGR projections, but no further comparisons are provided.

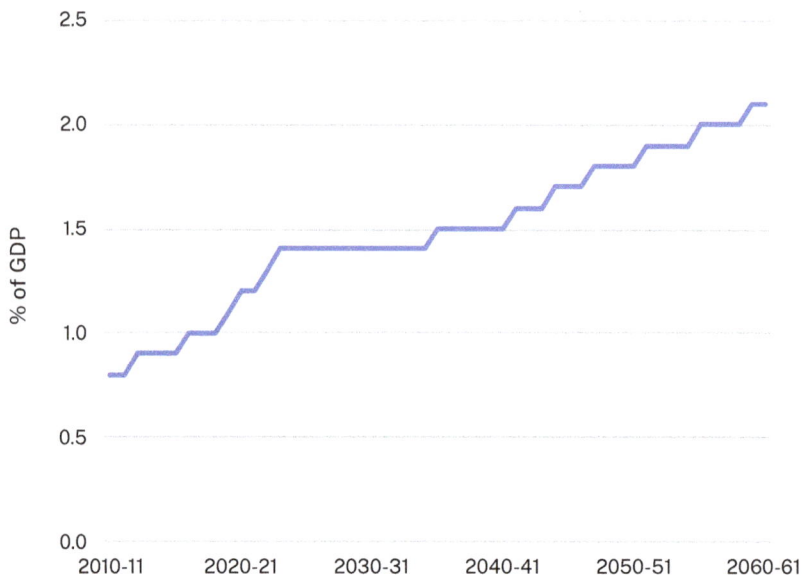

Figure 9.4: Australian government aged-care expenditure actuals (2000–01 to 2020–21) and IGR 2021 projections (2021–22 to 2060–61).

Source: Commonwealth of Australia (2021b:Chart 7.2.1).

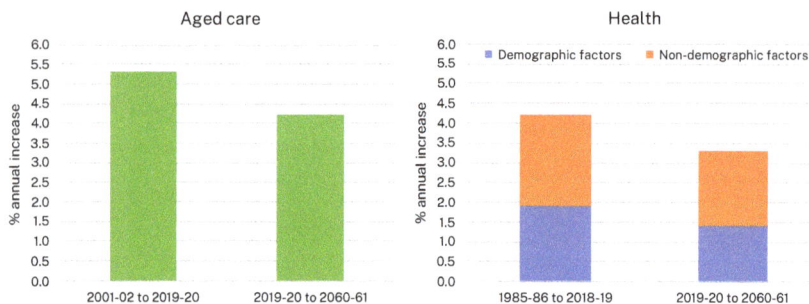

Figure 9.5: Australian government percentage annual increase in expenditure, historical trends (aged care 2001–02 to 2019–20; health 1985–86 to 2018–19) and IGR 2021 projections (2019–20 to 2060–61).

Source: For health expenditure: Commonwealth of Australia (2021b:Chart 7.1.5). For aged-care expenditure: author's calculations from Table 8 in Commonwealth of Australia (2002); Commonwealth of Australia (2007:Table A1); Commonwealth of Australia (2010:Table A3); Commonwealth of Australia (2015:Table A3); Commonwealth of Australia (2021b:Chart 7.2.1).

As Figure 9.4 shows, the $17.7 billion funding boost in response to the Royal Commission pushes the 2021 projections up in the short term, as projected spending increases by 0.1 percentage point per year from 1.1 per cent in 2019–20 until it reaches 1.4 per cent of GDP in 2023–24. It then remains relatively flat until 2034–35, dropping the projection series below all previous IGRs except for the 2015 report, before continuing to increase at a trajectory similar to the other series and reaching 2.1 per cent of GDP by 2060–61. By way of historical context, the data show Commonwealth government expenditure increasing at 5.3 per cent per year for the period 2001–02 to 2019–20, and by 4.2 per cent per year from 2019–20 to 2060–61 (see Figure 9.5).

The Royal Commission into Aged Care Quality and Safety provided extensive evidence that Australia's aged-care system was failing older Australians and their families. Based on an international comparison prepared for the Royal Commission, Australia spends markedly less on long-term care as a proportion of GDP (1.2 per cent of GDP) than countries such as the Netherlands, Japan, Denmark and Sweden (between 3 and 5 per cent of GDP) (Dyer et al. 2019). The cost of implementing the royal commission's recommendations has been estimated at $15.5 billion per annum, while the reforms recommended by the Grattan Institute in the wake of the royal commission would cost an estimated additional $7 billion per annum over current expenditure. Yet two years after our aged-care system was described as 'cruel and harmful' by the Royal Commission (RCACQS 2019), the 2021 IGR has produced only the most basic of projections for the future of aged care in Australia, and it almost certainly underestimates the expenditure that will be necessary to implement the Royal Commission's recommendations. While the IGR notes uncertainties in relation to future developments in labour productivity and wages, demand, consumer preferences and technological advances, the focus of this discussion is on the capacity to deliver downward pressures on government spending rather than on the risk that a status quo projection will underestimate future spending while simultaneously failing to address critical problems in the sector.

In the 2021 IGR projections for aged care, there is no separation of separate programs (residential care, home care packages and the Commonwealth Home Support Program). There is no attempt to separate demographic and non-demographic factors, and no publication of data separating demographic change into ageing and population growth. The text of the IGR indicates the potential importance of non-demographic factors as population growth in the over 70s age group slows but, as there is no decomposition of the growth into the demographic and non-demographic components, the point is rather lost. As is the case for health care, non-demographic factors need to be identified, including excess aged-care inflation, disease rate and disability prevalence, technological changes, shifts in models of care and the role of informal care.

Nor does the IGR projection include continuing shifts in policy away from residential aged care to community care, changing patterns of disability and disease, the impact of industry restructuring, the role of technology, labour force shortages or current shortfalls in the quantity and quality of services. These are the kinds of factors that the Deloitte Access Economics (2020) model explored in the projections undertaken for the Royal Commission, and the kind of modelling needed to understand the future policy directions for aged care. The baseline model prepared by Deloitte Access Economics incorporates (among other factors) continued reduction in age-specific disability rates, strong growth in home-based care, somewhat lower growth in residential aged care and a 5.5 per cent per year increase in wages for skilled staff in the sector, leading to projected expenditure under existing policy of just under 1.4 per cent of GDP in 2050. Their modelling of three alternative scenarios allowed for exploration of the progressive implementation of higher levels of staffing in residential care, equivalent to the 3-, 4- and 5-star ratings discussed in the Royal Commission report. With these increased staffing levels taken into account, expenditure was projected to reach 1.7 per cent, 1.9 per cent and 2.2 per cent of GDP for 3-, 4- and 5-star quality residential aged care respectively.

There are in-text references to some of these factors in the IGR, but even in the textual analysis there is insufficient detail and an over-reliance on generalisations. For example, in terms of need for care the report states: 'A key driver of aged care spending is the number of people over the age of 70' (Commonwealth of Australia 2021a:103). This perspective ignores reductions in age-related disability, the changing age structure of the 70+ population and the continuing policy drive to shift from residential to home-based care. The problem with this perspective can be illustrated by history—between 1981 and 2021 the number of people aged 70 and over more than tripled while the number of residential care beds barely doubled, and occupancy rates went down.

It is important to have better predictors of need for care, and hence better projections of the associated pattern of government spending. National modelling of future aged care must avoid the situation that arose in March 2019 when 129,000 older Australians were on a waiting list for an approved aged-care package. Projections based on a business-as-usual approach are wholly inappropriate for a sector that has demonstrably failed the Australian community over the past decade.

NDIS projections

The NDIS is jointly funded by the Commonwealth and state/territory governments and in this instance the 2021 IGR projections include expenditure by both levels of government. Total spending is projected to grow from 1.2 per cent of GDP in 2020–21 to 1.5 per cent, then level out at 1.4 per cent over the latter years of the projection period. Commonwealth spending on the NDIS is projected to go from 0.7 per cent of GDP in 2021–02 to 1.0 per cent by 2031–32, remaining at that level for the latter part of the projection. The projection assumes that state contributions will fall as a percentage of total costs of the scheme (see Figure 9.6).

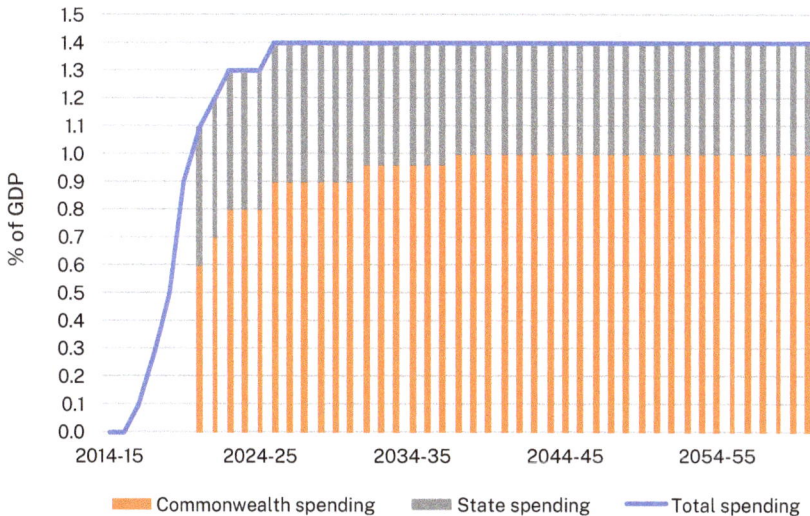

Figure 9.6: Total government NDIS expenditure (Australian government and state/territory contribution) actuals (2013–14 to 2019–20) and IGR 2021 projections (2020–21 to 2060–61).

Source: Commonwealth of Australia (2021b:Chart 7.3.1).

The NDIS began the transition to national coverage in 2016, and has only recently completed full national rollout. As is noted in the text of the 2021 IGR, there is consequently a degree of uncertainty around the full costs of the scheme, with unexpectedly high rates of growth in participant numbers and in average participant costs to date. As the rollout of the scheme matures, subsequent years of expenditure data will naturally provide a more robust basis for projections. Even when the scheme has stabilised, additional real growth could be expected associated with new technologies and new areas of demand. The uncertainties inherent in projection of NDIS future costs suggest that there would be significant benefits associated with undertaking sensitivity analyses or scenario forecasts of the kind undertaken by the Parliamentary Budget Office (PBO 2021). The PBO base scenario assumes a slowing of growth in participant numbers to match population growth by 2027–28, while the high scenario (see Figure 9.7) assumes growth at 4 percentage points above population growth per year. The high scenario includes higher rates of growth in per participant expenditure than the base scenario. This presentation of a range of future NDIS payment projections is arguably more suitable to a recent program such as the NDIS than a single line projection. The need for scenario-based projections is further underlined by the recent numbers released in the October 2022–23 budget forecasting a substantial increase over the medium term.

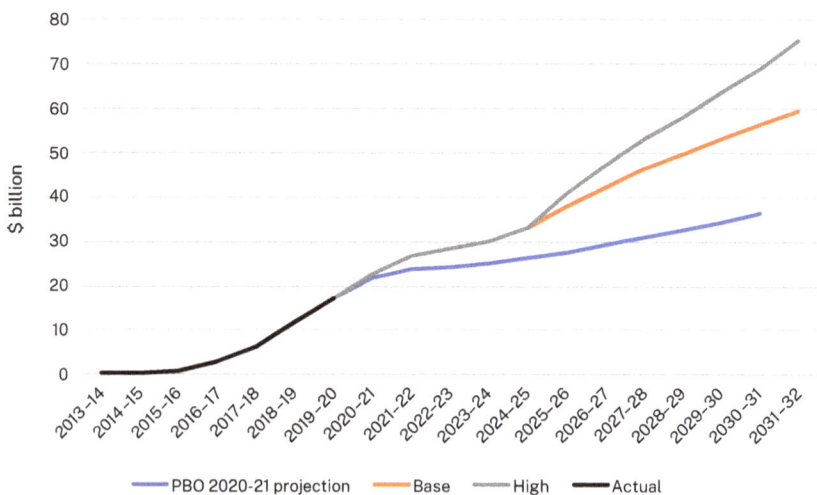

Figure 9.7: Total government NDIS expenditure (Australian government and state/territory contribution) actuals (2013–14 to 2019–20) and PBO projections (2020–21 to 2031–32).

Source: PBO (2021).

The key drivers of growth of health, aged care and NDIS expenditure

As outlined in previous sections, a number of drivers are in play when looking to the future expenditure on health, aged care and NDIS services. While the IGR relies largely on population growth, age structure changes and historical service trends, we have argued that a more nuanced analysis would draw attention to several important factors that are worthy of further attention in the future. An alternative approach would rely not just on historical trends but consider how recent and emerging trends are likely to affect morbidity, service use, patterns of care and prices in the future.

In this section, we focus on volume of services, changing disease patterns, expected excess health price inflation and the ageing of the population. There is also, of course, the role of population growth—more people means more expenditure on health services. In the period from 2011–12 to 2018–19, the decomposition analysis showed population growth to be the single largest driver (at 1.5 per cent per year) of increased health expenditure. Changes in non-demographic factors, discussed in terms of their specific components below, accounted for 1.2 per cent per year, and population ageing for 0.9 per cent per year.

But there are other factors worthy of attention, as set out in Table 9.2. The age-specific rates of disability (declining over time at older ages), the role of technology, shifts in models of care (increased primary care in the health sector, increased home-based care in the aged-care sector), the role of informal care and of labour supply, and the contribution of state/territory and private payments are all important factors as we look to the future.

Table 9.2: What is in the IGR and what could be in the IGR.

	Health system	Aged-care system
Demographic drivers		
Population growth		
Population ageing		
Non-demographic drivers	Best fit (for each of hospital, medical, PBS and private health insurance to 2031)	Best fit 'aggregate' non demographic drivers (expenditure per person)
Prevalence of disease		
Prevalence of disability		
Volume of services		

	Health system	Aged-care system
Excess health or aged-care inflation		
Technology		
Impact of income growth		
Models of care		
Informal care		
Labour force supply		
State payment share		
Private payment share		

Legend: green = what is in the IGR; blue = what could be.
Source: Authors' summary.

Growth in volume of services per case of disease

Volume of services delivered per case of disease has been a major driver of health expenditure in recent decades, though it is notable that the growth of this factor has moderated substantially in the most recent decade to 0.67 per cent per year (Table 9.1) compared to previous decades (Goss 2008, 2022). It is to be expected that, as income increases, more services will be delivered per case of disease. This is shown, for example, in the provision of more orthopaedic procedures to those with private health insurance (who have higher income/wealth). But this also illustrates the problem with understanding the drivers of increased service provision and the extent to which the increase leads to better health outcomes.

The 0.67 per cent annual growth rate in the period 2011–12 to 2018–19 represents a 7 per cent growth rate in services per case of disease when extrapolated over 10 years. The focus on the growth in services per case of disease does not address the extent to which there were gains in patient outcome: that is, whether the increase also delivered higher value. The availability of new technology is the major driver of increases in volume of services, and many new technologies are used in addition to the existing treatments but with better outcomes. New technologies often are more expensive replacements for older treatments. If new treatments and technologies deliver better patient outcomes, then there is the potential for improvements in productivity and participation.

From the perspective of a wellbeing framework, improvements in human capital associated with increased health and health-related expenditure could enhance social and economic sustainability rather than detract from it. From the perspective of the individual, a well-healed broken limb, a replaced disintegrating hip joint or the successful management of a chronic disease means not only enhanced quality of life, but the ability to continue to contribute to their families and their community.

Both the MBS and the PBS have established health technology assessment processes to establish value for money before new technologies are accepted for public funding. These focus on the technology in its recommended application; once listed, however, there is generally little constraint on the volume. In hospitals, technology assessments are not widely applied. The introduction of Activity Based Funding has constrained the cost growth per admission (casemix adjusted). But this is not an incentive to reduce low-value admissions. This may help to explain why the volume of services per case of disease growth is higher for admitted patient services than for the MBS. As a constraint on overall growth, the Commonwealth has also introduced a 6.5 per cent cap on the increase in its contribution to public hospital expenditure from 2017–18.

Expected changes in future expenditure for selected diseases

Changing patterns of disease have major implications for future service use and life expectancy, and hence for expenditure relating to both health and aged-care services. Looking back, for example, the dramatic reduction in circulatory disease from the 1970s has had dramatic consequences for life expectancy and health expenditure that were not even imagined in the 1950s (Gibson and Goss 2020). The COVID-19 pandemic provides a more recent example of how unexpected changes in disease can have significant consequences for the health system. By their nature, future disease trends are difficult to predict with any certainty—but there are indicators of future changes that may be taken into account. Box 9.1 sets out some of the possible futures relating to dementia, diabetes and kidney disease, mental illness and cardiovascular disease, and provides a valuable illustration of the case for sensitivity analyses or scenario modelling in undertaking projections in the health and aged-care sectors.

Box 9.1: Trends in disease patterns and implications for future expenditure.

Dementia

Dementia will continue to have a major impact on health and aged-care expenditure growth because of the ageing of the population and population growth. But it is expected that the age standardised rate of dementia will at least be stable and may well decline if the decline in the age-standardised incidence rate of dementia that has occurred in parts of the Western world in the last two decades continues (Wolters et al. 2020). If this happens, this will reduce pressure on health and aged-care expenditure growth. At the same time, there is good evidence from the Royal Commission that the quality of care being provided to people with dementia in aged care is well below community expectations (RCACQS 2021). If the recommendations of the Royal Commission area are actioned, there is reason to expect increased growth in the volume of services per person devoted to dementia.

Diabetes and kidney disease

There has been an increase in the prevalence rates of diabetes and kidney disease in recent decades due to the increase in obesity and this increase is expected to continue (AIHW 2021a). This will lead to a need for extra expenditure for diabetes and kidney disease. And if more untreated diabetes is treated, this will increase the volume of services delivered per case of disease.

Mental illness

There is no evidence the age-standardised rate of mental illness is either decreasing or increasing. And because mental illness is concentrated in the young and middle-aged, the ageing factor does not increase future expenditure on mental illness. The main factor to watch with regard to mental illness is the growth in volume of services delivered per case of disease. This may be an area where, like dementia, the volume of services currently delivered per case of disease is below community expectations. Therefore governments may decide to increase services that improve mental health. However, this may not lead to extra health expenditure, because, as the Productivity Commission has shown, increasing expenditure on programs directed at social determinants of mental illness like early childhood experiences and education, poverty and unemployment may be more cost-effective for the society than increasing expenditure on hospital interventions to reduce mental illness (Productivity Commission 2020:Tables I1 and I2).

Cardiovascular disease

The age-standardised burden of cardiovascular disease has dropped by 41 per cent from 2003 to 2018. What might happen from 2021 to 2061 with the burden of cardiovascular disease and what might be the consequent impact on cardiovascular expenditure growth? Based on the trend in the last two decades, it is likely that cardiovascular disease burden rates will continue to decline quite significantly, but at a somewhat lower rate than the 2.9 per cent per year decline seen from 2011 to 2018 (AIHW 2021b).

Expected excess health price inflation

Over the past decade, the negative growth rate of excess health price inflation for medical services (–0.5 per cent per year) has partially offset the excess health price inflation for admitted patient services (0.7 per cent per year). This excess health price inflation for admitted patient services is expected to continue in the future as the healthcare services sector is labour intensive. It is notable that the excess health price inflation for medical services in the period 2011–12 to 2018–19 was negative. The prices for Medicare medical services increased by only 8.8 per cent in the seven years to 2018–19 (1.2 per cent per year) in comparison to the increase in the GNE deflator of 12.6 per cent (1.7 per cent per year). This artificial holding down of medical prices due to government policy cannot be expected to continue for much longer (and has almost certainly contributed to increased private expenditure), so excess medical price inflation is likely to increase once more. The impact on government expenditure may be constrained if more costs are shifted to out-of-pocket expenses. The question of what might be involved in excess price inflation for aged care is yet to be scrutinised in the economic literature.

Ageing

Ageing is not the major driver of health expenditure growth. As shown in Table 9.1, it has been 0.9 per cent per year in the last decade for admitted patient and medical services. The fine print of the IGR always points out that the non-demographic growth rate (expected by the IGR to be 1.9 per cent per year in the next 40 years) is the larger driver of health expenditure growth, with demographic change accounting for 1.4 per cent per year. Of that 1.4 per cent, population growth rather than population ageing accounts for the larger share. Yet whenever the results are presented by politicians and reported on by journalists, there is always an emphasis on ageing being a major driver of health expenditure growth, and that ageing is a major challenge.

It is also frequently assumed that not only does the change in the age structure (that is, ageing) have a large impact on health expenditure growth, but also that a large amount of the increase in expenditure comes about because of a higher percentage increase in expenditure for the older age groups as compared to the young and middle-aged. Historically, however, this has not been the case. For the time period 2004–05 to 2012–13, admitted patient expenditure per person grew by 32 per cent for the age group 35 to 64 years, and by 17 per cent for the age group 65 years and over (see Figure 9.8).

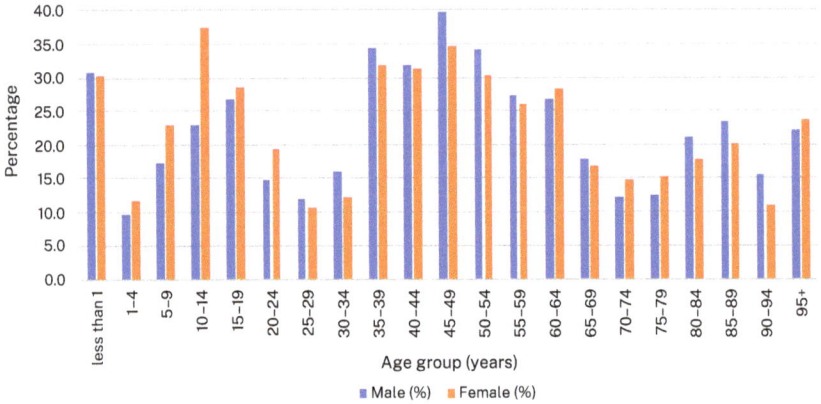

Figure 9.8: Growth in average total hospital admitted patient expenditure per person by age and sex, 2004–05 to 2012–13.

Source: AIHW (2017).

If the 32 per cent growth rate for the 35–64-year-old age group is not constrained in the future, this age group will become the predominant source of pressure on hospital admitted patient expenditure growth.

The impact of the growth in the aged population will be largely dependent on the health status of those older age groups; whether those longer lifespans will mean a longer period of poor health and disability or a healthier old age with a delay in the onset of disease and frailty. The impact of a change in these assumptions has quite a substantial effect, as shown in the New South Wales IGR (Cheung et al. 2021) (see Table 9.3).

Table 9.3: Sensitivity of total annual health expenditure growth to alternative morbidity scenarios calculated for the 2021 New South Wales IGR.

Expense category	Compression of morbidity		Expansion of morbidity	
	Percentage point change from baseline			
	Male	Female	Male	Female
Hospital	−0.17	−0.12	+0.25	+0.20
Outpatients	−0.19	−0.09	+0.20	+0.10
Community	−0.19	−0.13	+0.33	+0.25

Source: Cheung et al. (2021).

Impact of COVID-19

COVID-19 was an unexpected shock to the health system and indeed to the wider economy in 2019–20. We confine our comments to the health system, leaving others to comment on the broader economy-wide implications. The 2021 IGR shows a sudden large increase in healthcare expenditure for the years 2019–20 and 2020–21, then projects a return to pre-existing growth. There are several reasons why this assumption may not hold.

First, there may be a one-off but sustained increase in the cost of delivering health care. The need for increased testing and personal protective equipment can be expected to continue, even as case numbers decrease. The need to furlough infectious and potentially infected health staff will increase wage costs.

Second, there is already evidence of delayed diagnoses and initiation of treatment due to COVID-19. This can be expected to result in increased cases (the catch-up) and increased costs per case (more severe cases due to delays in diagnosis). In addition, the effects on the health workforce and other aspects of capacity will continue to stress the system.

Third, the current pandemic is not over, and there is every expectation that new variants and new infectious diseases are likely to arise. The likelihood of a pandemic is related to the size of the global population, and the extent of interaction (travel) between geographic areas. As both have risen enormously, the expected period of time until the 'next pandemic' is now much less than it was before.

Discussion

The genesis of the IGR is a concern with the implications of an ageing population. This concern has changed remarkably little over the two decades of producing IGRs; the projected growth in future expenditure is widely interpreted as due to ageing. For example, the former treasurer in his media release said one of the key insights of the IGR is that 'our population is growing slower and ageing faster than expected' (Frydenberg 2021). The ABC said, in its report on the 2021 IGR:

> A look 40 years into Australia's future shows that thanks in part to the pandemic the population is not going to grow as quickly as previously thought, meaning *a smaller economy will be tasked with managing the burden of a rapidly ageing population.* (Hitch 2021, emphasis added).

Later in the same report, the ABC states 'a large and ageing population that will continue to put greater stress on welfare and health services'.

Yet the evidence presented in this chapter finds population ageing is a modest driver of increasing expenditure, accounting for 24 per cent of health expenditure growth (Table 9.1).

Moreover, in a global context, Australia is projected to be 'the youngest among the English-speaking countries and the countries of Western Europe. It will also be younger than many of the current advanced economies in Asia' (McDonald 2016). An ageing population, rather than being seen as a difficulty that needs to be overcome, could be seen as an achievement as more people have the opportunity to live longer fuller lives. An older population contributes to the economy directly as older workers remain in the workforce, and indirectly through unpaid child care supporting greater female participation. The contributions made by older people are often underestimated. Drawing on the most recent Australian Bureau of Statistics data available, there were over 1 million employed persons aged 60 or over. Around one in five older people are volunteer workers up until age 80, when the proportion begins to drop. At age 65–69, 26 per cent were employed, 23 per cent undertaking volunteer work, 16 per cent caring for a person with a disability and 22 per cent providing child care (Gibson 2021).

The focus of the IGR on expenditure inevitably emphasises cost to taxpayers without acknowledging the benefits provided by that expenditure. Health expenditure must be understood as both an investment and a cost. Health benefits are improved length and quality of life. Health-related quality of life is more complex to measure than longevity, and even a higher prevalence of chronic conditions may reflect earlier diagnosis and treatment and improved rather than poorer functional ability. On the other hand, more health services may not always deliver better health outcomes. The quality of care in the Australian aged-care sector has been held up as a matter of national shame, and more aged-care expenditure is needed to deliver improved outcomes. While complex, more investigation of these issues is required to understand the value of a higher expenditure level, particularly as ageing is not the dominant factor behind projected expenditure growth.

The IGR estimates are based on a continuation of the growth trajectories of the previous two decades. Projections are most useful and policy relevant if they are based on a detailed understanding of the drivers of expenditure in the past. Moreover, patterns of change are not uniform across population subgroups. For example, in contrast to the standard assumption of greatest cost increases being incurred at older ages, the data show that the greatest impact of increased service intensity has been seen in the 35–64-year age group, rather than the post 70s and 80s.

This chapter also argues that changing prevalence of disease is an important consideration, as different diseases have different and likely changing treatment and expenditure consequences. A more sophisticated approach would use disaggregated information about recent trends in disease prevalence and treatment, and a more considered basis for projections than simple aggregate historical trends.

One of the missed opportunities of the 2021 IGR is that the analysis of drivers of health, aged care and NDIS expenditure in the past is inadequate. A more sophisticated approach would investigate how recent and emerging factors are likely to impact future expenditure and would provide a series of sensitivity analyses to allow more consideration of the robustness of the results.

The Commonwealth IGR presents only point estimates with regard to the drivers of health, aged care and NDIS expenditure growth. Yet the results are clearly sensitive to a range of assumptions about these expenditure growth drivers. In contrast, as shown earlier, the New South Wales IGR estimates how much projections will change if there is compression or expansion of morbidity, and the impact of using dynamic age cost indices rather than static age cost indices. The lack of accuracy in previous IGR projections in predicting actual growth is an indication that a more nuanced approach such as that employed in the New South Wales IGR is needed.

The 40-year projection period adopted in the first IGR remains unchanged and unchallenged two decades later. This long projection period is not well suited to the changing patterns of disability, disease, need for assistance and types of interventions available described in this chapter. The PBO focused on projections to 2031, while the Deloitte Access Economics scenarios undertaken for the Royal Commission project out to 2050. While a 40-year timeframe may have benefits for superannuation and income support planning, it is hard to see what the benefits are in planning for disability, health and aged-care services when the medium term of 10 to 20 years is so critical to current planning. Given the nature of compound growth, it is misleading to go beyond 20 years for projections, as small misestimations in parameters have major impacts 30 or 40 years into the future.

In the aged-care and disability systems, there is the additional problem that, because there have been such major policy upheavals in recent years, the historical trends, on which the IGR business-as-usual projections are based, are rendered almost obsolete. Scenario analyses—rather than just projections with sensitivity analysis—are needed to deal with this issue.

Finally, the 2021 IGR takes a very narrow focus by considering Commonwealth expenditure only. The other main sources of financing are state/territory governments and individuals (through out-of-pocket expenses and private health insurance). Other entities including state governments and the Productivity Commission have partially addressed this shortcoming. Despite these contributions, in the Australian government IGR we continue to have only a partial picture of the health, aged-care and disability sectors. What should matter to individuals—who are both taxpayers and service consumers—is the total amount they have to pay for adequate services, care and support.

References

AIHW (Australian Institute of Health and Welfare) 2017, *Australian health expenditure—demographics and diseases: hospital admitted patient expenditure 2004–05 to 2012–13*, AIHW, Canberra.

AIHW 2021a, 'Drivers of change in disease burden', in *Australian Burden of Disease Study 2018: Interactive data on disease burden*, AIHW, available at: www.aihw. gov.au/reports/burden-of-disease/abds-2018-interactive-data-disease-burden/ contents/drivers-of-change-in-disease-burden (accessed 21 September 2021).

AIHW 2021b, 'Comparisons over time', in *Australian Burden of Disease Study 2018: Interactive data on disease burden*, AIHW, available at: www.aihw.gov.au/ reports/burden-of-disease/abds-2018-interactive-data-disease-burden/contents/ comparisons-over-time (accessed 21 September 2021).

AIHW n.d., 'Health & welfare expenditure' (data set), AIHW, Canberra (scope: 2021 and earlier), available at: www.aihw.gov.au/expenditure-data#Public (accessed 21 September 2021).

Anderson, GF and Hussey, PS 2000, 'Population aging: A comparison among industrialized countries', *Health Affairs* 19(3):191–203, doi.org/10.1377/hlthaff. 19.3.191.

Cheung, J, Cheung, L, Ge, K and Zhang, C 2021, *2021 intergenerational report: Ageing and health expenses in New South Wales—revisiting the long-term modelling approach*, Treasury Technical Research Paper series 21-03, New South Wales Treasury, available at: nla.gov.au/nla.obj-2918574276/view (accessed 23 February 2023).

Clare, R and Tulpulé, A 1994, *Australia's aging society*, Background paper no. 37, Economic Planning and Advisory Council, Canberra.

Commonwealth of Australia 2002, *Intergenerational report 2002–03, 2002–03 Budget Paper No. 5*, Commonwealth of Australia, Canberra, available at: treasury.gov.au/ sites/default/files/2019-03/2002-IGR-report.pdf (accessed 13 June 2022).

Commonwealth of Australia 2007, *Intergenerational report 2007*, Commonwealth of Australia, Canberra, available at: treasury.gov.au/sites/default/files/2019-03/ IGR_2007_final_report-1.pdf (accessed 17 February 2023).

Commonwealth of Australia 2010, *Australia to 2050: Future challenges*, Commonwealth of Australia, Canberra, available at: treasury.gov.au/sites/ default/files/2019-03/IGR_2010.pdf (accessed 17 February 2023).

Commonwealth of Australia 2015, *2015 intergenerational report: Australia in 2055*, Commonwealth of Australia, Canberra, available at: treasury.gov.au/sites/default/ files/2019-03/2015_IGR.pdf (accessed 17 February 2023).

Commonwealth of Australia 2021a, *2021 intergenerational report: Australia over the next 40 years*, Commonwealth of Australia, Canberra, available at: treasury. gov.au/sites/default/files/2021-06/p2021_182464.pdf (accessed 13 June 2022).

Commonwealth of Australia 2021b, '2021 intergenerational report chart data' (data set), Treasury, Canberra, available at: treasury.gov.au/publication/2021- intergenerational-report (accessed 13 June 2022).

Commonwealth of Australia 2022, *Budget October 2022–23: Building a better future*, Commonwealth of Australia, Canberra, available at: www.budget.gov. au/2022-23-october/content/overview/download/budget_overview.pdf (accessed 29 October 2022).

Deloitte Access Economics 2020, *Aged care reform: Projecting future impacts. A report for the Royal Commission into Aged Care Quality and Safety*, research paper 11, available at: agedcare.royalcommission.gov.au/sites/default/files/ 2020-09/research-paper-11-aged-care-reform-projecting-future-impacts.pdf (accessed 9 February 2023).

Dyer, S, Valeri, M, Arora, N, Ross, T and Winsall, M 2020, *Review of international systems of long-term care of older people. Report prepared for the Royal Commission into Aged Care Quality and Safety*, research paper 2, available at: agedcare.royal commission.gov.au/sites/default/files/2020-09/Research%20Paper%202%20-%20Review%20of%20international%20systems%20for%20long-term%20care%20of....pdf (accessed 9 February 2023).

Frydenberg, J 2021, '2021 intergenerational report', Media release, 28 June, available at: ministers.treasury.gov.au/ministers/josh-frydenberg-2018/media-releases/2021-intergenerational-report (accessed 17 February 2023).

Gibson, D 2021, 'All the older people: where do they all belong?' *MJA Insight+* 4, 15 February, available at: insightplus.mja.com.au/2021/4/all-the-older-people-where-do-they-all-belong/ (accessed 9 February 2023).

Gibson, D and Goss, J 2020, 'Ninety and not out: Understanding our oldest old', *Australasian Journal on Ageing* 39(1):e62–e69, doi.org/10.1111/ajag.12695.

Goss, J 2008, *Projection of Australian health care expenditure by disease, 2003 to 2033,* Health and Welfare Expenditure series no. 36, cat. no. HWE 43, AIHW, Canberra.

Goss, JR 2022, 'Health expenditure data, analysis and policy relevance in Australia, 1967 to 2020', *International Journal of Environmental Research and Public Health* 19(4):2143, doi.org/10.3390/ijerph19042143.

Hall, J, Fiebig, DG and van Gool, K 2020, 'Private finance publicly subsidized: The case of Australian health insurance', in S Thomson, A Sagan and E Mossialos (eds), *Private health insurance: History, politics and performance*, pp. 41–64, European Observatory on Health Systems and Policies, Cambridge University Press, doi.org/10.1017/9781139026468.002.

Hall, J and Maynard, A 2005, 'Healthcare lessons from Australia: What can Michael Howard learn from John Howard?' *British Medical Journal* 330(7487):357–59, doi.org/10.1136/bmj.330.7487.357.

Hall, J and Savage, E 2005, 'The role of the private sector in the Australian health care system', in A Maynard (ed.), *The public–private mix for health*, Nuffield Trust, Radcliffe Publishing.

Hitch, G 2021, 'Intergenerational report predicts smaller population growth, rapidly ageing citizens', *ABC News*, 28 June, available at: www.abc.net.au/news/2021-06-28/intergenerational-report-ageing-population-growth-covid-debt/100248642 (accessed 17 February 2023).

McDonald, P 2016, 'Ageing in Australia: Population changes and responses', in H Kendig, P McDonald and J Piggott (eds), *Population ageing and Australia's future*, ANU Press, Canberra, doi.org/10.22459/PAAF.11.2016.04.

PBO (Parliamentary Budget Office) 2021, *Beyond the budget 2021–22: Fiscal outlook and scenarios* (data pack), Commonwealth of Australia, Canberra, available at: data.gov.au/dataset/ds-dga-b9af66c2-a69f-401d-a05e-0c6b428f9026/details (accessed 20 January 2023).

Productivity Commission 2020, *Mental health inquiry report*, report no. 95, Canberra, available at: www.pc.gov.au/inquiries/completed/mental-health/report (accessed 21 September 2021).

Productivity Commission and Melbourne Institute of Applied Economic and Social Research 1999, *Policy implications of the ageing of Australia's population: Conference proceedings, Melbourne, 18–19 March 1998*, AusInfo, Canberra, available at: www.pc.gov.au/research/supporting/ageing-population/ageing.pdf (accessed 21 September 2021).

RCACQS (Royal Commission into Aged Care Quality and Safety) 2019, *Interim report*, vol. 1, Commonwealth of Australia, Canberra.

RCACQS 2021, *Final report: Care, dignity and respect*, vols 1, 2, Commonwealth of Australia, Canberra.

Wiener, J and Tilly, J 2002, 'Population ageing in the United States of America: Implications for public programmes', *International Journal of Epidemiology* 31(4):776–81, doi.org/10.1093/ije/31.4.776.

Wolters, FJ, Chibnik, LB, Waziry, R, et al. 2020, 'Twenty-seven-year time trends in dementia incidence in Europe and the United States: The Alzheimer Cohorts Consortium', *Neurology* 95(5):e519–e531, doi.org/10.1212/WNL.00000000 00010022.

10

The Intergenerational Report and Climate Change

David Pearce

Key points

- The 2021 Intergenerational Report (IGR) provides a clear qualitative description of climate issues but does not provide any quantification or even orders of magnitude of the effects that it identifies.

- Because of the nature of the modelling that underlies the IGR—particularly the assumption that productivity growth returns to long-run values—it is not possible to judge whether the GDP scenarios in the IGR are consistent with the qualitative climate story.

- Indeed, the productivity assumption in effect assumes away any specific climate-related issues.

- This is a missed opportunity, as climate change is a genuine *intergenerational* problem—surely a convincing candidate for an IGR.

- A modest suggestion presented here is that, without requiring a full-blown modelling exercise, the IGR could significantly enhance its contribution to climate issues by using the social cost of carbon (SCC) as a framework.

- Just as the IGR has generated many useful insights through consistent use of a simple growth model (the so-called PPP or 'three Ps' model), with some analysis well within the scope of the IGR it could similarly provide useful insights on climate issues.

Climate change in the IGR

The 2021 Intergenerational Report (IGR) (Commonwealth of Australia 2021) contains a clear, qualitative discussion of climate change (in addition to other environmental challenges) along with a summary of key climate policy measures underway at the time the IGR was prepared.

It sets out some broad channels of climate impact, noting climate change could affect agriculture, the resources sector and the financial sector. It also notes the challenges from emissions mitigation.

Two quotes from the IGR serve to illustrate the broad tenor of the qualitative discussion:

> Rising global temperatures and other changes to the climate will impact locations, sectors and communities in diverse ways driving both structural adjustments and corresponding innovation. Connecting innovation and investment in climate-resilient development can significantly increase the adaptive capacity of our regions, towns and cities.
>
> …
>
> Mitigation efforts will require a step-change in innovation and global collaboration to make new energy technologies commercial and scalable. (Commonwealth of Australia 2021:57)

Importantly, the IGR distinguishes 'physical' effects (that is, the effects of climate change itself) from 'transitional' effects (that is, the effects of mitigation measures designed to reduce emissions). Transitional effects include costs of our own abatement, as well as the net effect of abatement in other countries. On these two effects, the IGR notes:

> A reduction in real GDP associated with climate change would have a fiscal impact through reducing taxation revenue, as well as increasing pressure on expenditure. Other revenue sources such as fuel excise and mining royalties could also be affected by changes in demand and consumption related to a global transition away from fossil fuel use. (Commonwealth of Australia 2021:59)

> Any reduction in GDP is likely to be unevenly distributed across sectors and regions. The agricultural sector is particularly vulnerable to the physical effects of climate change, the resources sector is particularly vulnerable to the transition effects, and the financial sector is vulnerable to both. (Commonwealth of Australia 2021:60).

The IGR implies a clear expectation that climate change (either in the physical or transitional aspects) is likely to reduce GDP (or at least to reduce GDP relative to where it might otherwise be, although the IGR is not clear on this).

Despite a large amount of information available from already existing studies, however, the IGR does not quantify or present orders of magnitude of the GDP effects of climate change through any of the channels it identifies.

Available information on transitional and physical costs

On the question of the costs of abatement (what the IGR calls transitional costs), the Centre for International Economics (CIE 2019) provides a detailed summary of a decade of detailed economic studies and what they imply for the cost of abatement (Figure 10.1 provides a summary of abatement cost from an ensemble of model results). A key point from the figure is that each plotted data point represents a different model outcome, with a large number of points representing a large number of studies (particularly for lower levels of abatement). Importantly, several of the studies reviewed were undertaken by the Commonwealth Treasury itself. Silence about the cost of abatement in the IGR is not a question of lack of readily available information.

Similarly, on the 'physical' cost of climate change, consider two impact examples (literally chosen at random for the purposes of the discussion here, and importantly studies that were available at the time the IGR was prepared. Since then, of course, more information is available from the most recent Intergovernmental Panel on Climate Change reports).

Kompas et al. (2018) use a large computable general equilibrium model to look at the overall economic impacts of climate change defined along a temperature dimension. Figure 10.2 illustrates the loss in GDP (relative to what would otherwise be the case) for different temperature increases over the long run (after 2067). For illustration, Australia's results are presented in comparison with Indonesia and China. The results show a significant loss for Australia (just under 2 per cent), but an even larger loss for neighbours and trading partners.

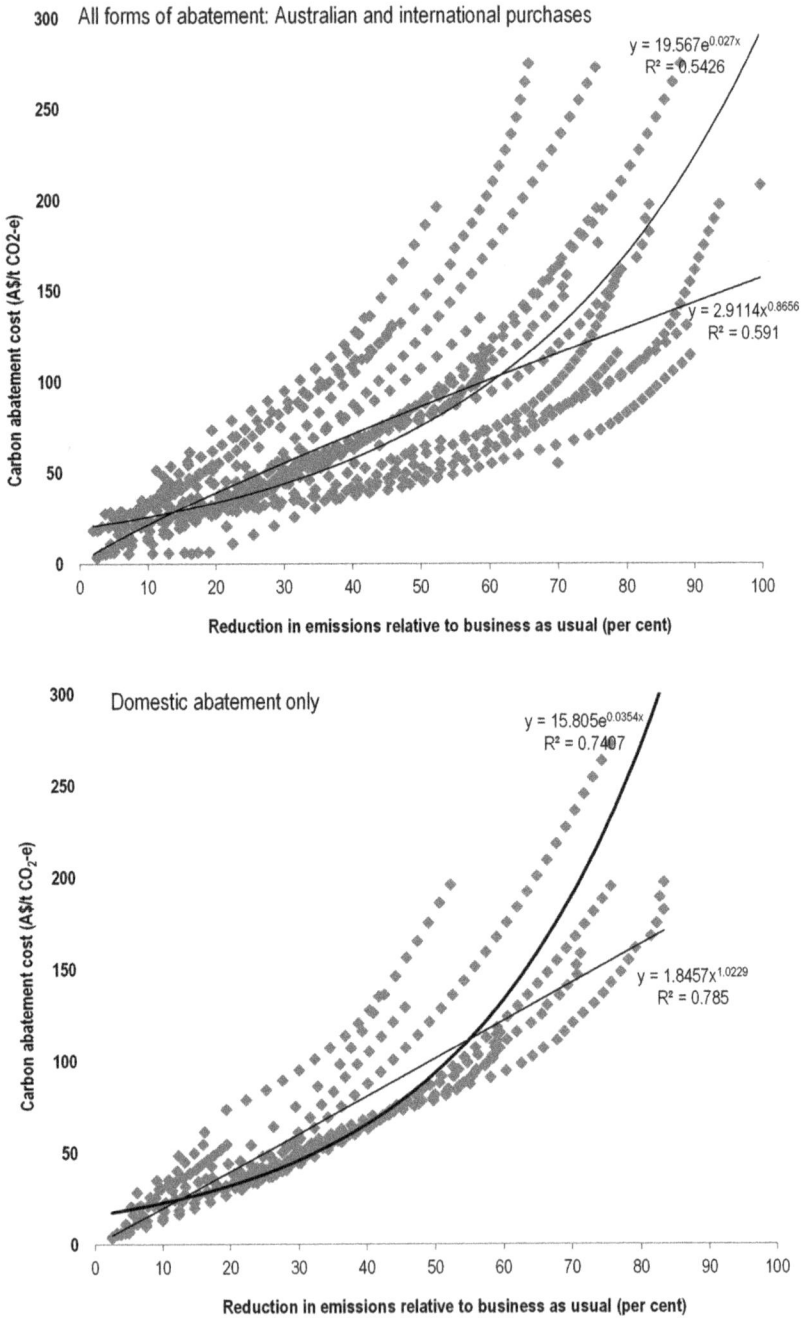

300 All forms of abatement: Australian and international purchases

$y = 19.567e^{0.027x}$
$R^2 = 0.5426$

$y = 2.9114x^{0.8656}$
$R^2 = 0.591$

Carbon abatement cost (A$/t CO2-e)

Reduction in emissions relative to business as usual (per cent)

300 Domestic abatement only

$y = 15.805e^{0.0354x}$
$R^2 = 0.7407$

$y = 1.8457x^{1.0229}$
$R^2 = 0.785$

Carbon abatement cost (A$/t CO$_2$-e)

Reduction in emissions relative to business as usual (per cent)

Figure 10.1: The marginal cost of abatement.
Source: CIE (2019).

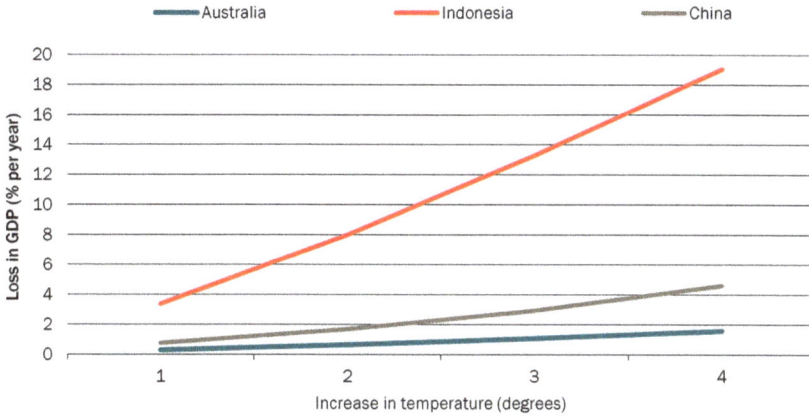

Figure 10.2: Loss in GDP for different temperature scenarios.
Source: Kompas et al. (2018).

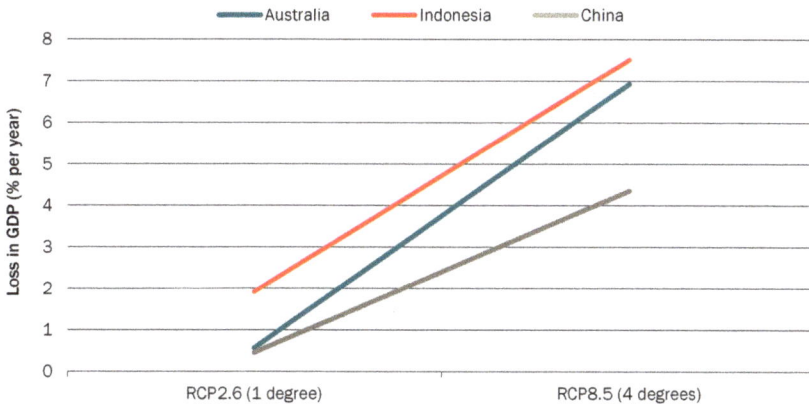

Figure 10.3: Loss in GDP for pathway scenarios.
Source: Kahn et al. (2019).

Along similar lines, Kahn et al. (2019), using a very different methodology (and defined against specific emissions pathway scenarios), look at the effects of climate change on a large panel of countries. Some key results are summarised in Figure 10.3. Again, there are significant potential losses in GDP for Australia and illustrative partners and trading countries.

Rather than explicitly using readily available information, the IGR implicitly assumes that despite climate change and the challenges it brings, (labour) productivity will converge to the long-run average under current policy settings. The modelling methodology used by the IGR does not allow us to assess whether this is reasonable or whether this is internally consistent with the qualitative story about climate change.

It's harder to go any further with the current IGR modelling framework

Put another way, it is hard to determine whether the qualitative discussion of climate change—and the clear expectation of structural changes and potential GDP loss—is, in any sense, consistent with the future pathway of GDP (and other aggregates) projected by the IGR.

This problem arises because of the very general nature of the methodology used by the IGR. Within the 'Population, Participation, Productivity' (PPP) framework the IGR uses, most of the impacts of climate change would appear in the 'productivity' component.

- For example, the net effect of unmitigated climate change could be to lower the productivity of agriculture (through reduced yields, more defensive expenditures on pests and diseases, higher infrastructure expenditure and so on).

- There are other effects of climate change such as sea level rise and tidal surges, which along with expectations of increased storms and flooding would either involve large recovery expenditures or defensive adaptation measures, all of which could appear as reduced economy-wide productivity.

In addition to these productivity effects, climate change and global climate mitigation policy are also likely to have a significant effect on Australia's trade composition and on Australia's terms of trade. Demand for Australian products is likely to shift away from fossil fuels, for example, and towards products that contribute to construction of renewable energy infrastructure.

In contrast to an approach of explicitly tracing through impacts that come along with mitigation and adaptation measures, a core assumption in the IGR (setting aside demographic considerations) is the expected pathway of productivity. The IGR states:

> This report, consistent with previous intergenerational reports, assumes that labour productivity growth converges to a historical average rate of growth. In this report underlying productivity growth converges to 1.5 per cent per year, the average growth rate in labour productivity over the 30 years to 2018–19. Given the current underlying productivity growth rate is below 1.5 per cent, it is

assumed that the transition to the long-term growth rate of 1.5 per cent per year will take place over the next 10 years. (Commonwealth of Australia 2021:46)

How the return to long-run productivity growth—given that it is currently lower than the long-term average—comes about is not made explicit in the IGR.

Thus, rather than examining the future issues involved, this assumption has the effect of assuming any particular climate problems away. Productivity is assumed to return to the long-run average under current policy settings, so (by assumption) nothing in future climate outcomes will change this.[1]

The modelling framework used by the IGR essentially only allows this sort of very broad assumption. Explicitly linking climate change impacts to the IGR projections would require a much more detailed modelling framework.

Such frameworks, of course, already exist and have been extensively used by Treasury and others to consider macro-economic and structural implications of climate change.

A missed opportunity

The minimal treatment of climate change within the IGR is a missed opportunity. Climate change is a genuine *intergenerational* issue— a candidate for an IGR if there ever was one. Climate change extends well beyond the usual scope of government projections and the IGR is one of the few government documents that considers the longer term. Careful consideration of climate change is also consistent with the stated aims of the IGR:

> The role of the Intergenerational Report is to examine the long-term sustainability of current policies and how demographic, technological and other structural trends may affect economic growth and public finances. (Commonwealth of Australia 2021:xvi).

Climate policy is not set and forget: it will require ongoing attention and development at least until 2050 (for the current Paris Agreement commitments) and then well beyond that because, even with the Paris

---

1   This brings to mind the 'assume a can opener' economist joke, which is so prevalent that it now has its own Wikipedia page (en.wikipedia.org/wiki/Assume_a_can_opener).

Agreement, the issues are not 'fixed' in any sense—the implications of increased greenhouse gas concentrations will continue for many years even once annual emissions are reduced.

This leads to the question of how policy focus can be consistently maintained over time; in effect of how it can be coordinated over time. This is particularly challenging as the full scope of policy response is well beyond the tenure of individuals currently in government or in business (this is not just a government problem):

> Emissions pledges often have agreeably long deadlines. The tenures of bosses have been shortening. The revolving doors of most C-suites will have spun several times before chief executives of multinationals are expected to keep promises made by predecessors. (Financial Times 2021)

Even today, there is limited coordination between different elements of climate policy. It is not unusual for analysis of the benefits of mitigation to use different values for each ton of carbon abated, and different policies have very different implicit costs of carbon. And, as is well known, Australian policy has been notably unstable over the past decade or so.

Is it possible for the IGR to make some contribution to dealing with these issues?

A modest suggestion

In between the current treatment of climate in the IGR and a comprehensive modelling effort, there is a modest possibility—well within reach of the resources available for the IGR—to enhance the analysis of climate change within the IGR to provide a role in the intergenerational understanding of climate change.

The suggestion is that the IGR uses the concept of the social cost of carbon (SCC) to draw together the current (that is, at the time of each IGR) quantitative understanding of key elements of climate challenges. This is not a suggestion for a full revamped modelling exercise. While this would be good, and appropriate, there is a risk that it will be seen as well beyond the scope of the IGR as currently understood.

The suggestion here is much more modest and easily achievable. Essentially, it is that the IGR use the SCC as a tool and framework to consider broader issues around climate change.

This suggestion comes by making an analogy with how the IGR works for other issues. In the current and past editions, the IGR has successfully used a simple PPP growth framework as a means to discuss future issues. Rather than being a complete or comprehensive modelling approach, it is, instead, a way of thinking through issues to help frame future problems.

The PPP framework is a decomposition of elements of growth from one particular perspective. It essentially involves pulling apart an identity and considering each piece of that identity. To be blunt, no one perceives the PPP framework as a sophisticated forecasting model. But it is a powerful 'pedagogical' tool to work through important determinants of future growth.[2]

As illustrated below, the SCC can be used as a framework to expose and think through a range of issues that need to be confronted—in exactly the same way that demographic changes, or participation or broad productivity issues, need to be confronted.

The social cost of carbon

According to William Nordhaus (winner of the 2018 Nobel Prize in Economics):

> The most important single economic concept in the economics of climate change is the social cost of carbon (SCC). This term designates the economic cost caused by an additional ton of carbon dioxide emissions or its equivalent. In a more precise definition, it is the change in the discounted value of economic welfare from an additional unit of CO_2-equivalent emissions. (Nordhaus 2017:1518)

The SCC of carbon is well embedded in the economic literature of climate change and has received considerable attention in the United States, where it forms the basis of a number of regulatory measures (as discussed in Nordhaus 2017). The SCC is, in effect, a measure of the benefit of abatement and provides a benchmark for how much abatement should take

---

2   Here I'm using 'pedagogical' in a loose sense referring to teaching people how to think through a particular problem. Thus, several iterations of the IGR have 'taught' the audience to think about growth in terms of its PPP components.

place given a particular SCC. It is a number that can enter into benefit–cost calculations around particular climate policies or projects, showing the degree to which benefits offset the costs of mitigation. At the same time, the SCC is closely related to adaptation in that adaptation (at a cost) lowers the future SCC. The SCC creates a pivot to compare both mitigation and adaptation.

The SCC has received less attention in Australia for a variety of reasons; in part because the large modelling exercises undertaken by the Australian government over the past 10 years (see CIE 2019) focused mostly on the mitigation costs of achieving a particular target and not on whether that target had benefits greater than costs.

Further, there is no point pretending that issues around the practical measurement of the SCC have been resolved—they have not. Indeed, there is considerable disagreement about the appropriate values for the SCC. Some have suggested abandoning it altogether (see, for example, Pezzey 2018), while others have noted serious problems with the integrated assessment models (IAMs) typically used to derive the SCC.

For example, work by Robert Pindyck critiques the use of IAMs.[3] He argues that:

> These models have crucial flaws that make them close to useless as tools for policy analysis: certain inputs (e.g., the discount rate) are arbitrary, but have huge effects on the SCC estimates the models produce; the models' descriptions of the impact of climate change are completely ad hoc, with no theoretical or empirical foundation; and the models can tell us nothing about the most important driver of the SCC, the possibility of a catastrophic climate outcome. (Pindyck 2013:860)

Cass Sunstein (who headed the White House Office of Information and Regulatory Affairs in the Obama administration) recently reflected:

> Working on the social cost of carbon, to produce a concrete number, may have been the most difficult task of my professional life. It was difficult in part because of the known unknowns, and the unknown unknowns, and the challenge of deciding how to handle

---

3   See in particular his 'Climate change policy: What do the models tell us?' and 'The use and misuse of models for climate policy', both available at web.mit.edu/rpindyck/www/papers.htm. The same arguments appear is his book, *Climate Future: Averting and Adapting to Climate Change* (Oxford University Press, 2022).

them. In some respects, we were flying blind. Dozens of people were involved; many of them were experts on science, economics, or both. They disagreed on fundamental issues. They disagreed vigorously about the magnitude of the harmful effects of greenhouse gas emissions. They disagreed about how much was known and how much was unknown. They disagreed about how to handle the possibility of catastrophe and whether to build in a large margin of error, which would produce a much higher number. We were able to reach agreement, but it took many months, and (to put it gently) not everyone who joined the agreement thought that the resulting number was the best choice. (Sunstein 2021:1–2)

Uncertainty (and disagreement) is the point

Despite these issues surrounding the SCC, for our purposes here—to propose a means by which the IGR can contribute to intergenerational climate issues—the SCC provides a useful framework to consider climate-related issues. Indeed, disagreements about the SCC tells us something fundamental about the nature of the climate problem. Examining the SCC and pulling apart its components provides a framework for thinking through the issues (directly analogous to the PPP framework).

Calculating and understanding the SCC requires:

- Modelling the link between emissions and greenhouse gas concentration levels (this is usually undertaken in large-scale climate models, and often summarised in IAMs).

- Establishing the link between greenhouse gas concentration and changes in temperature and other relevant 'physical' climate outcomes such as sea level rise, rainfall changes, frequency of storms and so on. (Again, this is usually undertaken in large-scale climate models, summarised in IAMs—although most IAMs focus on temperature change only.)

- Establishing a link between the climate outcomes above and relevant economic variables. This is often termed the 'damage function': for a given increase in temperature, how much is economic activity affected. These damages are usually measured in terms of GDP, but in principle there is no reason why any other relevant measure of economic wellbeing could not be used.

- Calculating future damages for each year, and then using an appropriate discount rate to bring these back to today's dollars.
- Confronting the uncertainty inherent in each of these steps and calculating how uncertainty itself affects the SCC.

It is true that every one of these linkages is uncertain. And it is precisely this uncertainty that provides the opportunity to confront a variety of perspectives and broaden the understanding within the IGR.

The argument put here is not that the IGR could, or should, resolve a single specific value for the SCC, but that the IGR could use the inherent structure of the SCC to further discuss the long-term implications of climate change. Subsequent analyses and tracking over time would institutionalise a substantive body of information that could extend well beyond any single report or administration. It would, over time, 'teach' readers how to think about quantitative elements of the climate issue (in the same way the IGR has already taught about the components of growth).

This suggestion would allow the IGR—within a constrained and manageable framework—to more explicitly confront trends that 'may affect economic growth and public finances' (Commonwealth of Australia 2021:xvi). It would allow, for example:

- **Explicit consideration of the 'damages function'.** This is an open area of research that is continually evolving. But being explicit about the damages function allows consideration of different views in policy development. A less steep damages function tends to lead to a lower SCC (all other things equal). Arguing for less (more) action on climate change is consistent with arguing for a less (more) steep damages function.
- **Explicit consideration of the discount rate.** This will help provide guidance on long-term coordination of climate policy. (As an aside, it is telling that the IGR does not mention the discount rate at all.) A lower discount rate tends to raise the SCC (all other things equal). Arguing for less (more) action on climate change is consistent with arguing for a higher (lower) discount rate. The discount rate is a central concept in all intertemporal policy, and explicit discussion in the context of the IGR would allow a lot more information to emerge than typically does in policy discussion.

- **Explicit consideration of uncertainty.** Uncertainty is often seen as something of a nuisance in climate policy. In contrast, *climate policy is actually about uncertainty*. Uncertainty is not a bug, but a feature. All other things equal, uncertainty tends to *increase* the SCC. That is, uncertainty implies doing more, rather than less (see, for example, Van den Bremmer and Van der Ploeg 2021).

Another perspective on lessons from the SCC

There is a final, slightly oblique take on the SCC that also helps clarify a question that currently confronts any analysis of mitigation measures. This question is whether any cost–benefit analysis looking to value mitigation should use a global SCC (that is, the cost to the whole world) or the Australian cost of carbon (cost to Australia only). These two provide very different answers. This is also related to the more primitive question of why we should worry about Australia's marginal abatement given that it has no effect on the climate.

This take comes from a remarkably useful article from the late Martin Weitzman. Published in *Economica*, Weitzman (2017) sets out a thought experiment (what he calls a parable) he had developed over time in a number of previous articles. He seemed to consider the *Economica* article a better presentation. The journal is probably not that widely read outside a circle of specialists, but the overall argument deserves much wider understanding.

The thought experiment is the idea of a World Climate Assembly (WCA), in which countries come together to vote on a binding global carbon price. This carbon price is imposed everywhere, and nations are allowed to keep the relevant revenue. The key element of Weitzman's paper is the analysis of the price that is likely to emerge from this process (under the conditions of the thought experiment, of course—Weitzman recognises the practical issues involved).

Consider thinking about what price to vote for from Australia's perspective. Australia might initially want to vote for a very low price, because every increase in the world carbon price imposes cost on us (as we reduce emissions in response), but with very little benefit because Australia's reduction in emissions are tiny compared with the world.

But at the same time, every increase in the world price also induces abatement everywhere else in the world, which compared with Australia's abatement is very large. From Australia's point of view, there is a large abatement 'multiplier' for every increment in the world price. Large global abatement is exactly what Australia wants as this reduces Australia's climate risk. Australia ends up with much more benefit from global abatement than our own abatement cost.

Thus Australia (and every other country) faces this interesting trade-off in choosing a price to vote for.

What Weitzman goes on to show—under simplifying but not unreasonable assumptions—is that the price chosen by a majority rule voting in the WCA is something very close to the global SCC.

The whole argument is subtle (typical of Weitzman's work) for it shows us that the *global* SCC is an appropriate metric for decisions within Australia because it is consistent in dealing with the global externality associated with climate change—the fact that Australia needs the whole world to abate in order to minimise our climate risk. Further, Australia should do at least the abatement consistent with that global SCC (despite our emissions being small) because that is again consistent with achieving global outcomes that are in Australia's interest.

In summary

The IGR currently has a minimal treatment of climate change; both in detail and in overall conception of how climate issues affect future outcomes.

One solution to this would be to fundamentally overhaul the modelling strategy underlying the IGR to include full modelled climate treatment. We know from past analyses that this is well within the capacity of Treasury (in combination with other Australian modellers).

If this seems too daunting, however, a minimalist suggestion is to upgrade the approach in the IGR by explicitly considering the social cost of carbon (SCC) as part of the analysis. Done properly, this could make a major contribution to long-term climate analysis.

As this chapter has tried to illustrate, this will bring both a means to reconcile diverse perspectives on climate issues as well as a way of confronting and managing issues to do with the climate damage function, the discount rate and uncertainty. Further, proper consideration of the SCC helps resolve some underlying policy disagreements as to the appropriate carbon price to use in benefit–cost analysis as well as the reasoning behind Australian action, even though Australia's emissions are globally small.

References

CIE (Centre for International Economics) 2020, *What existing economic studies say about Australia's cost of abatement*, Report prepared for Department of Environment and Energy, July, available at: www.industry.gov.au/data-and-publications/what-existing-economic-studies-say-about-australias-cost-of-abatement (accessed 6 February 2023).

Commonwealth of Australia 2021, *2021 intergenerational report: Australia over the next 40 years*, Commonwealth of Australia, Canberra, available at: treasury.gov.au/sites/default/files/2021-06/p2021_182464.pdf (accessed 17 February 2023).

Financial Times 2021, 'Net zero pledges: Not even next management's problem', *Financial Times*, 25 September, available at: www.ft.com/content/083c3972-d729-4867-82dc-a6806b83a7bd (accessed 6 February 2023).

Kahn, ME, Mohaddes, K, Ng, R, Pesaran, M, Raissi, M and Yang, J 2019, *Long-term macroeconomic effects of climate change: A cross-country analysis*, CAMA working paper 49/2019, Centre for Applied Macroeconomic Analysis, The Australian National University, Canberra, available at: cama.crawford.anu.edu.au/publication/cama-working-paper-series/14496/long-term-macroeconomic-effects-climate-change-cross (accessed 14 April 2022) (Note that other versions of this paper are available at: papers.ssrn.com/sol3/papers.cfm?abstract_id=3473108. There is also a published version at: www.sciencedirect.com/science/article/pii/S0140988321004898.)

Kompas, T, Pham, VH, and Che, TN 2018, 'The effects of climate change on GDP by country and the global economic gains from complying with the Paris Climate Accord', *Earth's Future* 6(8):1153–73, doi.org/10.1029/2018EF000922.

Nordhaus, WD 2017, 'Revisiting the social cost of carbon', *Proceedings of the National Academy of Sciences* 114(7):1518–23, doi.org/10.1073/pnas.1609244114.

Pezzey, J 2018, 'Why the social cost of carbon will always be disputed', *Wires Climate Change* 10(1):e558, available at: wires.onlinelibrary.wiley.com/doi/full/10.1002/wcc.558 (accessed 18 February 2023).

Pindyck, RS 2013, 'Climate change policy: What do the models tell us?', *Journal of Economic Literature* 51(3):860–72, doi.org/10.1257/jel.51.3.860.

Sunstein, CR 2021, *Averting catastrophe: Decision theory for COVID-19, climate change, and potential disasters of all kinds*, New York University Press, New York, doi.org/10.18574/nyu/9781479808496.001.0001.

Van den Bremmer, T and Van der Ploeg, F 2021, 'The risk-adjusted carbon price', *American Economic Review* 111(9):2782–2810, doi.org/10.1257/aer.20180517.

Weitzman, ML 2017, 'On a World Climate Assembly and the social cost of carbon', *Economica* 84(336):559–586, available at: onlinelibrary.wiley.com/doi/10.1111/ecca.12248 (accessed 18 February 2023).

11

The Future of the Intergenerational Report

Richard Holden

As the chapters in this volume individually and collectively make clear, the intergenerational report (IGR) is now part of the fabric of fiscal policy discussion in Australia. That said, this volume has also pointed out that a number of structural changes need to be made to the IGR to make it a central guide to the conduct of fiscal and perhaps wider policy.

Newly minted treasurer Jim Chalmers has announced that the next IGR will be published this year (2023) (Chalmers 2022). He has also argued for some time that annual budgets—and thus presumably the IGR—should adopt some form of 'wellbeing' framework. Exactly what such a framework will look like remains to be seen, and the details will matter for the usefulness of such a framework. The idea that economic measures of output do not provide a complete picture of social value is hardly a new one. It was known to the very economists who first constructed measures such as GDP (gross domestic product), but it was perhaps put most eloquently by Robert Kennedy in 1968:

> Our Gross National Product, now, is over $800 billion dollars a year, but that Gross National Product—if we judge the United States of America by that—that Gross National Product counts air pollution and cigarette advertising, and ambulances to clear our highways of carnage … Yet the gross national product does not allow for the health of our children, the quality of their education or the joy of their play. It does not include the beauty of our poetry or the

strength of our marriages, the intelligence of our public debate or the integrity of our public officials. It measures neither our wit nor our courage, neither our wisdom nor our learning, neither our compassion nor our devotion to our country, it measures everything in short, except that which makes life worthwhile. (Kennedy 1968)

Yet it is hard to deny that material wealth is important. It provides the resources to educate our children, care for the sick and infirm, to protect the natural environment and remedy existing harms caused by economic activity, and to provide the standard of living that permits human flourishing rather than constant toil for survival. There is also a spectrum of measurability running from the relatively easy to the ephemeral. Yet it is not only economic measures such as GDP that are easy to measure—so are life expectancy, infant mortality and a variety of other health measures. Various measures of human capital are slightly more challenging to measure well, but there are established and consistent ways to do so. At the other end of the spectrum are concepts like 'happiness' that are contested at best, and undefined at worst.

The challenge in using such wellbeing measures is to find measurable and meaningful measures that are stable enough across subpopulations and over time to make them a useful guide to what policies are 'working'. This is particularly important for the IGR, which, by its nature, takes a multi-decade perspective and is designed, in no small part, to act as a counterweight to the short-termism of annual budget and three-year political cycles. If the IGR is to incorporate a wellbeing framework, renewed investment will be needed into the capacity of the Australian Bureau of Statistics (ABS) to provide such measures.

Who should be in charge?

Indeed, the central purpose of the IGR is to focus the attention of both government and the public on the key long-term issues, particularly those that determine our fiscal sustainability. This can only be achieved if the authors of the IGR have the capability, freedom and incentives to identify these long-term issues. This raises squarely the question of who should be responsible for the report. The current practice is, of course, that the treasurer is responsible for the IGR. This inevitably constrains what is contained in the report and the government's response to it. If the chief failure the IGR seeks to address is excessive short-termism, then putting the same people, facing the same incentives, responsible for that short-termism in charge cannot magically lead to long-term thinking simply because the report is longer in focus than a federal budget.

One step away from this would be to make Treasury, rather than the treasurer, responsible for the IGR. To the extent that Treasury has some degree of independence this would be preferable. But there are good reasons to question that independence in modern politics. New Zealand provides a potential template for Treasury independence on these matters. But, as Podger, Hall, Woods and Trewin noted in the introduction to this volume, New Zealand has quite different institutional arrangements. There is legislation that requires the Treasury secretary in New Zealand to sign a statement certifying that Treasury has used its best professional judgement in preparing the report. Moreover, in New Zealand, departmental secretaries are appointed by the public service commissioner rather than being appointed by the prime minister.

An alternative is for the Productivity Commission (PC) to be given responsibility for the IGR, which would add a further degree of independence. One might also imagine a hybrid option where Treasury outsources part of the IGR work to the PC in order to give Treasury some degree of plausible deniability about responsibility for any politically inconvenient findings. The Parliamentary Budget Office is another option. None of these options offer a complete resolution to the problem of independence in preparing an IGR that provides an accurate and candid picture of Australia's long-term fiscal position.

What should the IGR cover?

This volume has also pointed to a series of other improvements that should be made to the IGR. The first is to properly incorporate state, territory and local government projections. This is particularly important in those sectors, such as health, where state and territory governments have major funding responsibilities; and it would provide a 'bottom-up' analysis that would complement the current 'top-down' approach. In so doing, this would offer an important check on the high-level assumptions made. This links to the second obvious improvement: incorporating more extensive sensitivity analysis to the critical assumptions that drive conclusions about fiscal sustainability. In particular, assumptions concerning migration, productivity and workforce participation are critical to the conclusions drawn by the report. Third, the IGR should take a less deterministic approach and incorporate the impact of possible future shocks such as pandemics, international economic crises, environmental crises and major trade disruptions, including from armed conflicts. Recent experiences with the health and supply-chain-disruption effects of COVID-19, the war in Ukraine and associated energy shocks, and the impact of bushfires and floods in Australia, all point to the impact of such events. Importantly, such events do not just have short-term impacts, but can have persistent effects through a change in net debt, long-run supply-chain changes, or workforce composition.

The various chapters in this volume, along with the experience of the 2021 IGR, point to a series of crucial long-term policy issues with which the Australian public and its political and civil society leadership need to engage. And this engagement needs to be informed by rigorous, independent, expert analysis—the type of analysis that differs from the type of think-tank lobbying and talking points that currently occupies a large portion of the public conversation about these issue.

Some of the most pressing issues facing the nation include the following:

1. Whether and how revenues should be increased to finance expenditure requirements in the most efficient, robust and transparent manner, while being sensitive to reliance interests.

2. The future direction of Australia's migration program, paying specific attention to the size and composition of skilled migration, and also the infrastructure needs to accommodate sustained increases in the population without undue impact on housing affordability, congestion and the provision of public goods.

3. How to continue Australia's proud tradition of a strong social safety net or, as Dixon and Holden (2022) put it, 'a generous social minimum', while maintaining the dynamism of Australian society and the Australian economy. The IGR has a crucial role to play in guiding the public narrative around issues such as inequality, for instance by pointing to Australia's post-tax-and-transfer Gini coefficient rather than the less relevant pre-tax-and-transfer version.

4. How best to manage the fiscal impact of projected growth in expenditures on health, aged care and disability support, while ensuring access. Given the projected growth in such expenditures, there will be an inevitable discussion of efficiency of provision and equity of access.

5. How best to respond as the direct impact of climate change becomes starker, including how to mitigate future climate change as well as adapt to the change that occurs.

6. Addressing education and training, labour force participation and productivity growth in an integrated fashion, taking account of all relevant policy areas across government departments.

7. Ensuring economic resilience in the face of possible future shocks.

In summary, the academy suggests the following changes to the approach Australia now takes to its IGRs.

• First, the IGR needs to be made more independent of the standard political cycle and political incentives so that it can provide a candid picture of Australia's long-term fiscal position and policy challenges.

• Second, the scope of the IGR should be national and not limited to the Commonwealth.

• Third, the analysis underpinning the IGR should be made publicly available in detail, including all data sources and code for any economic models used. Treasury or PC models should be viewed as open-source property of the Australian public, not proprietary intellectual property.

• Finally, the IGR should incorporate broader measures of so-called 'wellbeing' beyond purely economic measures such as GDP and net debt. But these additional measures should be tangible, easily quantifiable and comparable over time. The ABS should be asked to build such measures.

These reforms would help the IGR live up to its promise of providing a candid picture of Australia's long-term social and economic position that acts as a counterpoint to the short-term thinking that permeates our contemporary politics.

References

Chalmers, J 2022, Address to the Economic and Social Outlook Conference, Melbourne, 2 November, available at: ministers.treasury.gov.au/ministers/jim-chalmers-2022/speeches/address-economic-and-social-outlook-conference-melbourne.

Dixon, R and Holden, R 2022, *From free to fair markets: Liberalism after COVID-19*, Oxford University Press, New York, doi.org/10.1093/oso/9780197625972.001.0001.

Kennedy, R 1968, 'Remarks at the University of Kansas, March 18, 1968', Transcript at John F. Kennedy presidential library and museum, available at: www.jfk library.org/learn/about-jfk/the-kennedy-family/robert-f-kennedy/robert-f-kennedy-speeches/remarks-at-the-university-of-kansas-march-18-1968 (accessed 17 February 2023).

www.ingramcontent.com/pod-product-compliance
Lightning Source LLC
Chambersburg PA
CBHW060322310326
R18053000001B/R180530PG41927CBX00017B/3